Destiny and Deliberation

Destiny and Deliberation

Essays in Philosophical Theology

Jonathan L. Kvanvig

OXFORD
UNIVERSITY PRESS

OXFORD
UNIVERSITY PRESS

Great Clarendon Street, Oxford OX2 6DP

Oxford University Press is a department of the University of Oxford.
It furthers the University's objective of excellence in research, scholarship,
and education by publishing worldwide in

Oxford New York

Auckland Cape Town Dar es Salaam Hong Kong Karachi
Kuala Lumpur Madrid Melbourne Mexico City Nairobi
New Delhi Shanghai Taipei Toronto

With offices in

Argentina Austria Brazil Chile Czech Republic France Greece
Guatemala Hungary Italy Japan Poland Portugal Singapore
South Korea Switzerland Thailand Turkey Ukraine Vietnam

Oxford is a registered trade mark of Oxford University Press
in the UK and in certain other countries

Published in the United States
by Oxford University Press Inc., New York

British Library Cataloguing in Publication Data

Data available

Library of Congress Cataloging in Publication Data

Data available

Typeset by SPI Publisher Services, Pondicherry, India
Printed in Great Britain
on acid-free paper by
MPG Books Group, Bodmin and King's Lynn

ISBN 978–0–19–969657–4

10 9 8 7 6 5 4 3 2 1

To Don Baldwin and Edgar Lee, mentors unaware and yet unsurpassed

Omniscience - capacity to know everything there is to know

Omnipotence - having unlimited power

Omnibenevolence - unlimited benevolence - "good"

* Aseity - "from" "self" - the property by which a person/being exists in and of itself

Immutability - object cannot be modified after creation

Transcendence - existence or experience beyond the normal or physical level.

Libertarian - seek to maximise autonomy and freedom of choice, *political freedom

PREFACE

[handwritten: the study of / "end things"]

Introduction The following essays center thematically on the end points of time, with the doctrine of creation at one end and matters eschatological at the other. The latter focuses on the doctrines of Heaven and Hell, and the philosophical issues central to these doctrines. The former issue involves exploration of the nature of God's creative activity and the potential for understanding this idea in terms of the idea of deliberation itself. *[handwritten: natural or supernatural being, thought of as divine]*

The underlying theme of all the essays is the issue of developing a coherent theistic outlook that includes a high conception of deity together with a conception of human beings who are morally responsible because many of their choices are free; free in a sense incompatible with being causally determined. The high conception in question is associated most strongly with Anselmian perfect being *[handwritten: Philosopher]* theology, though my preferred formulation of the view derives such perfection from worthiness of worship, together with further assumptions. The conception of deity is thus one that involves omniscience, omnipotence, omnibenevolence, aseity, immutability, and transcendence.

I do not spend any time in these essays defending the libertarian theory of freedom assumed here, and won't pretend to a defense here either. Part of the reason is that both the philosophical literature and the common wisdom on the matter makes fairly obvious why libertarian freedom matters to us, but even given that assumed background, perhaps a hint at my own motivations for this assumption would be useful. In my view, freedom is essential to moral responsibility, and alternative conceptions of freedom are, somewhat surprisingly, insufficiently sensitive to the nature of science and a proper respect for its accomplishments. The story of science is the story of immense success at prediction, explanation, and control in terms of simpler and more elegant theoretical resources than previous attempts, and the story of the progress of science is a story that has not been kind to claims about what is knowable *a priori* by philosophical reflection alone. Philosophical arguments that determinism must be true or that some principle of sufficient reason must be accepted are some such arguments. In contrast, a deeper respect for science has to acknowledge that the story of scientific progress involves a recognition that causation might be merely probabilistic, in a way that never involves hidden variables which, when controlled for, would reveal some underlying deterministic system.

Moreover, the scope of the scientific enterprise is to accomplish the most with the least theoretical expense, and even for those who insist on a version of scientific realism in order to make sense of the success of science, the nature of the project cannot be understood properly without acknowledging the pragmatic dimension of the project. We need such an empirical approach to the universe precisely because we have only three-pound brains with limited cogni-

[handwritten: Sensible realistic practical]

[handwritten: Knowledge acquired by means of the senses — by observation and experimentation]

tive resources, and modeling systems in nature in ways that yield positive results in terms of explanation, prediction, and control cannot help but abstract away from certain features of those systems in order to generate the highest payoff at the least theoretical cost. Even apart from the variety of sociological evidence about the human foibles and flaws that, quite predictably, corrupt the history of science, the nature of the project itself and the capacities of those carrying out the project calls for circumspection in the face of outlandish expectations of some grand unified theory of/everything that will sustain the human desire to find a reason for everything. ₒ

Thus, a proper respect both for the accomplishments and limitations of the scientific enterprise nicely dovetails with the more common grounds for declining the offer to embrace determinism when thinking about human action. When such a refusal involves commitment to libertarianism, the view is usually portrayed as being unscientific, but the justification for this conclusion requires the libertarianism in question to be coupled with other commitments that place human behavior and human nature outside the nexus of naturalistic explanation that is the domain of science. Nothing of the sort is central to libertarianism, as embraced here, however. There is no assumption here that religious forms of materialism concerning human nature are false, nor that libertarian freedom is limited in nature to human behavior. In my view, if human behavior is distinctive in the natural order, it is because of moral responsibility, and libertarian freedom is necessary but not sufficient for that. If a philosophical theory of human nature and behavior is thought to be insufficiently scientific, the insufficiency in question will not be a result of any libertarian aspect to the theory, but rather to other features of the view. In fact, I offer the following alternative: perhaps only versions of libertarianism have the virtue of being sufficiently in step with a realistic appraisal of what a full scientific understanding of our universe involves.

These points are not intended to be an argument for the libertarianism I assume here, but are rather a confession of the stance from which that assumption is made. The essays here arise out of that stance rather than defending it, in large part because the case for libertarianism, whatever its defects, is widely known. The same cannot be said, however, of the other member of the twin engines driving these essays, which involves a conception to the high conception of deity characteristic of mature versions of the religions of the Abrahamic tradition. These essays assume the wisdom of this tradition without defending it, which explains why the focus here tends to be more on resisting approaches that tend toward abandoning the high conception of deity than on defending that conception. Moreover, these essays focus more on resisting those who see in libertarianism a reason to abandon the high conception of deity, revealing perhaps my own predilection to see the commitment to libertarianism as the deeper intellectual commitment of the two. The essays thus tend to address those with a similar strong commitment to libertarianism but who do not have as strong a commitment to a high conception of deity.

High conceptions of deity represent God as the most exalted, perfect possible

A preference or special liking for something.

being. God is thus portrayed as omnipotent, omniscience, omnibenevolent, and incapable of coming into being or passing away. Besides these intrinsic character-istics, the idea of a most exalted, perfect being has implications also for God's relational characteristics. First and foremost is that of being the sole creator of everything distinct from himself, in need of no cooperation from anything outside himself to accomplish his purposes in creation. This central aspect of God invites inferences that threaten much of our ordinary conception of the uni-verse and truths about it. First, it might appear to make the necessary truths of mathematics and logic dependent on God in a way that threatens their necessity. Second, to the extent that God's purposes are within his sole control, one might wonder what room is left for nature itself to play any causal role in explanations of how and why things happen as they do. This point extends to the causal contribution of human beings as well, but there is a further worry for those who think of human behavior as involving choices. If God's purposes are within his sole control, the appearance is quite strong that choices can only be conceived in a way that eliminates the plural: choice itself might be possible, but choices seem to put things in our hands to some extent rather than solely within God's control.

These essays are dedicated to the project of finding a logical interstice be-tween the high conception and these disturbing consequences. The point of view defended here agrees on the first point, that there is no future in a philosophical theology that undermines the necessity of mathematics and logic, but there is nothing in a high conception of God that need worry us here. For the most part, however, this point of view will be presupposed background, in order to focus on the latter two concerns above. The first is whether there is any room for causation and causal powers outside of God's power, and some of the essays touch briefly on this largely ignored issue in contemporary philosophical theology. Standard occasionalism embraces the concern in question, maintaining that all power is God's power and that nothing but God ever makes anything happen. Such news is hard to take: the sun surely seems to warm the air, and I seem to be able to raise my arm at will. Moreover, it is hard to see why God can't still exert sole control by distributing causal powers in nature as he wills. His sole control will thereby be indirect, rather than direct as it would be on standard occasionalism, but indirect control can still be sole control, it would seem.

But this point does not reach all the way to choices themselves. Granting such powers risks loss of control, since what is done must obviously be up to the individuals in question. Hence, the fundamental difficulty behind these essays: how is it possible for a philosophical theology to combine a high conception of God with libertarian freedom?

As noted already, these essays do not address the question of why one should find this high view of deity attractive, and given that the case for such a theol-ogy is considerably more opaque than that for libertarianism, it is appropriate in this introduction to indicate briefly what might attract one to such a position. A good way to focus this issue is by considering the feature of this conception that plays the central role in the following essays, the doctrine of full and complete providential control. According to this doctrine, God's plan in creating was *complete*, covering every detail of each moment of the existence of his creation. Even if we find it relatively easy to see why a conception of God in terms of the greatest possible being is appealing, we might still wonder why such control is an essential or even desirable feature of such a being.

Progress toward this conclusion arises initially, I believe, when thinking about divine engagement with human beings—an engagement prompted by divine love for his creation. The religions of the Abrahamic tradition all portray God as being interested in his creation in general and in human beings in particular. God thus makes commitments, both in terms of predictions about the future and in terms of promises regarding it, and reveals an unconstrained interest in the created order—an interest not limited by some power in nature to hide from God's presence nor one limited by what seems from a human perspective insignificant. Such commitments are compatible with a loving and perfectly good God only to the extent that sufficient providential control is in place to warrant such revelation. Broken promises, false predictions, and hyperbole concerning degree of interest are expected from the flawed and fallible, but not of the greatest possible being who is worthy of worship.

From this starting point arises the question of how much providential control is needed to sustain the divine predictions and promises. The answer here depends on scope—the range of these promises and predictions—and a central aspect of the religions of the Abrahamic tradition is that these promises and predictions extend into areas of human activity and destiny. So it would appear that there has to be sufficient providential control not only over nature itself, but also over human behavior. But here we encounter something like the *philosophical worst case* for the doctrine of divine providence: there is no aspect of creation harder to understand in terms of providential control than providential control of human beings assumed to be gifted with libertarian freedom. Hence, once one's theology involves divine commitments of the sort central to the religions in question, an account of providential control sufficient to preserve a high conception of God is needed for even the most difficult arenas for defending such control.

Even so, one might wonder why *full* providential control, extending to even the minutest aspects of creation, is required here. The answer is that there is no necessary connection here, but that one shouldn't be expected either. Good theorizing involves the development of a theory of explanatory power that is both adequate to the data and which outruns the data in terms of informational content. To require that the theory be entailed by the data is to require too much. Once we note this point, we can see that it isn't a defect of the doctrine of full providential control that it secures a ground for the divine commitments that goes well beyond what is required to ground those commitments.

Once we decline to overstate the requirements on an adequate theory, it is easier to see how the data to be explained incline strongly toward a doctrine of complete providence. If even the hairs on our head are numbered,[1] if even before on our tongue our words are altogether known,[2] if the activities of free individuals can be correctly predicted far into the future, if even the darkness is as light to the Creator,[3] what naturally comes to mind in contemplating such figures of speech is the idea of lack of limits. What explains these promises, predictions, and level of concern is precisely that there are no limits to what God knows and takes into account in undertaking the great miracle of creation. There is, thus, a presumption in favor of unlimited conceptions here because of their power to explain the variety and scope of the available data.

Presumptions can be overridden, of course, and hence one must also consider other ways to explain the data without involving such full and complete providential control. One might wonder why, for example, God couldn't let quantum indeterminacies abound that are outside of his providential control, so long as their outcomes never undermine the divine commitments. Or why God couldn't let freedom reign in human life in a way that is outside his control, so long as the promises and predictions made are generic enough to be sustained regardless of whatever variations might occur in this domain.

One might even think that there are theoretical benefits to allowing such free range in a creation. First, one might think that it a great-making property of a being to be able to orchestrate the uncontrolled so that one's overall plans are nonetheless achieved, when those plans are among the best plans there could be. Second, one might think there are benefits to such a theology when confronting those aspects of creation that, at least from our perspective, seem less than ideal. Not only are particular parts of nature surprisingly inefficient at pursuing their interests,[4] but death, disease, and destruction are rampant. Perhaps an account of the magnificence of the divine that made limitations on control central to a theology would be preferable in offering resources to explain these features of reality.

I believe there are two fundamental weaknesses with this idea. First, no such account has been developed in any detail, so we are not in a position to know whether such an account can be developed in a way that sustains the promise noted above. I note, in particular, that ruminations in this direction don't get to claim for free that what is outside of God's control can't or won't undermine the divine commitments—such claims must be earned by honest philosophical toil. I note as well that in the most direct engagement with this issue (van Inwagen 2008a), the results are not positive: it turns out that limited providential control goes hand-in-hand with having to hold that God overreaches by promising that

---

[1]Matthew 10:30

[2]Psalm 139:4

[3]Psalm 139:12

[4]The details of which are chronicled in various popular discussions of evolutionary biology, e.g. (Gould 1980) works that focus on the contrivances various life-forms display in managing to survive and reproduce—contrivances that do not show any obvious engineering perfection underlying them.

some will be saved.

Second, the promised benefits are largely illusory, especially the benefit of making it easier to address the problem of evil. The only evils that could be justified on such approaches are those that are *surprises* at the time they happen. With respect to vast arenas of suffering in our world, however, the suffering is not surprising, from the devastation wrought by hurricanes, tidal waves, tornadoes, and the like, to the horrific behavior of some human beings. Think, for example, of the angel staying the hand of Abraham before he plunges the knife into Isaac: apparently, signs were in place, prior to the plunging of iron into flesh, of what was going to happen. To the extent that there are signs of such impending doom for living creatures, a solution to the problem of evil is not helped at all by holding that God can't know prior to creation and, perhaps, can only know (just before the event in question) the likelihoods here and can't be certain. The point is that justified intervention doesn't require such certainty, and doesn't require knowledge prior to creation either.

The point here is that knowledge prior to creation isn't relevant. To secure an advantage here, either many evils, and many evils, would have to count as surprises from the divine perspective, or divine intervention can't be guided by mere probabilities. On the latter score, no Open Theist explanation of staying Abraham's hand can appeal to extreme probabilities (i.e., either 0 or 1), since Abraham's activity is clearly portrayed as free and self-initiated, and such features are Open Theist grounds for non-extreme probabiliities. On the former score, apparently non-extreme probabilities were enough to justify divine intervention, so a lack of certainty can't be a general strategy for Open Theists to use in blunting the apparent evidential force of evil, and horrendous evil, concerning the existence of God.

What can an Open Theist say here? We may presume that they have precisely the options that traditionalists have: they may appeal to standard theodical responses, such as free will, soul-making, greater good, etc. They may also appeal to the various versions of skeptical theism: that we are in no decent position to ascertain the range of goods that might justify the evils in question. It isn't important in the present context to sort among these options. The point is that there is nothing distinctively Open Theist among these options. They are, in brief, just the standard theistic options available. So the claim that Open Theism helps with the problem of evil is not defensible.

Moreover, it may be that the problem of evil is worse when the significant parts of the future remain unknown to God. Some interventions are required of agents even if a greater good would result from not intervening, as when the agent has no idea what the future holds. In such a case, intervention is appropriate. To the extent that God is ignorant of parts of the future, then, to that extent an explanation of divine non-intervention is going to be required in a great many cases in which it wouldn't be required if full and complete divine foreknowledge were present.[5]

In short, to help with the problem of evil, limitations on providence will not only have to hold that God doesn't know, prior to creation, the entirety of the future, but also that as time unfolds, the probabilities will hardly ever be in place prior to bad things happening to justify intervention. There is simply no evidence for such a posit, and a preponderance of evidence against.

Given these points, there is some justification for the historical predilection among those with an exalted view of deity to include a doctrine of full and complete providence in their theology. Moreover, if the case for libertarianism is strong, there is a serious philosophical conundrum taking shape—a conundrum about how God could both be in control of the future and yet it be up to us how we act.

This issue is pressing regarding both the beginning of the story at creation and the end of our story at the culmination. One might expect a symmetry here, so that any compromising on a high conception of God required by libertarian freedom would effect each part equally. Thus, if freedom eliminates the possibility of full providential control over the history of the universe, one might expect it to require also the possibility of eternal separation from God. And vice-versa: if eternal separation from God is possible, we might anticipate an account of creation according to which complete providential control is curtailed.

These essays, however, are a little surprising on this score. They address both the beginning and the end in a way that honors the importance of human freedom, arguing for an asymmetry that leaves separation from God forever a possibility but involves no loss of providential control in the story of creation. Along the way, those positions in philosophical theology that give pride of place to libertarian freedom are rejected. Open Theists openly embrace a loss of full providential control, while Molinists claim to have solved the problem of retaining a high conception of God together with libertarian freedom. There was a time when I agreed with them (Kvanvig 1986), but I now find the view ultimately unsuccessful, as these essays reveal.

I wish there were a standard philosophical term for the view developed and defended in these essays. For those willing to abandon libertarian freedom, there are the standard names of Thomism or Calvinism. For those willing to limit the high conception of God, there is Open Theism. In the history of Christian thought, the only widely-known position in between besides the Molinist position is Arminianism.[6] Arminianism is named after Jacobus Arminius, a Dutch

---

[5]On this point, see (Wierenga 1997).

[6]There is the entire voluntarist tradition in medieval thought that one might appeal to, including the voluntarisms of Henry of Ghent, Peter John Olivi, and, more prominently, John Duns Scotus and the entire Franciscan tradition with its emphasis on the primacy of the will. On this issue, it is worth noting the libertarian strain in some of Augustine as well. Calling one's view Augustinian, however, would mislead in the extreme, and referring to it using anything in the voluntarist tradition would obscure rather than enlighten for lack of general knowledge concerning the particular thinkers in question and the distinctive features of the Franciscan tradition. Thanks to Sydney Penner for a reminder concerning these possibilities, which are

pastor and theologian of the late 16th and early 17th centuries, who rejected the unconditional election doctrine of John Calvin and was posthumously declared a heretic by the Synod of Dort in 1618.

I hesitate to take on this label, however, since Arminianism is a position within systematic theology, and though systematic theology has some obvious philosophical dimensions to it, it also suffers from the Protestant affirmation of *sola Scriptura* that led to an aversion to and ignorance of the central philosophical dimensions of any careful thinking, including that involved in systematic theology. The most significant implication of this distaste for philosophy in our context is that Arminianism simply asserts the compatibility of freedom together with an exalted conception of God, with no explanation why or how these claims are co-tenable. That lack is, of course, the primary cost of Protestant thought, most egregiously displayed in the anti-intellectualism characteristic of American conservative Christianity. Even the most robust intellectual heritage within Protestantism—Calvinism (for philosophical substance, not so much Calvin himself but more by way of the great American thinker Jonathan Edwards)—adds little on the present issue to the massive achievement of Thomism. A significant motivation for the efforts represented by these essays is a recognition that there is no escape from the hard work of philosophical thinking, and this point is nowhere more obvious than in the issue of the compatibility of exalted conceptions of God with libertarian freedom. There is, to put the point bluntly, no alternative to philosophical work on this issue.

Another reason for reticence in embracing the label is that Arminianism is primarily a view affirming the significance of human freedom in a soteriological context having to do with the conditions that need to be met for salvation. There are obvious paths from this starting point to a more general view on human freedom, especially given its central role in accounting for moral responsibility, but those connections trigger more basic philosophical inquiry and thus tend to fall outside both the explicit focus and expertise of Arminian theologians.

The present essays, however, are unapologetically philosophical in orientation, and to mark this different starting point I will qualify the term, saying that the present essays can be seen in terms of a defense and articulation of Philosophical Arminianism. This position affirms the central importance of libertarian freedom in our understanding of human persons, but refuses to do so in a way that compromises a high conception of God. Moreover, this position insists that the fundamental work needed to sustain the intellectual respectability of Arminianism must be philosophical. In this respect, it shares a common theme with Molinist attempts to reconcile freedom and divine providence, but as I use the term, Philosophical Arminianism rejects Molinism, opting instead for an alternative explanation of the compatibility in question. Moreover, it affirms the Arminian standpoint while finding it intellectually inadequate to endorse

worth noting in their own right to avoid the inclination to think of traditional Christianity as uniformly determinist.

such compatibility without an account of how it could possibly be true: rampant and facile appeals to the mysteries of the faith when paradox threatens is just anti-intellectualism in sophist drag. In contrast, the defense of Philosophical Arminianism presented here arises in the context of a full commitment to pursue understanding rather than to settle for appeals to mystery.

These themes are pursued in the following essays, with Part One involving the end point of creation and Part Two involving the beginning point. The issues pursued in Part One focus on the question of universalism and its adequacy, together with a concern for how to understand the finality involved in the idea of an end point of creation. When afterlife possibilities are cast in terms of divine decrees, an answer as to how one's eternal destiny can be settled once and for all is simple: it is what has been decreed. For those inclined toward an account of eternal destiny that involves choices, however, the question of finality is more difficult. Moreover, this difficulty is central to the problem of Hell itself, conceived as a special instance of the problem of evil. Universalism offers some comfort here, but I argue that this comfort is ultimately illusory: it provides no escape from the problem of Hell and no adequate account of finality.

Part Two focuses primarily on the interplay between different ways of endorsing libertarian freedom in the story of creation itself. The first two essays in Part Two present a case against Open Theism—the view that limits providence and foreknowledge because of a commitment to libertarianism—and the next two essays detail my growing disenchantment with Molinism—the position commonly thought to be the only way to reconcile full providence and libertarian freedom. The final essay provides an alternative reconciliation—one which provides the linchpin for the claim that these essays constitute a defense of Philosophical Arminianism.

Here is brief abstract for each essay:

"Autonomy, Finality, and the Choice Model of Hell"

The Choice Model explains residence in Hell in terms of a transparent choice for such by those in Hell, but a problem arises for this model when one adds the notion of finality to a fundamental understanding of the nature of Heaven and Hell. If we think of Hell in terms of the contrast to Heaven, adding to this understanding the idea that at some point, one's eternal destiny is settled for all of time and eternity, how can the Choice Model explain such finality?

"Losing Your Soul"

The loss of soul theory attempts to solve the problem of the finality of Hell for the Choice Model by claiming that it is possible, through a series of free actions, to get oneself in a position where the choice of Heaven is no longer possible for one. I argue that this attempt to account for finality does not succeed.

"Universalism and the Problem of Hell"

A concise formulation of the problem of Hell is McTaggart's. He argued that if there is a Hell, one could have no good reason to believe it. He reasoned that there is no good empirical evidence to believe in Hell, so that if there is a good reason to believe in it, revelation must provide it. Yet, McTaggart continued, the infliction of Hell is very wicked, and so anyone who would send one to Hell must be vile indeed. In such a case, one could have no good reason to trust such an individual concerning anything of importance to our well-being, for as anyone familiar with the games played by schoolyard bullies knows, there is no telling why a vile person would say that something is good or bad for one. So if anyone, including God, tells us that there is a Hell to shun, McTaggart claims that we could have no good reason to believe that such an individual is telling us the truth. What such a person says, to put the point succinctly, undercuts the reliability of the testimony. Universalism—the view that everyone will ultimately be in Heaven forever—attempts to provide a response to this dilemma, but I argue that it fails in this attempt.

"Open Theism and the Future"

Open Theists affirm an Asymmetry Thesis, according to which the future is composed of two parts, one open to omniscience and the other not. The part of the future that is not open to omniscience is the undetermined part, with future free actions being the prime exemplar. The part open to omniscience is, then, the determined part. I argue, however, that such a position is untenable, and that the grounds given for the thesis by Open Theists commits them to nearly complete divine skepticism about the future.

"A Tale of Two Cronies"

Our tale involves three characters (Ott, Occ, and Moll), and a discussion about the relationship between God's power and the power of things in the created order. Moll and Ott agree that there are powers in creation, both deterministic and libertarian powers, while Occ claims that all power is God's power and the created order contains no entities with any power whatsoever. In the process of discussion, Moll forces a rethinking of what libertarian power involves, in such a way that actions by God that entail that an individual performs a certain action do not threaten the claim that the person displays libertarian freedom in performing that action.

"A Dead-End for Molinism"

Having argued elsewhere that Molinists have difficulty with embedded conditionals (Kvanvig 2002), this essay argues that an attempt to evade the problem fails. In particular, it is argued that Molinism cannot equate a counterfactual's being true in a way logically prior to God's will with the truth of that counterfactual being outside of God's control. The reason this equation must be forfeited is because of the logical behavior of embedded conditionals.

"Creation, Deliberation, and Molinism"

Molinism posits the existence of counterfactuals of freedom to explain how human beings can be free and yet God create in such a way that displays providential control over every aspect of creation. The point of such counterfactuals is thus the role they play in a deliberative model of creation—one that has a central place for deliberative conditionals. I argue that the types of Molinist views found in the literature do not provide conditionals which are capable of function in such a deliberative model of creation. I thus argue that Molinists need to develop a different approach to understanding God's creative activity.

"An Epistemic Theory of Creation"

This essay develops an alternative middle position between those who deny libertarian freedom in order to preserve a high conception of God and those who deny a high conception of God in order to preserve libertarian freedom. The key difference between this position and Molinism is that the present view relies on epistemic conditionals in place of counterfactuals, and thus substitutes an epistemic approach to creation in place of the more standard metaphysical and semantic approach relied on by Molinists and their opponents.

These essays in philosophical theology approach the issues in question from the perspective of Christianity, since it is in this context that the issues first became pressing for me, and the perspective from which the issues continue to be more than intellectual puzzles for me. The problems discussed and arguments presented reach well beyond this starting point, however, and are easily generalized to other religious perspectives. Any theistic outlook involving an afterlife must deal with the issues and arguments involved here, and thus Philosophical Arminianism is a position deserving attention in a broad range of religious traditions, in spite of the rather parochial character of the appellation.

My work on these essays has benefited enormously from comments and conversations with a number of friends and colleagues. There too many to provide a complete list of, but the following deserve special mention: Michael Hand, Scott Sturgeon, Mike Almeida, Hugh McCann, Linda Zagzebski, Wayne Riggs, Matt McGrath, Robert Johnson, Alex Pruss, Keith DeRose, Fritz Warfield, Tom Flint, Fred Freddoso, Dick Foley, Rich Feldman, Trent Dougherty, Ted Poston, Kenny Boyce, Justin McBrayer, Patrick Todd, Tom Talbott, Eleonore Stump, Steve Evans, Sydney Penner, Tim Williamson, Joe Salerno, Brit Brogaard, and Matt Weiner. Given my special competence at forgetfulness, I am sure there are many others equally deserving mention, and for the contribution of them all to my thinking on these matters, I am grateful.

I want to mention two other individuals as well, even though they had no direct effect on this volume: Don Baldwin and Edgar Lee. In different ways, they have both functioned as spiritual and intellectual mentors since my undergraduate years. They are, I am sure, in large part unaware of the important roles they have played in my career, and I here want to acknowledge these roles and thank them by dedicating this volume to them.

n though they had no direct effect on this volume: Don Baldwin and Edgar Lee. In different ways, they have both functioned as spiritual and intellectual mentors since my undergraduate years. They are, I am sure, in large part unaware of the important roles they have played in my career, and I here want to acknowledge these roles and thank them by dedicating this volume to them.

CONTENTS

PART I

HELL AND AFTERLIFE

1

AUTONOMY, FINALITY, AND THE CHOICE MODEL OF HELL

1.1 Introduction

In the context of traditional Christianity, the doctrine of the afterlife is pervaded with the concept of finality. Hell is described as the "second death", and the apocalyptic imagery includes a description of a Final Judgment involving a great white throne.

It is natural to think of such finality in terms of the language of "once and for all": there is a determinate consummation toward which history is aimed, a point at which one's fate for all eternity is settled once and for all. When clarified in such terms, contemporary philosophical thought about Hell seems seriously deficient, as will emerge in what follows. My purpose here is to investigate the issue of finality to determine whether and how contemporary thinking about Hell can be reconciled with it.

Before embarking on our journey, however, it is important to be clear about the language of Heaven and Hell and the precise nature of the problem I want to address. It is easy to think of these notions in geographic terms—that they are places, one where God is and one where God isn't. Such conceptualization will be avoided here given the serious problems with geographic conceptions. (In brief, the problem is that no matter what the actual character of any location, one can imagine people who find such an environment unpleasant. What makes Heaven Heavenly is the experience of the union with God it involves, not golden streets and the like. Moreover, it is incoherent to describe God as omnipresent and yet hold that Hell is a place where God isn't. What's lacking in Hell is, rather, the blessing and beauty of a joyful union with God for all eternity. The language of Heaven and Hell must be understood as relational, not geographic.)

So the language of Heaven and Hell should be thought of in terms of some ultimate good that is available to us, and my philosophical interest in the doctrine of Hell is driven by what I have called the problem of Hell, which is a version of the problem of evil. In order to appreciate the full scope of the problem of Hell, we need a more general understanding of the character of Hell than can be provided by any geographic conception of it. Once we have before us this more general characterization, we will see that adding the feature of finality to it exacerbates the problem of Hell rather than diminishes it. We can begin, then, by characterizing the fundamental distinction between Heaven and Hell that gives rise to the most general version of the problem of Hell.

Every religion posits some advantage to following its tenets, and some disadvantage in not doing so. It is this distinction that underlies the language of Heaven and Hell. In eschatological religions such as Christianity, the advantage in question is tied to God's purposes in creation—purposes that are complex and manifold, but which include an afterlife of joyous and eternal communion with God. In this way, the fundamental logic of Heaven and Hell is that Heaven is complete and total fulfillment in accord with God's purposes in creation and Hell is the loss of this unsurpassable good. To this negative characterization, various traditions add literary flare: Hell is the abode of the damned, a land of outer darkness, a place of fire and brimstone, of weeping and gnashing of teeth, where the worm does not die and the fire is not quenched; a place where one loses one's soul, where one becomes merely a war of strongest desires, a place where one is treated as one treated others, etc. These accretions to the fundamental character of Hell need to be added and defended only after the problem of Hell is answered in the face of the more fundamental distinction between Heaven and Hell. The reason for this priority is two-fold. First, if the fundamental problem of Hell cannot be answered, it is pointless to add to the description of Hell in any way at all. It is simply an untenable doctrine, for the same reason that adding further information to a contradiction doesn't make the inconsistency disappear. Second, if we find an acceptable answer to the fundamental problem of Hell, that answer may inform us as to what additional language can be allowed and how it should be interpreted.

This point is important, since it will help us avoid a common flaw in discussions of Hell. Some are given to making the following kind of contrast: "That guy doesn't believe in Hell; he thinks the unredeemed are simply annihilated!" Such a remark confuses the fundamental logical contrast between Heaven and Hell with some more particular conception of Hell. If Hell is defined in terms of fire and brimstone where even worms exist forever, then defenders of annihilationism do not think that people go to Hell. Such a way of defining Hell, though, simply confuses the philosophical issues surrounding Hell, since annihilationism is subject to the same general problem of Hell plaguing versions of the doctrine that imply eternal conscious existence. A better approach is to think of Hell as the negative complement of a doctrine of Heaven.[1] Then both the fire and brimstone crowd and the annihilation crowd oppose the universalist crowd, since the first two believe that some go to Hell and the third denies it. In short, Heaven is tied to the benefits of the religion, and Hell to the costs of rejecting the religion. In the context I'll presuppose here, that means that Heaven is understood in terms of God's goals in creation, and Hell in terms of the frustration of those goals.

This point is important in another way as well. Something akin to a doctrine of Hell is not optional for any religion, and there is no branch of Christianity involving a doctrine of the afterlife that can sensibly sing out, "No Hell, no

---

[1]On this account, limbo should be construed as a less severe compartment of Hell, and purgatory as a less comfortable part of Heaven.

Hell" (sung to chorus of "The first Noel"). Some Christians maintain that no one will ever be consigned to Hell eternally, but that is different from denying the doctrine of Hell entirely. Every religion must be able to make sense of the warnings it contains, and Christians need to make sense of warnings about the wide and narrow roads. To do so, an appeal must be made to the contrast between God's goals in creation and the results of the frustration of that goal. Various theories of Hell issue from descriptions of these results, but the logical core of the concept of Hell is the contrast it presents to the doctrine of Heaven. Failure to be sufficiently general in one's understanding of Hell makes it appear that the easy way out is to deny the doctrine of Hell entirely. But the problem of Hell, the problem of explaining how a perfectly good God could create a world in which there is a point to warnings about the consequences of failing to love God with one's whole mind, heart, and strength, would still remain. (One might think that this description is prejudiced against universalism, but that is not so. Universalists simply deny that anyone goes to Hell; they don't deny the existence of a logical or conceptual contrast to Heaven, nor should they be understood to deny that there is any point to the Biblical warnings. Hell does not cease to be real simply because unpopulated.)

What I'm interested in defending, explicating, and investigating is the idea that there is a doctrine of Hell that makes sense for God to author; not to give some exaggerated house of horrors description and then be put in the incoherent position of having to deny the doctrine. Such a position is incoherent in the following sense: it begins hoping to address the problem of Hell, but ends up only avoiding certain versions of that problem. Better to address the most general version of the problem and then determine which particular doctrines survive scrutiny than to proffer a particular doctrine and then watch it, to use an apt metaphor, go up in flames.

I've argued in print that there is a solution to this most general problem of Hell (Kvanvig 1993), but have not devoted much attention to the problem I will address here, the problem arising when one adds the notion of finality to a fundamental understanding of the nature of Heaven and Hell. Any traditional understanding of Hell in Christianity must honor the finality aspect with which I began. If we think of Hell in terms of the contrast to Heaven, adding to this understanding the idea that at some point one's eternal destiny is settled for all of time and eternity, what can we say about the problem of Hell?

1.2 Two Approaches to Hell

Recent thinking about Hell contrasts two quite different approaches to the subject. The traditional approach in Christianity involves retribution or punishment. More carefully, the traditional approach makes retributive punishment the core element in an account of Hell. In addition to this core element, various accoutrements can be added or left out. Traditional Christians typically add that escape from Hell is not possible, that the inhabitants of Hell include at least some human beings, and that Hell is a place of unending conscious suffering.

Mitigations of this traditional view of Hell are constructed by adopting the punishment model of Hell and dropping one of the latter requirements. Universalists deny that any human being will be in Hell, or at least that any human being will be in Hell forever. Annihilationists deny that Hell is a place of conscious suffering; instead, Hell is a description of non-existence: the unredeemed simply drop out of existence entirely. And second chance theorists affirm the possibility that once in the afterlife when the alternatives are finally clear to you, you'll have another chance to make the obvious and rational choice to avoid Hell.

In opposition to the traditional model of Hell and its mitigations is the more recent Choice Model, as articulated and defended by Lewis (1944), Swinburne (1977), Stump (1986), Walls (1992), Kvanvig (1993). On the Choice Model, people are in Hell because, to put it crudely, that's what they choose. As Lewis puts it, if the doors of Hell are locked, they are locked from the inside.

One of the problems with the Choice Model, however, is the problem of finality. If Hell is only locked from the inside, then those in Hell can unlock it and go to Heaven. Perhaps they won't, but the mere fact that no one ever goes from one eternal place to the other doesn't seem sufficient for the notion of finality involved in the idea of an eschatological consummation. Something stronger than a merely contingent fact seems to be required. The options here can be ordered in terms of modal strength: metaphysical, logical, nomological, etc. The very weakest we should be willing to accept here is counterfactual necessity: if you were to end up in Hell, you wouldn't ever leave; if you were to end up in Heaven, you wouldn't leave there either.

Perhaps I've been too hasty in dismissing a merely universal account of finality. Can't one insist that exceptionless universality itself is necessity enough? If we allow mere universality to count as finality in the intended sense, the Choice Model can easily account for finality simply by adding this contingent claim to whatever the details of one's favored embellishment of the Choice Model. I will return to this issue at the end of this paper, but for now I will table the suggestion, adopting instead the goal of taking on the harder problem for the Choice Model. So I will here assume that something more than mere universality is required for finality; that some real necessity is needed: counterfactual, logical, nomological, conceptual, or metaphysical.

If some kind of real necessity is needed, however, it is hard to see how the Choice Model can sustain any such necessities. If presence in Heaven or Hell depends on the exercise of free choice, conceived along libertarian lines, there are several lines of argument that cause problems. Against the ideas of metaphysical, logical, and nomological necessity is the plausibility of the Principle of Alternative Possibilities (PAP). And against the idea of counterfactual necessity is the problem of counterfactuals of freedom which Molinists posit and everyone else disputes.

1.3   Two or Three Problematic Possibilities

These points leave open three fairly obvious paths for a defender of the Choice Model to take in explaining finality. The two I'll spend a little more time on concern PAP and Molinism, but there is also the path of adopting a compatibilist account of freedom alluded to above in noting the libertarian conception of freedom typically associated with the Choice Model. By adopting such an alternative conception of freedom, finality could be achieved in virtue of God's activity itself, since God could bring about conditions that cause one to be in whatever internal states cause such a permanent choice. The idea of this position is that God can't directly cause one's presence in Heaven or Hell, but indirect causation of the right sort is perfectly fine.

Compatibilist freedom, however, is not the only commitment needed for this approach. The list of commitments becomes quite large, and, at least to my mind, a bit philosophically unwieldy. Let me point out what I think are the most problematic elements. The view has to hold that we live in a deterministic world as well (a view that does not cohere well with the available scientific evidence, by the way). Moreover, there is a loss of univocity in the account of freedom, since God's freedom in creation cannot be understood in compatibilistic terms, on grounds of explanatory circularity (God chooses the laws, so they better not be needed to explain God's choices). The best option here is to explain God's freedom in terms of being unconstrained by factors external to Himself, but then divine and human freedom are construed differently (compatibilist freedom defenders cannot avoid the claim that free actions are nonetheless constrained by external factors).

These issues are deep and difficult and we could get lost in them for nearly an eternity, and since my intention is to focus on other issues, I'll rest content with noting that most versions of the Choice Model assume a libertarian conception of freedom, and that is the version I want to focus on here (at least in part because it is the view of freedom I find most congenial). As my remarks above indicated, there are two other paths to consider, one concerning PAP and the other concerning Molinism. I'll discuss the PAP route first.

The argument against the possibility of finality on the Choice Model appealed to PAP, but PAP has come under fire ever since the attack on the principle in Frankfurt (1969).[2] Frankfurtians hold that an action can be free and the agent responsible for it even if the action itself is necessitated. The usual formulations of PAP say that one is free, or morally responsible, for bringing about a certain state of affairs A only if it is possible for one not to bring about A. To undermine this principle, Frankfurt's demon is ever watchful to see if you'll do some dastardly deed, and leaves you alone as long as you go through with it. But he'll intervene

---

[2]Frankfurt's argument is against a principle of alternative possibilities for moral responsibility rather than for freedom, but since libertarians typically connect freedom with moral responsibility, even if indirectly as in Kane (1996), it is relatively easy to adapt his objections to the context of freedom itself.

should you show any signs of not following through, leaving it impossible for you to avoid it.

The failure of PAP, however, doesn't seem to help the Choice Model with finality. What is needed is an explanation of how some choice of eternal destiny is *permanent*, in the sense that it cannot be revoked. Frankfurt's demon only gets permanence as a result of an ever-watchful being who will secure a given outcome if the agent in question won't. The Choice Model, however, needs an explanation in terms of choices of the agent, not one depending on coercive outside forces.

Deniers of PAP will protest this characterization, however. The language of coercion is appropriate in contexts where a person is forced to do what they do not choose to do, but in the case in question, the person does choose. It is the choice itself that is necessitated, so even if it is necessitated by God's intervention, one's eternal destiny is a function of one's choices and the language of coercion out of place.

There are two points to make to this line of argument. The first is that such an approach to the Choice Model eviscerates it in order to preserve its vestige. Philosophical accounts of Hell are motivated by a desire to be able to explain how each individual is morally responsible for their eternal destiny. To adopt a version of the Choice Model that explains eternal destiny in terms of individual choices, but in such a way that the individual is not morally responsible for those choices, would be disastrous for an account of Hell. Moreover, Frankfurt's counterexample to PAP is meant only to show that one can be responsible even if one couldn't have done otherwise because the demon may need to do nothing at all. Frankfurt's example would lose all of its appeal if it involved the actual intervention of the demon to produce the desired behavior. Moral responsibility exists in Frankfurt examples only when the demon idly observes, not when the demon actually has to intervene. So if one preserves the Choice Model by appeal to Frankfurt counterexamples to PAP by applying Frankfurt's technique to the choices themselves while admitting that in some cases intervention is required, one will have preserved the Choice Model only by abandoning its connection to moral responsibility. That theory would be only a shadow of a substance we can't do without.

It is here that careful attention to the formulation of PAP is instructive and relevant as well, since the usual attacks on PAP woefully underestimate the resources available to a defender of PAP. Once this point is appreciated, we will see that little hope remains of grounding finality in some necessity based on a denial of PAP.

The crude formulation of PAP uses the ambiguous phrase "could have done otherwise." Frankfurt's attack on PAP assumes that this phrase should be understood so that, where the action in question is A, the "otherwise" locution refers to the absence of the action in question: one could have done otherwise in a situation in which one A's if and only if one could have failed to A. That's only one possible interpretation of the phrase, however. Here's another. One can talk about what one intends rather than what one does: one is free, or morally responsible, in bringing about A only if it was possible for one to fail to intend to bring about A. The demon may be able to force you to do the deed, but not to intend nor try to do it. Perhaps moral responsibility depends on some optionality with respect to the intentional realm, with respect to what we might call "tryings". Maybe Adam had to eat the apple (at least he seemed to claim Eve made him do it), but he could have tried not to and he didn't.

This response helps to defend PAP, but it is not by itself sufficient. For any action that is not an instantaneous action, including intendings and tryings, the demon can see the first signs of failure to perform the action and intervene at that point (if we imagine him prescient enough). So if your intending not to A takes more than an instant, the demon can see its beginning and prevent its completion. In order to fix this problem, we'll have to posit instantaneous "flickers of freedom," which the demon can't extinguish.[3] Maybe Frankfurt's demon can prevent a full trying or intending from occurring, but he can't prevent the beginning of such, and maybe that flicker of freedom is all a defender of PAP needs.

I'm not certain that there are any such things as instantaneous actions, but if there are no such things, it is hard to see why. If we admit the possibility of instantaneous actions of this sort, however, the possibility of defending finality by denying PAP along this route is lost. There remains the possibility of other routes to a denial of PAP, and on this point there is a vast literature, usefully summarized in Timpe (2008). It is safe to say, however, that there is no growing consensus in favor of denying all interpretations of PAP.[4] Given these points, together with acquiescence on the possibility of instantaneous actions, defenders of the Choice Model would be best advised to take a different route in looking for a solution to the problem of finality.

An alternative way to build the Choice Model so as to include finality is the way of the Molinist. The Molinist holds that there are true counterfactuals of freedom, counterfactuals of the form "if S were put in circumstances C, S would freely do A," where the kind of freedom in question is assumed to be libertarian freedom. The doctrine of Molinism refers to God's knowledge of such counterfactuals as "middle knowledge," coming logically after his natural knowledge (i.e., his knowledge of necessary truths) and before his free knowledge (knowledge of contingent matters of fact true in virtue of God's creative activity) (de Molina 1988).

If we suppose that there are such true counterfactuals of freedom, we need only add one further element to build the notion of finality into the Choice Model. That further element is that any omniscient being knows which counterfactuals of freedom are true and which antecedents will actually obtain. Given this knowledge, it is relatively simply to explain how it could be that one's afterlife destiny is counterfactually final: there only needs to be a true counterfactual

[3]The phrase "flicker of freedom" is borrowed from Fischer (1994).

[4]"Perhaps the debate is ultimately over which set of intuitions is more plausible, in which case we should not be surprised by the lack of a clear victor." (Timpe 2008, p. 67)

of freedom to the effect that whichever afterlife situation one finds oneself in, one would never freely choose the changes needed to move from one situation to the other.

This is a neat package if there are true counterfactuals of freedom. It is the "beautiful game" of philosophical theology, since it incorporates a commitment to libertarian freedom while at the same time refusing to compromise on the question of God's providential control of all of time and eternity. The hitch, however, is whether there are true counterfactuals of freedom. On the side of the existence of such is the intuitive argument: we use subjunctives in a variety of contexts, especially when deliberating, and would have no problem including the language of freedom in them if asked about it. Think of "He wouldn't have signed even if we'd offered him ten thousand more" to explain why we should give up on trying to buy that house; "If he'd hung that curveball again, I'd have hit it out of the ballpark" to lament striking out again; or, the ignored academician's lament, "If they'd only read my stuff, they'd see..." In each case, a counterfactual is expressed by a sentence in the subjunctive mood, and even though none are counterfactuals of freedom, we wouldn't balk at inserting the language of freedom into the sentences in question. The reason we don't has to do with Gricean maxims[5] to the effect that one's contribution to a discussion should be informative and relevant, so that including items that everyone will legitimately assume to obtain is tedious and overdone. So, don't mention the language of freedom when speaking of human action unless it is somehow in question in the conversation.

On the other side of the coin are the worries about how to explain the truth of a counterfactual of freedom. This concern is sometimes called the grounding objection, but I find that language puzzling and unhelpful. When someone asks what grounds the truth of a certain claim, they've waxed metaphorical in a way we should move beyond.[6] Giving up the metaphor can be done, however. Just ask about the truth conditions, or truth-makers, for counterfactuals of freedom. I'll

---

[5] Gricean maxims are principles about communication that go beyond semantic content. See Grice (1968).

[6] For a recent defense of the centrality of the notion of grounding to metaphysics, see Schaffer (2009). Schaffer defends an Aristotelian approach to metaphysics on which the central questions concern what is fundamental, what is derived, and the grounding relation between the two. But he also notes in passing that this same grounding relation, which is first and foremost a relationship between substances (what is fundamental) and every other thing that exists, may be just what is needed by truthmaker theorists to explain what grounds the truth of a proposition. Here I doubt we have anything more than homophony for the two grounding roles: ontological dependence relations are one thing and are theoretically independent of whether there even are such things as truthmakers for every truth. Moreover, appeals to the grounding relation face a dilemma that Schaffer notes in passing: if the grounding relation itself is fundamental, it gets confused with substances, and if it is not fundamental, it reflects some theoretical disunity to insist that it is nonetheless not in need of grounding by whatever is fundamental. For these reasons, I remain convinced that talk of grounding, especially in the context addressing the truth of various counterfactuals, cannot be rescued by any appeal to advantages of an Aristotelian approach to metaphysics.

focus on truth conditions. It is here that formal semantics can give us some insight into the truth conditions of sentences, in terms of the logical form of the sentences and the satisfaction conditions for sentences having that form. Since the 1970s, the standard, albeit not wholly satisfactory, semantics for counterfactuals has appealed to possible worlds and some ordering of such at least weakly centered on the actual world (Lewis 1973). What this means, in non-technical language, is that some ways of imagining the world to be different than it actually is are less similar to actuality than others. For simplicity, assume that for each particular way of imagining the world to have been different, there is one world that is most similar, though not identical, to the actual world (involving this particular imaginative difference). Then a counterfactual with that imagined difference as antecedent is true just in case the consequent of that counterfactual is true in this most similar world. A quick example may help. Consider the claim that if I'd been offered $100,000 to write this paper rather than doing it on my own, I still would have written it. Imagine the world changed to accommodate this wholly undeserved possibility, and then ask yourself, "Would Kvanvig be writing in such a situation?" The answer is, obviously, "Yes;" in fact, I not only would have written the paper, I'd make a standing offer for a free lunch to all who read it! So the counterfactual in question is true.

"But wait," you say. "You could have refused the offer, couldn't you?" The answer is, again, "Yes." So now there are two worlds in which the offer is made—one in which I give the lecture and one in which I don't. If the first is somehow more similar to the actual world than the second, what explains this difference? The usual answers by defenders of the standard semantics cite features such as: same laws of nature, same history up to the point in question, small insignificant miracles favored over large ones, and so on. (These items are ordered in terms of importance: same laws trumps same history which trumps miracles, etc.)

The problem is that this account doesn't help with the example, assuming as I am that I have libertarian freedom with regard to writing. In one world I write and in another I don't. Each of these worlds have the same laws and same history up to the time of writing. We assume the same panoply of miracles in each world up to that time as well, so the only differences in the two worlds are future differences. So which world is more similar to the actual world? On all these criteria, the worlds are tied.

What might we try here? I'll not go into the technical details needed to provide an answer here, but there are a couple of general points worth making. The standard semantics is particularly well-suited to accounting for the truth of counterfactuals under the assumption of determinism, for then, once you freeze the laws and the history of the world, the only thing that can get things to be different from the actual world is a miracle or some change to the past. But, to put the point tendentiously, nobody should assume determinism any more, and if we don't we have one of two options. The first is to find a semantics for counterfactuals that is more at home with denials of determinism, or adopt the view that our counterfactual talk is really best understood as a stand-in for more precise talk about probabilities.[7]

Here's how things might go on the probabilistic story. Instead of holding that it is strictly true that if circumstances C were to obtain, S would freely do A, one should hold that the strict truth is something like: "it is probably true that in C, S would freely do A," or "the probability of S's freely doing A, given C is very high". There is a deep problem with such views, however. Suppose you say to me "if you were to utter a profanity during your talk, I'd get up and leave." This is a claim I know how to test. And I know what circumstances would constitute a decisive refutation of your claim, and so do you. Here they are: I utter a profanity and you stay where you are. But notice that this set of circumstances does not constitute a decisive refutation of any probability claim. The point to notice is that no matter what semantics we adopt for subjunctive conditional, that semantics had better honor the sacrosanct principle that such a conditional is always false when it has a true antecedent and false consequent.

We are left, then, with the option of finding a replacement for the standard semantics in question, and the demand for an explanation of what grounds the truth of counterfactuals of freedom is best understood in terms of a complaint that we have no idea what an adequate semantics would look like that has the required conditionals coming out true. On that point, I acquiesce: Molinists need a better semantics for counterfactuals, and there is no clear possibility in sight. To that extent, the Molinist approach to finality is discomfiting.

1.4   Choice and Finality

I will not press the case for Molinism further here, however, in order to focus on the question of what happens if the beautiful game of the Choice Model plus Molinism collapses. Here's what we're left with if we stick with the Choice Model. Either some other intermediate position must be found—a position that retains full providence and libertarian freedom, and does so in a way that avoids whatever difficulties arise for Molinism because of the grounding objection— or full omniscience has to be abandoned, since exhaustive foreknowledge of the future will no longer be within God's reach.[8] And once we have a Choice Model tied to a lack of omniscience, it looks like the idea of finality is lost, since there

[7]This probabilistic interpretation is now standard for indicative conditionals; see what has come to be called the Jeffrey–Adams–McGee (JAM) tradition of providing a probabilistic semantics for indicative conditionals (See Jeffrey (1964), McGee (1989), Adams (1975)). Various problems plague this account, to my mind the most important being that conditional probability is too coarse semantically to account for semantically distinguishable conditional sentences (see Suppes (1994)) and that this interpretation of JAM-conditions does not properly accommodate *reductio* arguments expressed using conditional sentences (see Levi (2004)). This approach is instructive in the present context, since a probabilistic approach to subjunctives faces a version of the latter problem (a refutation of a subjunctive conditional occurs when its antecedent is true and its consequent is false), but also because the truth conditions for indicatives differ from the truth conditions for subjunctives, so there would need to be some difference in the conditional probability semantics for each.

[8]I resist strongly the idea that there aren't any truths about the (undetermined) future— that's a failure to appreciate the significance of tense (present tense sentences allow us to say

might be people in Hell for whom there exists forever the open-ended option of changing so as to get out of Hell.

To use a common term for a view such as this, let's call the position that combines the Choice Model with loss of omniscience "Open Theism". To put the point as starkly as possible, must an Open Theist deny the coherence of the Final Judgment, the coherence of eschatology conceived as the doctrine of the Last Things?

To try to account for finality, the defender of openness will have to place restrictions on the range of autonomy. One's presence in Heaven or Hell might initially be something we choose, but the inability to leave will not. One might imagine a position where the option of leaving Hell is closed off, but it is hard

---

true things about the present, past tense about the past, and future tense about the future). The best reason to succumb here is a failure to see what's wrong with the argument for logical fatalism that appeals to such truths. Once we see what's wrong with that argument, there's no reason to think the openness of the future requires absence of truth-value for certain claims about the future.

Moreover, we should also resist temptation to run an analogy with omnipotence so that omniscience requires only knowing all that is knowable just as omnipotence only requires being able to do all that is possible. Proper care in developing the analogy with omnipotence takes one to the conclusion that omniscience doesn't require a being to know everything, only everything true, so a failure of exhaustive foreknowledge is simply a failure of omniscience. In brief, here's why. Omnipotence is a modal notion while omniscience is not. When the idea of doing everything is proposed as a requirement for omnipotence, two responses can be made. The first is that an omnipotent being only needs to be able to do what's possible, and the other that an omnipotent being only needs to be able to do what's actually done. Why prefer the former to the latter? The answer is simple: omnipotence is a modal notion, so the modal account is preferable. (Besides, the non-modal version gives us no reason to think that there are miracles God has the power to perform but doesn't.) So when the idea is proposed that an omniscient being has to know everything, two responses can be made as well. Well, actually three. One is in terms of knowing all that can be known (a modal restriction), and the other two are non-modal: knowing all that is true or knowing all that is actually known. Since omniscience is, in the relevant sense, a non-modal concept, we should prefer one of the latter two over the former. Knowing all that is actually known is too weak—God could be omniscient just by knowing the sum of everything his creatures know. So if we want a non-modal restriction, we should prefer the requirement of knowing all truths. (For a fuller statement of this argument, see Kvanvig (1989*b*).) Such a conclusion has a happy result in the face of the specter of skepticism. If we conceive of the gloomy scenario in which Peter Unger is right, that knowledge is really an absolute concept that cannot be instantiated, then everything is omniscient on either of the other two accounts, since everything would know everything that is known and everything that is knowable. Omniscience is supposed to be awe-inspiring, but if somehow it is philosophically conceivable that my coffee cup, without alteration of its intrinsic nature, displays it as much as God, then we have failed to grasp the nature of omniscience. (For a way of avoiding this nasty consequence, but without addressing the difficulties the analogy faces, see (van Inwagen 2008*b*).)

All this without yet mentioning the implications for those of us retaining a high view of Scriptural authority. Here I think especially of Psalm 139, and the most difficult part of it to explain away: "My very self you knew; my bones were not hidden from you, when I was being made in secret, fashioned as in the depths of the earth. Your eyes foresaw my actions; in your book all are written down; my days were shaped, before one came to be." The author may be waxing hyperbolic, of course, but the language is just the awe-inspiring sort any adequate account of God's nature ought to include.

to see how any point chosen will make the position better at dealing with the problem of Hell than the traditional retributivist understanding for which an alternative is thought to be needed.

To see why, consider the following attempt. We hold that presence in Hell is a result of one's choices, and in the process of choosing in such a way as to end up there, one turns oneself into the kind of person for whom it is psychologically impossible to choose to leave. This account of finality, however, has no advantages over Molinism. Either the impossibility in question is sufficient to imply Molinist counterfactuals, or it isn't. If it implies that one gets oneself into such a state that one wouldn't choose otherwise, then the view has no advantages over standard Molinism (unless, of course, it posits that there is no possible world with the history in question in which the person chooses otherwise—a claim fraught with explanatory problems of its own[9]). If, however, it posits a type of impossibility compatible with the claim that one counterfactually might still choose otherwise (i.e., the denial of a Molinist counterfactual), the sense of impossibility seems to lose all force whatsoever. What more could such a claim mean beyond the claim that one will permanently refuse the choice to leave? And if that is all there is, we have no finality beyond that posited by a merely accidental general truth concerning the future.

A more attractive option, then, is the universalist view, according to which God finally decides that if one has not freely chosen Heaven, there will come a time where one will be brought to Heaven against one's will. One will experience, in this sense, coercive redemption at some point.

This option allows that autonomy is valuable, but not so valuable as to allow the befalling of utter ruin. It achieves a mitigation of Hell by defending a mitigation of the value of autonomy.

There is a question here about whether this position counts as a version of the Choice Model, though ultimately the answer doesn't tell one way or another against the position. My initial inclination is to think it abandons the Choice Model. Even though initial presence in Heaven or Hell is a matter of what one chooses, one's eternal destiny may not be a matter of what one chooses. There is a way for the Open Theist to retain the Choice Model, however, by objecting to my description of their viewpoint given above, according to which we may be saved against our will. In place of my description, they might prefer to contrast libertarian freedom with its close cousin, compatibilist freedom. When God's patience with one's misuse of libertarian freedom is exhausted, they might say, he needn't act against our will. Instead, he might allow freedom to be retained, though in a different sense. He might remove libertarian freedom and replace it with compatibilist freedom, and put us then in the position that we will freely choose Heaven. "Choose," not in the libertarian sense, but in the compatibilist sense.

---

[9]These problems are discussed in "Losing Your Soul," this volume.

If universalists take this route, they will need to claim that the value of libertarian freedom exceeds that of compatibilist freedom. Without this addition, there is no reason to resist compatibilism from the very beginning. Given this value claim, however, this universalist does not need to say that God will ultimately save us against our will, or that autonomy will ultimately give way. Instead, only the most valuable sort will if need be, and since God does not know in advance whether any such need will exist, it remains an open question whether he will have to limit freedom in this way. Whether or not he does remove the most valuable freedom, however, it remains the case that one's eternal destiny is a matter of one's choices.

One ought to have some hesitation in thinking this way of retaining choice makes any difference if one has libertarian sensibilities. For such people—me, for example—the difference between doing something against one's will and doing it with compatibilist freedom is a difference that makes no evaluative difference. That is, libertarians may tend to view anything less than libertarian freedom as equally lacking in value, no matter how described. It might sound better to the ear to be able to describe it as if it were a kind of freedom, in the way that describing death in terms of going home is found comforting, but there is in fact no evaluative difference between doing something against one's will and doing it with compatibilist freedom.[10] But I will not press this point further.

There is a different point I want to press, however, and it is the point that this position confuses the fundamental distinction between Heaven and Hell. To move toward this conclusion, note first what this view will need to say about people who view Heaven as abhorrent and union with God as a loss of all that matters to them. The universalist who wishes to preserve finality says that God has a recipe for that. He can wipe out the present views and replace them with new ones and eliminate affective states and replace them with states of pure joy. The hope of the universalist is that God can do this indirectly, by exposing the individual to experiences aimed at prompting such responses in the way libertarians cherish. But since there is no guarantee that such will work, the only guarantee available is to do it more directly, by bringing about compatibilistically free responses of the sort in question.

Here's the fundamental problem with the view, and it arises from returning to fundamental distinction between Heaven and Hell, with the second being properly characterized in terms of a loss of the goods proffered by the first. On the present picture, the first involves the union and intimacy with God for which we were created. So the second involves a loss of this possibility. On the picture

---

[10]To say nothing, either, about the gross philosophical mis-step of taking various theories of X, turning the term for the theory into an adjective, and pretending as if there are now various kinds of X identifiable by prefacing 'X' with that adjective, thus getting, e.g., foundationalist justification and coherentist justification, real properties and nominal properties, as well as libertarian and compatibilist freedom. I understand such adjectival temptations, and also how to interpret them in terms of theories of the thing in question, but as used in the text, such an interpretation is barred. But then it is simply a confusion: the existence of a compatibilist theory of freedom does not at all imply that there is such a thing as compatibilist freedom.

just imagined, there are two classes of people. Both are described as being in
Heaven, but it is not clear why. There is no language of fire and brimstone, of
punishment and desert for the lesser crowd, but there is loss. There is the loss
of the pure and total fulfillment of the union of libertarianly autonomous being
with the Creator, the admitted goal of creation by both sides of the debate. Both
sides agree, that is, that the goal is a union with God that has its source in the
autonomous expression of the created in pursuing union with the divine, where
the notion of autonomy is understood in libertarian terms. Once this option is
foreclosed, something less valuable is put in its place, according to this version of
universalism, and thus this universalist says there will be second-class citizens in
Heaven. They, perhaps, won't be able to tell that they are not experiencing the
goal for which they were created, but the fact of the matter is that they won't
be experiencing the goal. This version of universalism is one in name only. It is
really a position that describes a much less troubling doctrine of Hell. Those in
Hell are not in pain; they are not tormented day and night forever. They may
not even understand their loss. But they have suffered a great loss—one that
falls outside the primary intention of the perfectly good and wise Creator. It is
incorrect to describe them as experiencing the joy of the beatific vision, since that
experience requires autonomous surrendering to the will of the Creator. Even if
they can't tell the difference between their experience and the experience of the
blessed, there is one, and at least God knows it. So this version of universalism
is not universalism at all; it is simply as strong a mitigation of the experience
of Hell that can be imagined. Much as the denizens of Descartes' evil demon
world cannot tell the difference between their world and ours, between their
illusory experience and our veridical experience, just so, those in Hell can't tell
the difference between their experience and the experience of the redeemed. But
those of us being presented with the two options know the difference. They have
suffered a great loss, but they just may not be able to tell that they have. When
we identify Heaven properly in terms of the obtaining of the great good for
which we were created, they are not in Heaven. They think they are, perhaps;
they can't tell that they are not, perhaps; but they are not in Heaven.

The only way to try to avoid this result is to deny that the goal of union with
God involves (libertarian) free choice at all. But then the question is why God
would have wanted freely chosen union in the first place. If it makes union more
valuable, more worthwhile, then there is a reason, and it would be hard to see
why God wouldn't have made that the goal. If it adds nothing to union, then
it is an arbitrary accretion. I have no objection to arbitrary elements in action,
but it makes no sense to cause pain and suffering to an individual for the sole
purpose of achieving some arbitrary goal that adds no value whatsoever to the
resulting end-state.

1.5   Ersatz Universalism and Quasi-Annihilationism

As a result, the Open Theism position described is not a version of universalism;
I'll call it *ersatz* universalism, or EU for short. EU admits that some are saved

and some are lost. It is just that the loss isn't experientially appreciable in the way conscious burning in a fire where the worm dieth not and the fire is not quenched would be.

Elsewhere, I've argued for a different picture where people ultimately get what they want, which is, for the damned, total and complete separation from God, which is annihilation (Kvanvig 1993). Which of these two views better addresses the problem of Hell? In my view, both rob the problem of Hell of its bite, differing only on the value question regarding libertarian freedom. The annihilation view of Hell treats the creation of libertarian freedom as completely serious; the Open Theist view of Hell treats it as less serious, viewing preference-satisfaction as outweighing it on the scales of value. Perhaps the difference here is between those of Kantian intuitions in the theory of value and those with utilitarian intuitions. From the perspective of those concerned about the problem of Hell, however, this is a pleasing result. The solution to the problem depends on the solution to the axiological dispute between Kant and his opponents: does value ultimately trace to the value of a good will, properly understood, or to the value of preference satisfaction? Here I'm with Kant, though naked of argument.

There's one difference though, a difference concerning the issue of finality with which I began. Ersatz universalism accounts for finality by allowing freedom to run loose only up to a certain point. At that point, God ends the openness of the future, and the fate of all is determined by his decree. The annihilation view does not have this option without embracing either the denial of PAP route or something like Molinism route. In this respect, it appears that EU has an advantage over annihilationism.

It is important to see where exactly the loss of finality happens on the annihilation view. Central to the view, as I've defended it, is the point that one should not always honor the choices of human beings, even when they are full adults. People are sometimes depressed, sometimes careless, and when they make momentous choices afflicted in these ways, intervention is surely warranted. As a result, merely choosing separation from God is not sufficient, on this view, for the choice to be honored. That leaves open the possibility that individuals might choose separation from God and yet never satisfy the conditions necessary for their choice to be honored, leaving the possibility of unending separation from God short of annihilation. Moreover, the unending separation would never, at any point, be final in any modally strong way. Finality results only when union with God is achieved or annihilation occurs; short of that is the intermediate state of, to put it a bit misleadingly, never-ending uncertainty.

The objection this view must address is whether, so conceived, this position founders on this failure of finality. All that is left is what I termed earlier "mere universal finality." It is not metaphysically impossible to leave Hell once there, nor logically, nor nomologically, nor even counterfactually impossible (given the assumption that Molinism won't work). All that remains is a mere accidental generalization—that those in Hell will never leave.

Merely universal finality can, of course, be added to the Choice Model, since it is compatible with it. The disturbing question, though, is on what basis it can be added. Given the assumption of the failure of Molinism, not even God can know what choices would result from presence in Heaven or presence in Hell. It may be a fact of the matter that no one will ever leave, but we couldn't have Molinist-like grounds for thinking so. So what grounds could we have? All that seems left is the mysterious position of David Hunt that God has simple foreknowledge, knowing the complete future as it actually is, but not knowing it on any Molinist basis (see Hunt (1993) as well as his contribution to Beilby and Eddy (2001)). Here the question of how God has such exhaustive foreknowledge is not answered. Perhaps it can be answered by endorsing the doctrine of God's eternity, supposing God to be outside time, so that there is no more perplexity about God knowing the future than about God knowing the past and present. We will all be forgiven for thinking of this option akin to having our complaints about being stuck in the dark answered by being forced to look directly at the sun.

1.6 Conclusion

We are left, then, with an unfortunate set of options. The Choice Model needs an account of finality, which can be secured by limiting the role of libertarian freedom in the story of our destiny or by losing libertarian freedom altogether. In this way, Calvinists and Open Theists are more like bedfellows than proponents of the extremes on the spectrum of positions on human destiny and its relationship to God's decision framework prior to creation. Without such limit or loss, we are left only with an Open Theism that offers nothing more than a shrug in response to the question of how finality is possible.

Molinism offers hope of something better. It needs no loss or limitation of libertarian freedom, and yet can offer an explanation of why and how such finality might obtain. In the past, I have defended this approach to issues involved in the freedom/foreknowledge controversy (Kvanvig 1986) as well as to questions concerning human destiny (Kvanvig 1993), but considering the difficulties cited above for the view, as well as other issues,[11] I am no longer convinced that Molinism is the solution to the problem raised here.

Even so, it is an example of the type of theory that provides the best hope for a satisfying solution to the problem of finality. What we need is some modal strength in the account of finality, not a mere accidental generalization. A satisfying account, we might put it, is one that maintains that we have a *destiny*, not merely a run of good or bad fortune. Moreover, in order to give libertarian freedom its due, this destiny cannot be one imposed by some outside force. And all this without forcing qualification on the idea that God knew what he was doing when he created the universe.

We thus stand in need of a better theory—a theory that can preserve the idea that we have a destiny, without limiting the scope of God's discernment of the

---

[11]These other issues arise in a number of other essays here, most especially in "A Dead-End for Molinism" and in "Creation, Deliberation, and Molinism," this volume.

decision framework involved in creation. I believe such an account can be found, though a full defense goes beyond the scope of this present essay.[12] A sketch of the approach, however, may provide some indication of how one can secure all the advantages of Molinism without the metaphysical and semantic quagmire where counterfactuals of freedom are found.

The key is to descend from the grand metaphysical mountaintop where Molinism is found to the more everyday environment of epistemic inference. Instead of worrying about the possibilities that Suzie might do a given action and might not as well, we might focus instead on whether a given set of circumstances provides adequate evidence for the conclusion that she will do one of the two. Only an overreaching skepticism would insist that because human beings are free in the libertarian sense, we can never have adequate grounds for concluding something about what a free individual will do in a given set of circumstances.

Moreover, only an indefensible limitation on a high conception of deity would insist that even though we can have such grounds, God cannot. One might legitimately worry that one will not be able to bridge the gap between the ordinary knowledge derived from everyday epistemic inference to the high and exalted infallible knowledge befitting a divine being, but two points are in order about this concern. The first is that this worry shouldn't be turned into a kind of "sour grapes" epistemology for the divine, according to which if infallible knowledge can't be had, better to have no knowledge at all. In short, failure to secure the essential omniscience of God (that it is simply impossible that he lack omniscience) should not be turned into an argument for abandoning omniscience itself. Second, there is some ground in the following for hope of being able to move from ordinary fallible knowledge for human beings to infallible knowledge for the divine. The story of human fallibility is intimately wedded to our cognitive limitations and the way in which, no matter how careful our inquiry, much remains beyond the purview of what is discovered. In this landscape of the undiscovered are found epistemic dragons galore, leaving in place the possible defeat of any opinion we have formed. But for a divine being with unlimited intellect, there is no such region in the epistemic landscape. Hence, any piece of information that could undermine the confirming power of some evidence on behalf of a given conclusion is information a perfect intellect will have already taken into account.

Such remarks do not come even close to providing an adequate answer to the worry in question, but they are offered only to provide some hope that an adequate answer can be developed. For those who have lost the Molinist faith, such a path is the only one left for maintaining that human beings have a destiny of their own making. To see more than darkly how this might be, we must move from the standpoint of the present essay, which is at one end of the story of creation, to the standpoint of the decision framework prior to creation itself.

We conclude, then, by noting what we must investigate in order to determine

---

[12]See "The Epistemic Theory of Creation," this volume.

whether a satisfactory account of human destiny can be developed. For libertarians, there is no satisfaction in approaches that require jettisoning a libertarian account of freedom. Nor is there any philosophical comfort in positions that insist on a destiny not of our own making. What remains is a land that Molinists claim and claim to have mapped. I doubt both the entitlement and the mapping skills, however, and thus hang my hopes on an epistemological approach that contrasts with the metaphysical machinations of Molinists.

ian account of freedom. Nor is there any philosophical comfort in positions that insist on a destiny not of our own making. What remains is a land that Molinists claim and claim to have mapped. I doubt both the entitlement and the mapping skills, however, and thus hang

2

LOSING YOUR SOUL

2.1 Introduction

The danger of losing one's soul so poignantly contrasted by Jesus with gaining the whole world has been put to philosophical use in recent times to help address the problem of Hell. That problem is a special case of the general problem of evil, and one way of formulating it concerns how an infinite punishment could be deserved for each and every wrongdoing, no matter how small or insignificant. The idea behind this appeal to Jesus's language is that one can lead a life that results in a loss of soul, and with this loss, comes the incapacity to escape Hell. This incapacity is the result, not of punishment imposed, but rather a straightforward consequence of the things people do to themselves. Our choices form a bent of character in us, and continual patterns of behavior in a certain direction can harden one to the point, one might claim, that certain choices are no longer open to one. Instead, in the arena in question one has become nothing more than a stimulus-response mechanism, where the mechanism always and forever is inclined in a certain direction. If that direction is hardened in opposition to God, this loss of soul would be responsible for the permanence of Hell, for in losing one's soul one has intentionally become the kind of person for whom no alternative choice is any longer possible. Since this incapacity is self-imposed, a solution to the problem of Hell in terms of what people freely choose might be able to be combined with an account of Hell that involves suitable finality, thus blocking one of the deepest difficulties facing approaches to the problem of Hell that focus on free choice.

Such a theory attempts to supplement the most popular way of abandoning the traditional conception of Hell. The traditional conception of Hell conceives of it fundamentally in terms of punishment, thereby yielding a straightforward (albeit troubling) account of why Hell is permanent. It is permanent because that is the form the punishment in question takes. Accounts that attempt to avoid this punishment model of Hell prefer to explain the nature of Hell in terms of the free choices of an individual among the available alternatives. If, however, presence in Hell is a result of choice, it becomes much more difficult to generate any permanence regarding presence in Hell. If being in Hell is a result of a choice, then a natural view to hold would be that residence in Hell is no more permanent than one's choices are, and those are open to change. In order to avoid this result, the Choice Model must be supplemented in some way or other, and one way to supplement it is in terms of the idea of losing one's soul.

The loss of soul theory, as I will construe it here, is an ambitious approach to the problem of explaining the falsity of universalism and the permanence of Hell. While it is true that any account of Hell can be supplemented with the idea of loss of soul, the theory I am concerned with here attempts to use the idea of loss of soul to shore up a difficulty faced by the Choice Model when universalism is rejected. To some, this problem has appeared to be so severe that it requires a limitation on the explanatory scope of the Choice Model, so that permanence is accounted for in other ways, even if initial presence in Hell is a matter of choice. A full defense of the loss of soul explanation insists that no such limitation is warranted, and that a better explanation of permanence is found in full commitment to the Choice Model combined with the loss of soul idea.

I will argue that the loss of soul theory has fairly good prospects for defending the insistence on a full commitment to an anti-universalist understanding of the Choice Model, but that it is less successful in defending the idea that loss of soul provides a good account of the permanence of Hell. I will begin, then, by defending the full commitment to the Choice Model that the loss of soul theory needs. After doing so, I will explain more precisely the idea of loss of soul that is needed by the theory in question, and then my reservations about it.

2.2   Limitations on the Choice Model

The loss of soul theory maintains a full commitment to the Choice Model while embracing an anti-universalist understanding of the implications of that model. In order to defend this stance, the loss of soul theorist needs to argue that universalism can't be defended without a limitation on the Choice Model, and that no such limitation is defensible.

The easier task would seem to be the first, given the understanding of freedom involved in the Choice Model. The notion of freedom involved is that of libertarian freedom, understood to involve some form of alternative possibilities available when one is free. In slogan form, the libertarian notion of freedom embraces the idea that to have a choice, one must have choices.[1] But as long as choices remain, one such option would seem to be interminable stubborn resistance to the end. The possibility of such sheer rebellion is difficult to resist.[2]

One might grant the force of this argument and still resist on epistemic grounds, allowing the possibility of sheer rebellion while arguing for the surety

---

[1] In the sense, of course, of free choices. Throughout, I ignore the idea of coerced choices and their relation to freedom, since that issue isn't involved in the appeal to choice involved in the Choice Model. There is a complication that could be introduced each time the notion of a choice is used here, to take account of Kane (1996), where some choices can be determined so long as they trace to sources which are not. This indirect connection between libertarian choices and choices for which we are responsible in spite of being determined is hereby noted, but I will not note this possibility in the text, since my discussion will always be compatible with this extended connection between free choices and choices for which we are responsible.

[2] The best attempt to resist this argument is developed by Thomas Talbott. See Talbott (1990, 2001, 1999). For counterargument, see Kvanvig (1993) and Walls (2004*a,b*).

that it won't happen.[3] Such an epistemic version of universalism begins by noting the deep love of God for his creation, and the lengths to which he will go to secure our salvation. These facts make it incredibly unlikely that any given person will resist God forever, it might be claimed, for given the resourcefulness and power of God, how could it be otherwise? If the likelihood of destruction is vanishingly small for each individual, it can also be vanishingly small for all, in which case it would follow that it is overwhelmingly likely that all will be saved. How likely? Well, nearly certain, or as close to certainty as most anything we believe. So it is as well-substantiated epistemically that all will be saved as most anything we believe, thus rendering universalism as a good a theological position as any reasonable person could ask for.

This account depends centrally on a detachment rule for probabilities. The idea is that in certain cases we can go from a justified belief in a high probability for p to a justified belief in p itself. I believe, however, that there is a defect in appealing to such a detachment rule. One can have adequate evidence for there being a high probability for p, and one can have adequate evidence for p itself. But there is no adequate rule that allows one to conclude that p is true based only on adequate evidence that the probability of p has exceeded a certain high threshold. No matter how high the threshold, so long as the probability is less than 1, it is possible to have adequate evidence for believing that the probability of p has exceeded that threshold and yet lack adequate evidence for p itself.[4]

This point should not be taken to imply that there can't be situations in which one both has adequate evidence for a high probability for p and for p itself. Nor does it imply that a given body of evidence can't be evidence for both a high probability for and for p itself, for that can happen when one has direct evidence for p itself of such a nature that allows us to infer a high probability for p from p itself. But when one gives an essentially statistical and probabilistic argument for a high probability for p, one can't rely on any general detachment rule that allows one to infer p from such a high probability. The failure of such a rule is one of the lesson of the lottery paradox: even if one's ticket will lose, remonstrance is the proper reaction to anyone asserting or believing that their ticket will lose on the basis of the probabilistic information alone. So, on the basis of the probabilistic argument above, the Limited Choice Theorist is not entitled to endorse the universalist conclusion, even if the argument shows that the universalist position is highly likely to be true.

It is true, however, that knowing that the probability of p is high, together with the absence of any defeating information for the inference from this high

---

[3]Here my understanding of the variety of universalist positions and the arguments for each have benefited from Keith DeRose's work on the subject and to conversations with him about his views. His work on the subject is available on his website.

[4]Standard approaches to the lottery and preface paradoxes note that while high probability alone is not sufficient for rational belief in the content in question, it is sufficient provided no defeating information is present. For discussion of this point, see Williamson and Douven (2006).

probability to p itself, would allow one to rationally believe p on the basis of its high probability. So the defender of this probabilistic route to universalism could revise the argument to add the codicil that there are defeaters for the inference in question.

This addition, however, adds a premise to the argument to which the universalist is not entitled. We can see this point by considering possible lotteries that differ from typical ones. In typical lotteries it is known that there will be exactly one winning ticket, but we can imagine a lottery in which all that is known is that nearly all of an extremely large number of tickets will lose. The lottery is set up in a way that leaves it an open question whether any ticket will win, but it is guaranteed that there will be very few winners, perhaps only one winner, if there are any winners at all. Even in such a situation, asserting or believing that one's ticket is a losing ticket is still unwarranted, so the inference from high probability to the claim that one's ticket is a losing ticket must be subject to defeat (on the assumption that high probability plus lack of defeat allows the inference to go through). These features of the unusual lottery situation mimic precisely the features present in this latest attempt to derive universalism from its high probability plus absence of defeat, so this latest attempt must contain a false premise as well. In particular, it must be false that there is no defeating information present regarding the inference from high probability to truth.

There is another problem with the argument that the loss of soul theorist may note as well. Note that the argument begins by concluding something about a given case, to the effect that in any given case, the likelihood of unending rebellion is very low. The loss of soul theorist may point out that estimating these chances is perilous. We may properly recognize the resourcefulness of God in accomplishing his purposes, but the extent of depravity at the core of the human heart is difficult to comprehend. Without assessing its contribution, we run the risk of drawing a probabilistic conclusion on the basis of mere partial information. We know of stories–in Scripture, for example—of God accomplishing his purposes using those obstinately opposed to these purposes, but the extent to which these examples are representative remains inscrutable to us.

Moreover, even if we grant the claim of low probability in a given case, there is still the agglomeration step that is needed. That is, we must get from probability in a given case to probability for the conjunction of all cases as well. As is well known, it is rare for the probability of a conjunction to be as high for a conjunction as for the conjuncts. It is possible that it is as high, but it is not likely to be as high.

So the probabilistic argument faces three issues. The first is the inscrutability problem for probability in a given case. The second is the need for a defense of the agglomeration step. These two difficulties do not present the kind of case against the argument that arises from the third difficulty, however. The third difficulty arises concerning a needed detachment rule—a rule that allows us to detach p from a high probability for p, and such rules founder because of the epistemic paradoxes such as lottery and preface. The problem is that such a justification for p is not strong enough to allow asserting or believing p because, as we may put it, it is not strong enough to put oneself in a position to know that p is true (even when it is true).

One may try to escape this last problem by remarking that theology is not a domain in which knowledge is possible anyway, so we should allow the detachment rule in spite of having insufficient grounds for epistemic justification—the justification necessary for knowledge. Or perhaps one might try to hold that one's attitude toward theological propositions is not one of belief at all, but some weaker state, so that one shouldn't be held to any strict rules about propriety of belief.

Regarding the former maneuver, I don't think it will help. Even in domains where skepticism is appropriate, arguments that must use the detachment rule in question are inadequate. The domain in question sets the standard of adequate defense for claims in that area, and any defense relying on a detachment rule will fall below such a standard. The rule for assertion and for the kind of justification needed for it may depend on context in this way, but it doesn't change the way in which arguments that rely essentially on the detachment rule are not good enough arguments in the context. Remonstrance will still be a legitimate response to the assertion or belief of such a conclusion, when it appears to rely on such an unrestricted detachment rule.

Perhaps if the issue were one of hope rather than belief, this difficulty would disappear. For the standards that need to be met to make hope reasonable are much lower than for belief. But the issue here isn't so much which psychological attitude is in question regarding theological propositions. Instead, we are interested in the question of which theological propositions have adequate arguments for them and which do not. We are not inquiring about the justification of particular psychological states of any individual at all. What it takes for an argument (or body of evidence) to be adequate may depend on the particular subject matter in question, but once that issue is settled, the issue of justification is one concerning the claims in question, not the psychological attitudes of those endorsing or denying the claims in question.

As a result, we should conclude that this epistemic defense of the surety of universalism fails, and with it the attempt to keep universalism without imposing some limits on the Choice Model. Restricted appeals to the Choice Model admit that though the ideal is for an individual to cooperate freely with God in the process of redemption, the nature of choice is such that no guarantee of success is possible. As such, for finality to be achieved, God must at some point end the uncertainty either by damning some forever or choosing to redeem a person against their will if need be. The former options include consigning some to permanent existence in Hell forever or annihilating them. But since an attraction to the Choice Model is motivated by dissatisfaction with the more traditional Punishment Model, these views do not sit well with many who endorse the Choice Model, leading some to prefer coerced redemption over coerced damnation for those who refuse to cooperate. The value of freedom is outweighed by the disvalue of eternal separation from God, and so redemption may occur against our will.

Loss of soul theorists join other anti-universalist adherents of the Choice Model in rejecting this limitation on the role of freedom in an understanding of the afterlife, claiming that whatever conditions allow justified overriding of human freedom, they are not conditions present in the story of salvation. All such anti-universalist theories need to be able to give grounds for rejecting such limited endorsements of the Choice Model, and loss of soul theorists need such grounds in order to motivate the explanatory role they see for the notion of a loss of soul in explaining the permanence of presence in Hell. Here I believe they have two bases from which to develop such an argument. The first issue concerns the respective values of freedom and existence, and which takes precedence when they conflict. In Kvanvig (1993) I argued that there is intuitive support for freedom taking precedence over that of existence when we are considering fully autonomous individuals. It is instructive to note in this regard that those who argue for preservation of being over honoring freedom often resort to examples involving children and their parents, where it is obvious that parents ought to prevent utter ruin from befalling their children rather than allow them full freedom of choice. Once we reach the level of full autonomy, however, the demand for intervention is no longer universal and unqualified. Instead, there is strong support for non-intervention in the plans and purposes of other individuals in certain circumstances, even when they are mistaken and when disaster is quite predictable. The mere fact that disaster will ensue justifies persuasion and intervention, but it is far from clear that it justifies outright coercion in those who have rational and firm opinions that their lives are their own and any disaster that results is one they are willing to embrace.

There is a second argument as well—one concerning the relationship between sin, salvation, and the will. The condition of humankind to which God's redemptive plan is aimed is intimately involved with our will, with the story of the fallenness of humanity intimately connected with an inclination to take the love, honor, respect, and devotion that rightly belong to God and attach it to other things instead, most especially to attach it to self. The solution to this problem requires a change in human beings that results in the fulfillment of what the Westminster Catechism describes as the purpose for humanity: to love God and enjoy Him forever. The story of Scripture is, of course, that in a very real sense we cannot do anything to accomplish such a change, and that the direct intervention of God is required in order for this purpose to be fulfilled. The important question, however, is not whether we have the power to accomplish such a change, but whether the change can be accomplishment independent of any activity of our wills. It is true that if one refuses to endorse a libertarian conception of freedom, one can speak of God's causally necessitating the will in a certain direction and insist that no contradiction results. In the context of the Choice Model, however, such talk cannot be tolerated: we here assume a libertarian understanding of the will and so cannot speak of such necessitation. If the Heavenly experience, the beatific vision, involves loving God and enjoying him forever, it is very hard to see how properly to conceive of this love apart from some free exercise of the will, at least in terms of our acquiescing to the aims and purposes of God. Central to the fallenness of humanity is our rebellion against God, and reconciliation is not a concept that makes any sense apart from some role for the will to play in the process, even if only in terms of acquiescing to the grace offered. Even when the conversion experience is modeled on that of St. Paul on the Damascus road, there is still the acquiescing of the will displayed in asking, "Who are you, Lord?" and getting up from the ground to go into the city as directed. Any love that doesn't involve its source in some such expression of autonomy is not, it would seem, the proper sort of love of God.

We reach the same point when we ask what is involved in loving God with one's whole heart, soul, mind, and strength. Those who refuse to endorse a limitation of the Choice Model in order to secure the truth of universalism can maintain plausibly that there is no beatific vision, no Heavenly experience, apart from such love of God, and such love is impossible without the engagement of the will, at least in terms of acquiescing to the impulse to adore and worship the source of all goodness, beauty, and truth. No contradiction results from adding to the positive story concerning the conditions that lead to total conversion that these conditions may be accompanied by sheer rebellion to the end. If so, however, the conditions themselves do not explain the Heavenly experience apart from the activity of free will. Such a conclusion should not surprise in the least for those of libertarian inclinations, since it should not surprise us at all to discover that the turning from a focus on oneself to a focus that includes another, a turning that is central to the nature of love, involves an expression of ourselves conceived as autonomous beings. This point about love is true at the most mundane level, whether the love is directed at a pet, or one's children, or more abstractly at the environment of our planet. Love, or at least the kind of love most worth experiencing, is by its very nature an expression of autonomy. Hence, love of God, of the exalted sort involving one's whole heart, soul, mind, and strength, paradigmatically requires such a source in autonomy.

There is an alternative account that contrasts with this one, however. The Calvinist picture takes us in an entirely different direction, toward the language of vessels created for redemption and destruction (and universalism when we add that God is soft-hearted in love toward humanity rather than hard-hearted). It is instructive to note, however, that Calvinism does not pretend to any attraction for libertarianism. Theological determinism is the coin of the realm as far as Calvinism is concerned, and the argument above about the nature of love and its relationship to autonomy will be either denied or recast in compatibilist terms by Calvinists. But the loss of soul theorist in search of an argument for refusing to place limitations on the Choice Model can take refuge here in pointing out that one shouldn't waver between two opinions here: one should either cleave to the truth of libertarianism and its understanding of human nature and the autonomy central to meaningful relationships or it should deny this truth and cleave to the other. Hate the one and love the other, or despise the one and be devoted to the other.

The double-minded might press harder, however, insisting on a more compelling argument why we can't have it both ways. Why can't we have autonomy connected with love *in the usual and ordinary case*, but deny that the connection is essential, as the loss of soul theorist needs to claim? The proper response here is that once a plausible account connecting autonomy and love has been presented, an opponent of the view needs to present an alternative account of what it means to love God with one's whole heart, soul, mind, and strength that doesn't involve autonomy if a limitation on the Choice Model is going to be sustained. Merely suggesting that the connection between autonomy and love is common but inessential doesn't give any reason to doubt the account of the relationship between the two that the loss of soul theorist needs. Moreover, the loss of soul theorist can take solace in the following thought experiment. If we can be saved against our will, why not picture Heaven to include the moral equivalent of the sullen teenager, stuck in the perceived unhappiness of home but lacking the resources to leave? Why, that is, must those in Heaven *enjoy* it? The answer to these questions, the loss of soul theorist will plausibly insist, is that the central fact about the language of Heaven and Hell is that it is about an unsurpassable quality of experience rather than inhabiting a certain locale, and that the experience of Heaven requires turning from self toward God. Such turning is essentially an expression of an autonomous agent rather than that of an automaton.

This position, the loss of soul theorist can plausibly insist, limits the significance of freedom does not actually succeed in getting to the conclusion of universalism, but instead only minimizes the disaster that befalls those in Hell forever. To see why, a bit of background is necessary. Note first that one way to approach the problem of Hell is to minimize the nature of the disaster that befalls an individual who ends up in Hell forever. One primary attempt at such mitigation is annihilationism, which holds that one doesn't suffer in Hell forever and ever, but instead ceases to exist altogether. Such a position counts as a *mitigation* of Hell only by way of contrast with a truly horrible description of Hell such as is found in Jonathan Edwards' sermon "Sinners in the Hands of an Angry God." Notice that if we contrast capital punishment with life in prison, the usual moral judgment is that the first is by far worse than the second. So if annihilation is preferable to eternal, conscious existence in Hell, it must be so because of special features associated with the kind of eternal existence in question.

So one way to try to make progress on the problem of Hell is to re-describe the disaster of ending up in Hell. One might describe Hell in less horrific terms, or one may hope to find some third state that counts as being in neither Heaven nor Hell. When a theorist talks of forced presence in Heaven, the loss of soul theorist may claim, the proper way to understand such language is in one of these two ways, either as a re-description of Hell or as an attempt to find some third alternative that involves neither the full joy of Heaven nor the disaster of

Hell.

It is not hard to see why we should reject both such possibilities. The latter understanding can be resisted by insisting that a proper understanding of the logical space of possibilities finds only two: one is either united with God forever or one isn't. The first is Heaven, the second Hell. When one thinks of Heaven and Hell in geographic terms, it is easy to see how to generate the desire for a third alternative to Heaven and Hell, since if these are but two postal addresses, the possibility of other postal addresses is easy to imagine. But when one's conception of the afterlife is a relational matter with Heaven involving a beatific vision and enjoyment of the divine, Hell is properly understood as the contrast of such a relationship. Hence, even if Heaven is a place with pearly gates and streets of gold, one still can't be in Heaven by passing through the gates and walking on streets of gold.

Given these points, the loss of soul theorist can point out that the temptation to talk of necessitated presence in Heaven is the temptation to try to solve the problem of Hell through mitigation. Being in the land of pearly gates and streets of gold isn't Heaven, but it is a place where God could, perhaps, put those who reject him. In such a case, Hell wouldn't be the horrific place of the language of weeping and gnashing of teeth, but it would still be Hell. For it wouldn't be the Heavenly experience of the beatific vision, of eternal union with God that involves loving him with all of one's heart, soul, mind, and strength.

So a limited appeal to the Choice Model is one a loss of soul theorist can find substantial arguments for rejecting. Moreover, these arguments are not limited in their appeal in such a way that one would already need to be a card-carrying loss of soul theorist to accept them. Once we secure this conclusion together with the earlier conclusion that universalism can't be secured without some limitation on the Choice Model, the loss of soul position is especially attractive, since it hold forth the promise of explaining why presence in Hell is permanent even though such presence is not a matter of an imposed punishment on a person but rather a consequence of the choices made by such an individual. Central to this explanation is the idea of loss of soul, to the clarification of which I now turn.

2.3   The Idea of Losing One's Soul

Whereas in the words of Jesus the idea of losing one's soul is contrasted with gaining the whole world and is thus best understood in terms of a contrast between a focus on temporal versus eternal goods, the loss of soul theory attempts to characterize the idea of loss of soul in more personal and psychological terms involving the notion of libertarian freedom. It maintains that, through a series of choices, one can get oneself in a position where one no longer has choices, where all options but one are impossible. As such, it is important to distinguish the loss of soul explanation of permanence in Hell from other accounts. Molinist accounts, for example, will appeal to Molinist counterfactuals of freedom in order to explain permanence in Hell. Both accounts agree on full commitment to the Choice Model, but the Molinist explains the permanence of Hell in terms that the loss of soul theory rejects. The Molinist claims that for each person, and each possible set of events and experiences, there is a fact of the matter about whether that person would acquiesce to the Divine invitation were that person and set actualized together. Permanence in Hell is thus explained in terms of the truth of what we might call *disheartening* counterfactuals of freedom: counterfactuals about eternal resistance to the divine invitation, counterfactuals shown to be true by one's actual resistance.[5] There is a form of Molinism, according to which maximally effective efforts to secure presence in Hell are not needed, but only God's knowledge of the disheartening counterfactual itself, but there is also a more defensible form of Molinism that involves conditions as effective as any could be for securing acquiescence—a form that is, in my opinion, much easier to defend.

The loss of soul theorist (the LOST), however, eschews appeals to counterfactuals of freedom in favor of the idea that a person can lose their soul and thus become incapable of leaving Hell. Such a theorist maintains that an account of Hell is unacceptable on which it remains an open question whether or not any remain in Hell forever. The loss of soul theory takes Scriptural authority seriously when it speaks of the final judgment, of the final separation of sheep and goats, of the final *eschaton* toward which all of history is headed. Such a teleological conception of the universe is at odds with a picture of an afterlife that is simply unending and on which the elevator between Heaven and Hell sits forever with open doors to allow one-way, and perhaps two-way, traffic.

For such an explanation to succeed, we need an account of the notion of losing one's soul that makes it impossible for one to leave Hell once there. According to the loss of soul theory, freedom always operates within a limited sphere, and the sphere can expand and contract, based on prior history. For example, without athletic training, deciding whether or not to dunk the basketball after leaping toward the basket from the free throw line is not open to us. Needless to say, for nearly everyone the decision isn't open even with athletic training, but for some it is. In this way, prior history can expand the range of free action available to a person.

The range of free action can contract as well. Some obvious ways in which this is true involve the process of aging. Even the most gifted athletes suffer decline of abilities, and thus come to lack the capacity to dunk a basketball. Moreover, not just degeneration can be responsible for lost abilities, but sequences of choices can be as well. Those whose lifestyle is nearly completely sedentary are in the process of making physical activity of various sorts more and more difficult, and the process in question leads to a point where many common physical movements have become impossible.

---

[5]This is the explanation I proposed in Kvanvig (1993, pp. 156-158). I no longer endorse this account, and would substitute for it an account in terms of the epistemic conditionals central to the theory of creation presented in the essay contained in this volume, "The Epistemic Theory of Creation."

Loss of soul theorists claim that what is true of external, physical reality is also true of the internal psychological realm. The process of character formation can make it easier to desire the good and the right, but it can also make it easier to resist. As the process continues, a description just like that given above about sedentary lifestyles is appropriate: the end point toward which the process is headed is one where the patterns of desire and preference have become hardened to the point that any other desiring or preferring is impossible.

The loss of soul theory results from applying this general idea to the afterlife itself. Regarding the greatest good possible for humans being, the experience of Heaven, we may conceive of the situation in which a hardening of desire and preference has occurred to such an extent that the choice of Heaven is no longer possible. To be in such a position is to have lost one's soul. In that situation, there is nothing one can do or choose or decide or intend, including no sequence of choices, that would make possible the experience of Heaven. That option, because of what one has become, is foreclosed forever. One has lost one's soul, and in losing one's soul one has become a person for whom Hell is eternal and the Final Judgment final in terms of something persons do to themselves.

This characterization of the idea of loss of soul must be refined in order to avoid an obvious objection. The objection begins by noting that in the physical realm, if an ability is lost through disuse, it can be restored by miraculous intervention. Just so, if one's character development has led one to the place where one can no longer desire a certain thing or prefer it to something else, miraculous intervention could restore such a possibility. So when it comes to the point of trying to explain the finality of Hell, loss of soul alone seems an insufficient explanation, since it would seem to need to be accompanied by the additional claim that God refuses to intervene miraculously to restore the lost possibility.

To avoid this objection, the loss of soul theory must distinguish between two ways of arriving at the end point at which the ability is lost. One way to progress toward that end is to make certain choices that lead, via the laws of nature and logic, to the end point in question. In such a case, one need not be choosing the end point as the intentional object of one's behavior. It is not the goal toward which one is aiming, but is rather the consequence of a sequence of such choices. In other cases, however, one's choices aim directly at such an end point. The loss of soul theory must focus on the latter possibility in order to avoid the objection just voiced, for if the result is unintended it is hard to see how the choices alone can explain finality. If, however, the loss of capacity in question is an intended consequence of the sequence of choices, if it is part of a person's plan, then the loss of soul theorist can appeal to the value of autonomy to complete the explanation of why divine restoration of the possibility in question would be inappropriate.

The idea of such intentionally chosen loss of possibility is difficult to imagine, and one may resist the theory simply because it is so difficult to imagine. To rebut such resistance, it is worth taking a look at an example that comes very close to this possibility; an example found in Cormac McCarthy's recent novel in dramatic form, *The Sunset Limited*. The novel is a dialogue between a black minister and a white professor—a professor whose suicide attempt has been thwarted by the rescue efforts of the minister. The minister views it as his mission from God to help the professor. In the end, the minister fails, and is left perplexed and in emotional turmoil. After being pressed persistently by the minister to talk, the professor finally agrees to talk and explains his decision for suicide, which he does in a sequence of remarks:

> Well, here's my news Reverend. I yearn for the darkness. I pray for death. Real death. If I thought that in death I would meet the people I've known in life I don't know what I'd do. That would be the ultimate horror. The ultimate despair. (McCarthy 2006, p. 135).

When the preacher asks whether he wants to see his own mother, the professor answers,

> No I don't. . . . I want the dead to be dead. Forever. And I want to be one of them. Except that of course you can't be one of them. You can't be one of the dead because what has no existence can have no community. No community. My heart warms just thinking about it. (McCarthy 2006, pp. 135-136).

In order to understand the professor, it is crucial to note that he welcomes the loss of community, and does not think of his view of things as pessimistic at all. There is a kind of existential despair that is based on the belief that we are alone in the universe and that death is preferable to it. The professor does not suffer from such despair. To spend eternity in community, with his mother and other acquaintances, would be the ultimate despair, for it would involve "start[ing] all of that all over, only this time without the prospect of death to look forward to." (McCarthy 2006, p. 135).

The professor longs for a church that would, instead of preparing one for more life, prepare one for death (non-existence). He suffers from alienation, saying about other humans, "Do I see myself in him? Yes. I do. And what I see sickens me." (McCarthy 2006, p. 138). But it is an alienation, not in opposition to his fundamental desires, but rather an expression of them. All fellowship is, for him, a fellowship of pain: it is its intrinsic character, not an unfortunate accretion to something good in itself. He says,

> And if that pain were actually collective instead of simply reiterative then the sheer weight of it would drag the world from the walls of the universe and send it crashing and burning through whatever night it might yet be capable of engendering until it was not even ash. (McCarthy 2006, p. 137).

The professor thus claims to have achieved the insight that the goodness of community and fellowship is but an illusion, not in some contingent fashion but by its very nature. It is for this reason that he seeks a community, a "church", that prepares one for death.

Here is a depiction of the sort the loss of soul theorist takes to exemplify the possibility in question. It is a possibility of self-chosen ends—ends which result in the loss of the possibility of choosing otherwise. What the minister encounters is an individual who has become immune to the efforts of the minister, since for every good thing or rewarding experience the minister can point to, the professor has an interpretive scheme and nature that leads to aversion. A central part of this possibility is conceptual, for the professor has come to view things in a certain way and has developed a conceptual framework that is completely resistant to the goods of which the minister speaks. But another part is affective. The professor is not in a state of resignation regarding his preference for death. He doesn't partly want to cease to exist and somehow wish it were otherwise or in some way regret the desire at the same time. His alienation from things is not tinged with any such sense of loss. His despising of community, whether with other humans or God, is complete and thorough. Nor are these affective and conceptual features of his condition one's that surprise him or were unintended in any way: they are aspects that he embraces with his whole being, viewing them as central to what he is rather than as some optional accretion to his fundamental nature. The minister laments the professor's sad condition, but the professor says the worst thing should not be thought of as the situation the professor is in, but something else instead.

The minister finds this remark perplexing and inquires about what could possibly be worse. The professor replies, "Rage is really only for the good days." (McCarthy 2006, p. 139). What upsets the professor is not being in the condition he is in, but in experiencing good days that, presumably, present temptations to think and feel otherwise. Attempts to get him to see the error of his ways lead to rage, and anything suggesting that he is wrong in thought or attitude is interpreted as fundamentally misleading.

Such a character at least comes very close to exemplifying what the loss of soul theorist needs—a character whose resistance is complete and the elimination of which would violate his autonomy. I offer the example as an example only, and not as a decisive argument in favor of the position the loss of soul theorist needs. Moreover, those who remain unconvinced either that the dispositions in question are unalterable or that autonomy need not be honored in this particular case will find fodder for their view in some of the remarks that the professor makes.[6] The professor is alienated, especially from his own mother, and opponents of the lost soul description here may suggest the need for counseling (though, of course, the professor has already tried counseling, to no effect). In addition, there are still a few signs of affective dissonance. The professor's heart "warms" at the thought of non-existence, and yet he describes his view as one of having recognized the "futility" of everything. He is also firmly committed to atheism, and one might insist that it is open question what would become of the professor

---

[6] It is worth noting that interpretations that look for such in the professor do some violence to authorial intent. The minister laments at the end that God has not given him the words to help the professor, but has instead given the words to the professor. The minister pleads for reassurance from God, then claims that no response is fine as well, but succumbs again to the need for an answer. It is fairly clear that the "professor of darkness" is the hero here and not the minister—a point of view consistent with the McCormacian corpus, which is nothing if not full of darkness.

if this viewpoint were to change. Such points would certainly be well taken, and further discussion could go on quite a bit about what the professor would be like once efforts at therapy and removal of cognitive and affective dissonance had occurred. But the point of the example is to give some substance to the idea of how a person can come to be in the position that the loss of soul theory claims is possible, and the example does a good job of generating some plausibility for the claim that such a possibility exists, even if it does not fully establish the existence of such a possibility.

It is on this idea of losing one's soul and the role it is claimed to be able to play in accounting for finality that I wish to turn a critical eye. I will argue in the next section that the theory fails.

2.4   Problems for the Loss of Soul Theory

The idea of losing one's soul is a special case of the idea of lost abilities, and the relevant lost ability in the present context is the ability to *choose*. The loss is a loss of freedom, rather than the loss of an ability to express the will in a given way. The will itself becomes constricted in its domain of operation, unlike cases of other lost abilities, such as the ability to dunk a basketball. That ability is lost, even though the ability to try, to will, to choose, is not. To have lost one's soul is to have lost the ability to choose in favor of God and against whatever focus on self (or nothingness, as in the case of the professor discussed above) results in the ultimate disaster of losing out on the greatest good of loving God and enjoying him forever. This idea of losing one's soul involves two aspects—one being the conclusion that one's history can take a shape such that the choice for God is foreclosed forever, and the other being the explanation of how a history can take such a shape. The former aspect we have already seen; the latter aspect involves an appeal to psychological realities. These realities, unlike the physical, degenerative story about losing the ability to leap, involve a story about how habits of choice develop, about how a sequence of choices can make a further choice psychologically impossible, and how acquiescing to the force of strong desires can make one's subsequent behavior nothing more than a war among desires, with the strongest always winning.[7] So there is both the conclusion claimed about what happens when one loses one's soul—that losing one's soul implies a restriction on the range of freedom so that the choice of Heaven is no longer available—and the argument or explanation as to why losing one's soul implies this conclusion.

A good place to begin critically assessing this approach is at the end. The end point in question, is, of course, the point at which the individual *can't* choose any more for Heaven. There are two points worth questioning about this end point. We should note first that the loss of soul theorist is assuming that the end point can actually be reached, but the description given of how this end

---

[7]This latter notion of behavior being nothing but a war among competing desires for those who have lost their soul is Richard Swinburne's. See Swinburne (1983).

point can be reached doesn't guarantee that it can be reached. Consistent with the description of habit formation and increasing difficulty of certain choices because of the effects of prior history is the idea that such a process can bring one closer and closer to such an end state, making it increasingly difficult to choose to act out-of-character, but that the possibility of acting out-of-character always remains, regardless of how unlikely it has become. In short, we should wonder why the end point cited isn't simply a boundary that can be approached but never reached, instead of a point that can be reached.

One might attempt an argument for the logical or metaphysical possibility of losing one's soul by insisting that there is no contradiction implied or entailed by the idea of character fixation progressing to the point of impossibility rather than merely approaching it. Such a claim would have to be pitted against the alternative claim, that no contradiction is implied or entailed by the claim that the possibility of acting out-of-character always remains, no matter how unlikely. One of these claims must be false, since they contradict each other, and hence the appeal to the failure to imply some obvious contradiction in each case cannot be judged to be decisive in favor of either claim.

This concern may seem to be overdone philosophical nitpicking, but it is not. Merely describing a process that has as its logical end point the loss of soul doesn't properly explain the finality of Hell unless those in Hell have actually lost their souls. And, as is obvious, one hasn't lost one's soul unless it is possible to do so. Moreover, the history of mathematics ought to have sensitized us by now to the possibility that a sequence can approach a certain end point but never actually get there. For example, the sequence of fractions having the same number as numerator and the denominator squared as the next step in the sequence approaches zero but never gets there. Finally, an intentionally chosen progression aimed at achieving such an end point is not anything we've ever witnessed, and so the interpretation of the process in terms of the possibility of achieving the end point is in need of defense.

Moreover, there is a way of modeling the idea that the end point can be approached but not achieved. On this model, we organize affective (or cognitive) states into levels, with base-level states being the typically outward-directed desires, preferences, etc. of ordinary experience, such as the desire for chocolate, a good espresso, or a nice evening with friends. Meta-level states would then be states that involve lower-level affective states, such as the desire to desire to be good.

In the case of ordinary human beings, the hierarchical structure of levels of affective states is quite limited. Perhaps the ordinary human being has two levels of affective states, and perhaps some even have three, but it would be implausible to suggest that every human being has affective states of every level whatsoever. Central to our intellectual capacities, however, is the capacity to reflect on our own affections, to take attitudes both cognitive and affective toward items lower in the hierarchical structure in question. In so doing, we begin a process with the possibility of altering the items in the hierarchical structure. In reflecting about our desires, we may come to see them as perverted or as lacking in some other way, and in so seeing them, begin a process of extinguishing them. Part of the process of extinction may require assistance from others, either human or divine, and recognition of this fact may prompt requests for such help. This point, however, doesn't undermine the characterization given above of the process, but is rather just a particular instance of it, since what is possible to change needn't be the same as what is possible to change given help from others.

Such a model provides resources for resisting the idea that the end point of impossibility toward which the process of character entrenchment is directed can ever be reached. For the entrenchment in question is not plausibly thought of as functioning in such a way as to preclude forever some critical reflection assessment of the items in the hierarchical structure itself. No matter how much reflection has occurred and no matter how much integration and coherence among the items in the hierarchy, the possibility of reflection on such items always remains possible, and no matter what efforts of habituation and entrenchment have occurred in a person, they cannot have occurred intentionally with respect to anything more than levels in the hierarchy that are non-empty (since the intention in question would populate any level at which it aims by falling into the next meta-level). So whatever entrenchment we aim at can only close off options within the presently existing realms of the hierarchy, and thus cannot succeed in closing off further "metamind" possibilities. So long as such higher levels of reflection remain possible, even processes that get closer and closer to the end point of impossibility of choosing otherwise cannot actually arrive at that end point, for that would require foreclosure of further metamind operations.

I do not offer this model as an obviously correct account, or even one that I've provided an argument for. I offer it for purposes of illustration, to forestall the idea that only persnickety quibbling could lead one to claim that the end point of impossibility could be approached but not reached. Such an account has some attractions, and that is all that is needed at this point to make the worry in question a substantial one.

The loss of soul theorist might insist, though, that even given this hierarchical story, the possibility exists of getting oneself in a position where choices become impossible in part because one has devoted oneself as well to realizing the loss of metamind reflective capacities. On this scenario, one gets oneself in the position of being able to choose union with God by a history of such choices together with a history of choices aimed at extinguishing any possibility of second-guessing concerning the future one aims to create for oneself.

Such a response reveals some strain on the loss of soul theory, since the individual pursuing this strategy is so highly unusual. All of us are familiar with the way in which habits foreclose possibilities, but the type of reflective attempt needed to sustain the loss of soul diagnosis is highly contrived at best. It isn't hard to see how to extinguish particular types of reflection—just think about training regimens aimed at extinguishing obsessive/compulsive behavior patterns. If a person can't leave the house without checking the lock on the front door dozens of times, one might attempt to restore ordinary behavior patterns by extinguishing the habit of reflecting on the state of the front door. Doing so will involve higher-order metamind processing, such as noticing immediately when thoughts about the front door are beginning to creep into one's thinking, and consciously choosing to stop thinking about such things. Such a way of proceeding, however, won't help the loss of soul theorist, since the loss of soul theorist needs extinction of the entire hierarchy of metamind operations regarding the issue of union with God. Even if we can make sense of patterns of choices aimed at extinguishing any particular reflective level in the hierarchy, that doesn't show that we can make sense of the idea of a pattern of choices aimed at extinguishing the entire hierarchy. Since it is this latter possibility that the loss of soul theorist is invoking, it is fair to conclude that much more by way of argument is needed to sustain the hope that there is a series of choices that can explain both the loss of an ability to choose union with God while at the same time explaining the loss of an ability to reflect, at any level whatsoever, on the wisdom of the path one has chosen (and on the wisdom of losing this ability to reflect, etc.).

Here it is worth pressing a point about the epistemology of modal claims. One doesn't become entitled to a possibility claim simply because no contradiction has been shown to result from a claim made. Clearly, the loss of soul theorist is entitled to claim that no contradiction has been shown regarding this complicated claim that I'm calling contrived. Loss of soul theorists cannot rest content with claiming only that no contradiction has been uncovered in their position. What they need is a positive defense of the possibility that they claim exists, and the difficulties cited in the last paragraph count as some evidence that the theoretical apparatus envisioned may be nothing more than an impossible figure of the sort featured in many Escher drawings. In short, possibility claims don't come free. Moreover, the contrived nature of the speculation, failing to fit with the ways in which conditioning can stop higher-order metamind processing, counts against the modal claim, providing inductive grounds for thinking that isn't such a possibility of the sort needed by loss of soul theorists. Hence, whatever probative value is found in noting that no contradiction has been found is defeated by inductive evidence that no such possibility is there to be found.

This point leads to my second complaint against the view. Even if we grant the possibility claim in question, we should ask what sense of possibility is involved. The description is that, at the end point, one can no longer choose for Heaven, but what kind of 'can' is this?

The kind that comes to my mind first is psychological impossibility. Weaker notions of impossibility surely won't do, as when our students say things like, "I just can't learn to do proofs." It isn't psychologically impossible for them to learn, and maybe what they say simply isn't true at all. But there is a charitable reading of what they say, that given all of their other interests and desires, and their lack of interest in learning proof theory, it can't be done. Since all of these factors could change, however, the kind of impossibility won't be of any use to the loss of soul theorist. So a better suggestion is that the choosing in question has to become psychologically impossible for the individual in order for that individual to have lost their soul.

The problem here is that psychological impossibility isn't the right sort of impossibility. For it to be the right kind of impossibility, it would need to be true that if it is psychologically impossible to choose to leave Hell, then a person is no longer free to do so. The notion of freedom that is relevant here is that of libertarian theory, and the relevant contrast to libertarian freedom is causal determination.

The inference from psychological impossibility to causal impossibility is, however, invalid. Here's why. In the special sciences, every law will have to have a *ceteris paribus* clause to cover cases where interference occurs on the basis of factors outside the system being characterized by the laws in question. For example, whatever laws govern the operation of an ordinary television set do not take into account what happens when the TV is hit with a sledge hammer. Instead, they describe how things operate, holding fixed non-interference from forces outside the systemic factors involved in the ordinary operations of such entities. So when it is electromagnetically necessary that the television respond in a certain way when the power cord is plugged in and the power switch is pushed, it doesn't follow that this response is causally necessary, since the same response would not occur were the antecedent of the law combined with intemperate use of a sledge hammer.

We should expect some connection between such special electromagnetic necessity and causal necessity, however. Perhaps the connection is as follows. Perhaps the laws of the special sciences are derivative in some sense from the fundamental laws of physics, and these laws need no *ceteris paribus* clause requiring non-interference from other factors within the natural order, since the fundamentality of such laws implies that they already take into account all such forces.

Assuming this picture, the psychological impossibility of opting for Heaven won't imply the loss of libertarian freedom to choose Heaven. The laws of chemistry are more fundamental than the laws of psychology, so even if making a choice is psychologically impossible in certain circumstances, maybe the *ceteris paribus* clause leaves open the possibility that if you eat more broccoli, you'll be able to opt for Heaven. No one would think that freedom is lost simply because you can't make a particular choice without eating broccoli first, and the reason is straightforward: the trying in question isn't causally impossible even though it is psychologically impossible.

Of course, the broccoli example is just an example–I don't know what exact chemical conditions might be involved in the *ceteris paribus* clauses of psychological laws. For those whose humor inclines to the dark side, maybe they involve the laws of attention for donkeys, involving contact between lumber and head. The point, though, is that one cannot glibly associate loss of libertarian freedom with just any kind of necessity to one's behavior. The only kind of necessity that could imply the loss of libertarian freedom is the necessity associated with the fundamental laws, the laws which are *ceteris paribus* clause-free for factors from within the natural order.

So the lost soul theorists will have to come up with an entirely different line of argument than the one proposed concerning the continuum involved in the process of character formation and transformation. For even if this process is assumed to be able to result in putting oneself in a condition where trying to do otherwise is psychologically impossible, that one's desires and preferences and dispositions to behavior are so fixed that no choice of Heaven can be made for an individual with such a psychological makeup, that conclusion isn't strong enough to undermine the presence of libertarian freedom. In order to undermine freedom, the lost soul theorist will have to claim that it is possible to put yourself in conditions governed by the fundamental laws (of physics, presumably), so that no analog of eating broccoli can arise, and thus making it nomologically necessary that one can no longer make a certain choice.

The loss of soul theorist, though, may simply ask that we revise the description of loss of soul to accommodate this point. Instead of claiming that the process of character development can reach the point at which it has become psychologically impossible to choose otherwise, they can claim instead that the process can reach the point at which it becomes causally impossible to choose otherwise.

Doing so, however, enhances the need for an argument, for it was already unclear that the claim of impossibility was justified regarding the claim of psychological impossibility. If we strengthen the claim to that of causal impossibility, the argument must be correspondingly stronger. So while it is true that the objection just raised can be sidestepped in this way, it doesn't much help to avoid an objection by strengthening a claim without providing an argument for the stronger claim.

Moreover, to the extent that we have evidence for the process of hardening that leads to loss of ability to choose, the evidence we have is evidence about psychological realities and not about causal necessities. The process of character formation is capable of producing ossification of such hardness as to preclude, perhaps, any possibility of acting out-of-character, but the possibility in question here is psychological possibility. We are familiar with the pronounced effects on behavior by various techniques of intervention, including pharmacological and even shock treatments, to say nothing of natural catastrophes such as the results of a stroke. The changes in behavior induced by such factors is remarkable, and provide strong evidence that even the most entrenched behavior patterns are causally open to revision even if not psychologically open to such revision.

Here, of course, the loss of soul theorist will appeal to the unwarranted nature of such intrusion from any third party. But such an appeal is not to the point here, since many of these techniques can be self-administered or self-requested in the basis of meta-mind reflection as discussed earlier. It is not a question of who does the intervention, but a question of whether the possibility of such intervention exists. The use of such techniques provides evidence that the idea that hardening can make behavioral changes psychologically impossible, but not causally impossible.

The story told by lost soul theorists is thus weak. It needs a defense of the claim that one's character can be so fixed that it becomes causally impossible to act out-of-character. Merely citing such a state as the boundary of the process of character formation doesn't show that it is a state that can be reached through the process in question. It is more plausible to claim that acting out of character can become psychologically impossible, but even granting that point doesn't help, since loss of freedom is not implied by such psychological impossibility. The relevant kind of possibility needs to be causal impossibility, and lost soul theorists have provided no clue whatsoever as to how to get from psychological to causal impossibility. I conclude, then, that the inferences needed by lost soul theorists do not sustain the conclusion that losing one's soul is possible or that this possibility implies the loss of freedom central to the lost soul explanation of the finality of Hell.

2.5   Conclusion

The proper conclusion to draw, then, is that so far the only version of the Choice Model of Hell that can account for the finality of Hell is a position of the sort that Molinists aim at: one which involves full providential control with a recognition of the value of freedom that allows no limitation on the Choice Model. In light of the difficulties facing Molinism, many will view this conclusion as a deep problem for the Choice Model. If these difficulties are surmountable, or if a suitable substitute for Molinism can be found, however, there is hope that such an unlimited Choice Model can be defended.

Such an approach to afterlife issues will not allow defense of strong versions of universalism, according to which it is logically impossible for anyone to be separated from God forever. Hope remains, however, for more attenuated versions of universalism, from simple contingent universalism, according to which it is simply a contingent truth that no one will be separated from God forever, to slightly stronger modal versions of universalism that do not imply the logical necessity of the view. Here Molinism offers an instructive example. If Molinism is true, then, for all we know, some might be separated from God forever. Equally true, however, is that if Molinism is true, then, for all we know, there may be no feasible world in which anyone is separated from God forever. This latter possibility involves a modal strength that ought to satisfy even the most ardent universalist tendencies, and even the most ardent anti-universalists should hope that it is true. For those for whom freedom has such a high value that no limitation on the Choice Model should be tolerated, a middle position that can preserve both providence and freedom while leaving open such a modally strong version of universalism is a position uniquely positioned to meet the variety of philosophical constraints on an adequate account of these matters.

pe that it is true. For those for whom freedom has such a high value that no limi

UNIVERSALISM AND THE PROBLEM OF HELL

3.1 Introduction

A concise formulation of the problem of Hell is given by the British metaphysician John McTaggart (1906, section 177). He argued that if there is a Hell, one could have no good reason to believe it. He reasoned that there is no good empirical evidence to believe in Hell, so that if there is a good reason to believe in it, revelation must provide it. Yet, McTaggart continued, the infliction of Hell is very wicked, and so anyone who would send one to Hell must be vile indeed. In such a case, one could have no good reason to trust such an individual concerning anything of importance to our well-being, for as anyone familiar with the games played by schoolyard bullies knows, there is no telling why a vile person would say that something is good or bad for one. It may be for amusement, it may be to see one suffer, or it may be for any of a host of other reasons which are compatible with the falsity of what is being said. So if anyone, including God, tells us that there is a Hell to shun, McTaggart claims that we could have no good reason to believe that such an individual is telling us the truth. What such a person says, to put the point succinctly, undercuts the reliability of the testimony.

We can put this argument in the form of a dilemma which, in honor of its source, I will call "McTaggart's Dilemma". Either there is good reason to believe in Hell or there is not. If there is no good reason for belief in Hell, no one should believe in it. After all, without some reason to believe in Hell, the option of believing in Hell is no better than any other merely conceivable catastrophe (such as the catastrophe of accepting the view that committing suicide immediately is the only way to escape an eternal medieval torture chamber). The point is that there are too many mere conceivables that our lives end in ruin and too many merely conceivable routes to avoid these conceivables to make belief in any one of them plausible at all. So, if the doctrine of Hell is to be respectable, it must be because there is good reason to believe in it. The difficulty for this option, according to McTaggart, is that the only kinds of reasons there might be are self-defeating. For the only evidence there might be for Hell is on the basis of revelation from the one who can consign one to Hell, and yet no one of that sort who claims that Hell exists and outlines conditions for avoiding Hell can be trusted. So, on either horn of the dilemma, the conclusion to be drawn, according to McTaggart, is that belief in Hell is not intellectually respectable.

McTaggart's Dilemma shows, I will assume here, that an adequate version of Christianity must include a doctrine of Hell on which it would not be wrong for someone to end up in Hell. That is, I will assume here that there is no adequate version of Christianity without some doctrine of Hell. That may seem to be a large assumption, but since I have argued for it elsewhere (and argued that it is, in fact, not a large assumption when Hell is understood in a minimal way in terms of the logical contrast to Heaven) (Kvanvig 1993), I'll merely assume it here. For those inclined against this assumption, the argument here can be conceived in terms of answering the following conditional question: if Christianity is to contain a doctrine of Hell, what must that doctrine be like? The argument McTaggart gives would not be rhetorically interesting were it not for the fact that the traditional conception of Hell is plausibly held to succumb to that dilemma. According to traditional Christian teaching, Hell is a place where some people are punished eternally with no possibility of escape. We can analyze this traditional conception, which I term "the strong view," into four separate components:

(H1) The Anti-Universalism Thesis: some persons are consigned to Hell;

(H2) The Existence Thesis: Hell is a place where people exist, if they are consigned there;

(H3) The No Escape Thesis: there is no possibility of leaving Hell, there is nothing one can do, change, or become in order to get out of Hell, once one is consigned there;

(H4) The Retribution Thesis: the justification for and purpose of Hell is retributive in nature, Hell being constituted so as to mete out punishment to those whose earthly lives and behavior warrant it.

As already noted, this doctrine has appeared morally objectionable to many individuals, and I do not intend to dispute that claim here. My interest is rather in an alternative which has become increasingly popular over the past few centuries. This position, universalism, maintains that the basic structure of Hell is as the strong view maintains, but claims that the population statistics the strong view implies are mistaken. Where the strong view goes wrong, universalists maintain, is in thinking that Hell is populated at all. All will in the end be saved, according to universalism, and once we accept their viewpoint, universalists maintain, the problem of Hell disappears.

Universalist views, though traceable to the Alexandrian school of theologians founded by Clement and Origen, have become increasingly popular in the last three to four hundred years.[1] Though orthodoxy has never wavered since condemning universalism at the Fifth General Council at Constantinople in 553 A.D.,[2] a revival of interest in universalism began in the late seventeenth century with the Cambridge Platonists and carried into the eighteenth and nineteenth

---

[1] For an historical account of the beginnings of the popularity of universalism, see Walker (1964).

[2] An exception may be taken here concerning the controversy in England in the eighteenth century surrounding the "Damnatory Clause," Article 43 of the Athanasian Creed. The clause reads, "And they that have done good shall go into life everlasting; and they that have done evil into everlasting fire," and Article 44 reads, "This is the Catholic Faith, which except a man believe faithfully, he cannot be saved." The controversy continued sporadically, and when the Episcopal Church in the United States separated from that in England it deliberately omitted the Athanasian Creed as a standard of faith in ratifying the Prayer Book in 1789. This concern over the Damnatory Clause, however, was not so much an affirmation of universalism as a rebellion against the traditional doctrine of Hell.

centuries in the work of Swedenborg, Tennyson, Kant, Schleiermacher, Ritschl, and in the rise of the Unitarian and Universalist denominations in America (Walker 1964, esp. Part Two). Universalism continues into the twentieth century, though the rise of the influence of existentialism clouds what might otherwise have been a complete embracing by many of the most influential theologians of our century.[3] In addition, the demythologizing program of Bultmann and the reinterpretation of salvation in terms relating to social, political, and economic affairs have all done their part both to undermine the traditional understanding of Hell and to mask universalist tendencies. In those for whom the afterlife is taken seriously and one's fate in it of importance, however, it is fair to say that universalism presents by far the most attractive alternative to the strong view.

Just endorsing the view, however, isn't sufficient in itself to provide a solution to McTaggart's Dilemma. The view must be developed in a way that implies some mistake in this dilemma but which is also satisfactory philosophically and theologically. The prospects for universalism are intertwined with such thorny problems as the nature of human freedom and the conditions for salvation, and no breezy and shallow sentiment in favor of the idea that everything will work out for the best in the end can be thought adequate here.

We can begin entry into these issues by first distinguishing versions of universalism in terms of modal status. *Contingent universalism* holds that, though it is possible that a person end up in Hell as described by the conjunction of (H2)-(H4), as a matter of contingent fact every human being will end up in Heaven. *Necessary universalism* holds that it is not only true but necessarily true that every human being will end up in Heaven; it is simply impossible that anyone be damned. I will argue that both versions fail to solve the problem of Hell; that contingent universalism is too weak to solve the problem and necessary universalism is too strong. I will then turn to the question of whether there is any adequate middle ground between these two positions.

3.2 Contingent Universalism

According to contingent universalism, the possibility exists that some people end up in Hell, but as a matter of contingent fact, no one will. In the end, God's saving grace and power win out over the forces of evil, and the entire created order is reconciled to God through Christ Jesus.

This position is quite common among contemporary theologians. One example is John Macquarrie. His understanding of Hell is in terms of annihilation; he says, "If Heaven is fullness of being and the upper limit of human existence, Hell may be taken as loss of being and the lower limit. . . This utter limit of Hell would be annihilation, or at least the annihilation of the possibility for

---

[3]See, for example, Brunner (1954) and Barth (2004, Vol. IV), each of whom apparently affirm universalism, but where the stress on 'apparently' must be strong. Other recent theologians given to such tendencies include Karl Rahner, Paul Althaus, and Hans Urs von Balthasar. A notable on this list here is Robinson (1950), which shows obvious signs of the influence of existential thought and yet clearly embraces a version of universalism.

personal being." (Macquarrie 1966, p. 327). Given this understanding of Hell, Macquarrie goes on to suggest a version of universalism. He says, "If God is indeed absolute letting-be, and if his letting-be has power to overcome the risks of dissolution, then perhaps in the end . . . no individual existence that has been called out of nothing will utterly return to nothing. . ." (Macquarrie 1966, p. 322). To drive home his rejection of traditional conceptions of Hell, he says, "Needless to say, we utterly reject the idea of a Hell where God everlastingly punishes the wicked, without hope of deliverance. Even earthly penologists are more enlightened nowadays." (Macquarrie 1966, p. 327).

So Macquarrie holds that the strong view of Hell and its associates are at best unenlightened (elsewhere he terms such views "barbarous"), that Hell is best thought of in terms of annihilation, though the concept is a limiting one, in the realm of mere possibility rather than the destiny of some human beings. Of special interest in the present context is the juxtaposition of universalism with the strong view of Hell and its associates. This juxtaposition suggests the possibility that the inadequacies found in traditional conceptions of Hell can be thought of as being overcome by a doctrine of universalism.

It is the motivation behind the affirmation of universalism that is important here—a motivation having to do with the need to solve the moral problem of Hell. This theoretical motivation can be found even in some of the more conservative Christian groups. Clark Pinnock, a conservative evangelical theologian, claims,

> If the doctrine of Hell is taken to mean (as it so often is) that God raises up the wicked to everlasting existence for the express purpose of inflicting upon them endless pain and torment, universalism will become practically irresistible in its appeal to sensitive Christians . . . If the only options are torment and unversalism, then I would expect large numbers of sensitive Christians to choose universalism. (Pinnock 1987, p. 40).

Pinnock goes on to defend the annihilation view, but in the present context, what is of greater significance is that he sees in universalism a solution to the moral problems facing the strong view of Hell and its associates. According to Pinnock, if the conservative Christian faces the options of a morally problematic view of Hell on the one hand and universalism on the other, it would be fully understandable if the conservative Christian opted to embrace universalism.

The pressing question in the context of McTaggart's Dilemma is how endorsing contingent universalism is supposed to block the dilemma. We may presume, I think, that the idea is as follows. Central to McTaggart's Dilemma is the idea that sending someone to Hell would be an incredibly wicked thing to do, and so if no one is sent to Hell, the wickedness claim that is central to that dilemma should be rejected. So the dilemma disappears.

The problem with contingent universalism is that the wickedness claim involved in McTaggart's Dilemma doesn't turn on population issues concerning Hell. The claim in the dilemma is that the infliction of Hell involves wickedness. What follows from such a claim is that if God sent someone to Hell, he would have done a wicked thing. But suppose God doesn't actually send anyone to Hell, as contingent universalists claim. Even so, the wickedness charge doesn't disappear. For God is not only perfectly and wholly good in this world, He would be perfectly and wholly good no matter what the course of affairs took. He is not just contingently morally perfect; rather, His moral perfection is essential to His character. So, suppose no one actually is sent to Hell, but had things been slightly different, God would have sent someone to Hell. Then the dilemma becomes pressing again, for such a counterfactual possibility would involve wickedness, according to McTaggart, and nothing the contingent universalist has claimed has any power to show that McTaggart is mistaken. If the wickedness claim remains unscathed by contingent universalism, the trust issue about whether to trust the word of someone who tells us about Hell is still in place. Since we are assuming that a doctrine of Hell is central to Christianity, contingent universalism would leave us with McTaggart's Dilemma in place and thus with no good reason to think that an essential part of Christianity is true. So, if the worry is that the infliction of Hell is wicked, affirming contingent universalism will not solve that problem. At best, it only modally masks it, with the hope that McTaggart doesn't have the insight to see that it is only a mask.

3.3 Necessary Universalism

If contingent universalism fails to engage the dilemma by undermining the claim that the infliction of Hell involves wickedness, necessary universalism appears much better off. Necessary universalism holds that it is impossible that Hell is inflicted on anyone, and if that is true, no threat to God's perfect goodness remains. One might try to reinstate McTaggart's Dilemma by insisting that it nonetheless remains true that if God were to send someone to Hell, a wicked thing would have been done, and that if this conditional is true, there is still a worry about anyone warning us to avoid something that would be wicked to impose on us. In support of this claim, we might be reminded that threatening to do something wicked is itself wicked.

Here we need to be reminded of the defeasible relationships that typically hold in moral and epistemic reasoning. To learn that a given threat is a threat to do something wicked is a defeasible reason for thinking that the threat itself is wicked, but it is no logical guarantee that the threat itself is wicked. Adopting a policy of mutually assured nuclear destruction is to threaten to do something wicked, but if it is the only way to prevent a nuclear attack by an enemy, the consequences of such an attack are so severe that only the most recalcitrant deontologists will insist that it is not justified. If only rabid Kantians can press the point, necessary universalists are on safe enough ground that we can push forward considering their proposal, leaving what to say to, and what to do with, rabid Kantians to another time and place (perhaps hoping for enough insightful critique from gifted ethicists to relieve us of further argumentative burden). Further, we might also note that the worry about the wickedness of Hell is clearly a worry deriving from the consequences of suffering eternal damnation rather than some feature more plausibly appealed to by strict Kantianism, so relying on such a strong deontologism at this point will undercut the basis of the dilemma (to say nothing of the fact that cases in which real disaster looms unless Kantian strictures are violated look like clear counterexamples to those strictures).

So necessary universalism, unlike contingent universalism, offers some hope of avoiding McTaggart's Dilemma. Among the philosophically unsophisticated, one often hears the worry that such a view compromises the very heart of Christianity, according to which we are all headed for Hell apart from the redemptive work of God in Christ. But such a worry is confused. The claim in question—that we are all headed for Hell apart from God's intervention—is no less true should the intervention in question be necessitated by God's nature.[4] So we need not balk at necessary universalism on these grounds.

There are grounds, however, for worrying that the position of necessary universalism is indefensible. Some worries are theological in nature, claiming that an adequate soteriology requires a role for faith that the appropriate kind of faith can obtain only if one has knowledge of the existence of a first-century Jewish man named Jesus. There is even a proof-text for the view: "Salvation is found in no one else, for there is no other name under Heaven given to me by which we must be saved."[5] According to such individuals, it would not be sufficient, for example, to have faith in God himself in order to be saved, nor would it be sufficient to recognize one's own inability to achieve salvation and to trust in what God has and will do for one. The conceptual contents of faith in these latter examples are too general; in order to be *saving* faith, the conceptual content of faith must involve particular reference to an historical individual of the first century, Jesus of Nazareth.

Once this soteriological position is adopted, necessary universalism appears very hard to defend. For it is hard to imagine how any such piece of human knowledge could be necessary. In fact, it appears not even to be true, say nothing of necessarily true, that every human being knows who Jesus is.

---

[4]Such a position is committed to the possibility of some counterfactuals with necessarily false antecedents failing to be only trivially true, in contrast to what the standard semantics for such counterfactuals implies. The standard semantics for counterfactuals proceeds in terms of finding a "close" world in which the antecedent of a counterfactual is true, where the notion of closeness is a technical notion the explication of which is deeply problematic. For our purposes, though, the rough idea is that one world is closer to the actual world than another just in case the first is more like the actual world than the second in terms of which causal laws are true and which events occur and in what order. Now, if there are no worlds in which the antecedent is true, there will be no close worlds in which the antecedent is true; and, on the semantics in question, a counterfactual is true just in case there is a closer world in which both antecedent and consequent are true to any world where the antecedent is true and the consequent false. Thus, when there are no worlds in which the antecedent is true, the counterfactual is trivially true. For more on the semantics for counterfactuals, see Stalnaker (1968), Lewis (1973).

This commitment of necessary universalism should not be thought damaging to the position, however, for the implication of the standard semantics for counterfactuals is one of the least attractive features of that semantics. Thus, it is appropriate to treat necessary universalism as unscathed in its conflict with the semantics for counterfactuals.

[5]Acts 4:12, NIV.

There are, however, serious difficulties with this soteriological position and the use of this passage as a proof-text for the view. For one thing, this objection must assume that the knowledge in question has to be knowledge in this life, prior to death. Without this assumption, it is much harder to insist that such knowledge would have to be contingent. For another thing, those who hold this view would also agree with the apostle Paul that Abraham was righteous by faith, and yet it is quite implausible if not nonsensical to hold that Abraham was aware of the existence of a first-century Jewish man named Jesus. A full exploration of this topic is required if our goal is a complete soteriology; but given our present purposes it is sufficient to note that the view of faith that requires conceptual content referring to Jesus of Nazareth is far from obviously correct (even given quite conservative assumptions about doctrinal matters). Exactly what kind of conceptual content is required is an interesting question to explore, but it is beyond our present purposes.[6] Even if there is some way to formulate this objection to get around the problems it faces, I will not here rest a rejection of this universalist solution to McTaggart's Dilemma on this sort of objection, for I believe there is a much more serious one.

This more serious problem arises from what I will call "the free will argument." In succinct form, it claims that God cannot guarantee the presence of all in Heaven without being willing to violate the freedom of some individuals to choose otherwise. Fundamentally, this argument concerns the relationship between God's moral perfection and human free will. First, note that God's moral perfection, His holiness, requires His participation in the moral perfecting of fallen human beings. In particular, those who will be united with God for all eternity must become morally perfect (otherwise God would be either unconcerned about moral imperfection or unmotivated to help correct the defects, and either supposition is not befitting an adequate conception of God). This fact is consonant with the Biblical view that the effects of the Fall are to be done away with through the redemptive work of Jesus Christ. It is not just that, according to Christianity, the life of Jesus makes it possible to go to Heaven rather than Hell, but that through the work of Jesus, the redeemed shall be changed "from glory to glory," coming to participate fully in the nature the One who redeems.

So if necessary universalism is true, it is simply impossible that anyone fail to be conformed to the image of God's Son, given that such a failure is incompatible with God's holiness. Yet, such conformance, it would seem, cannot be imposed on us; we must either undertake the task ourselves, or at the very least, acquiesce

---

[6]One standard way out of the problem I am raising is that of dispensational theology, according to which the conditions for salvation differ according to whether one lived before or after Christ. On this view, the conceptual content of Abraham's saving faith could differ from the conceptual of any person's saving faith after Christ. This view deserves exploration, but the important point to note about it here is that it is not immediately implied by anything in any of the sacred writings of Christianity. So if it is to be acceptable, it will have to be so on the basis of its theological adequacy. That is an enormous task, well beyond the scope of this work; hence any argument against universalism which relies on this theological standpoint is much too complex to generate a succinct argument against universalism.

to the Divine solicitation to aid in the formation of our character. Still, if our cooperation is important, it will also be possible that a person freely choose not to cooperate and forever maintain this uncooperative stance. What possible grounds could be given for thinking that eternal rebellion is impossible?

This argument is, I believe, telling against necessary universalism, at least when the type of freedom in question is assumed to be incompatible with determinism. Regarding this assumption, we may note the following. If a defense against McTaggart's Dilemma only succeeds on the assumption that libertarian accounts of freedom are mistaken, we do not have a full response to the dilemma. Hence, even if a defense of necessary universalism were available by employing some other account of freedom, such a defense would be less than satisfactory here. In what follows, then, I will assume a libertarian conception of freedom.

I will also assume that some formulation of the Principle of Alternative Possibilities (PAP) correctly describes this notion of freedom (the principle claims that in order to act freely one must be able to do otherwise). There are challenges to PAP stemming from Frankfurt's seminal paper on the subject (Frankfurt 1969), but the challenges threaten particular formulations of the principle only, leaving open the possibility of reformulating it to avoid the challenges. For example, the original challenge involving a meticulous individual with the power to coerce you to do A, but merely observing your doing A of your own free will, attacks only the version that interprets the phrase "can do otherwise" in terms of refraining from the action in question. The intuitive response to such counterexamples is to insist that the ability to do otherwise in question must involve something internal rather than external, something like the intention in question. There are complications here that could distract us for a considerable time, but it is sufficient to note what was pointed out earlier regarding the libertarian assumption itself. If we were to adopt an account of freedom that denies PAP, we would have at best a partial solution to McTaggart's Dilemma, since it is far from clear that there is no defensible version of PAP. So here we will assume not only a libertarian account of freedom, but will assume as well that such an account involves some formulation of the principle that in order to act freely one must have been able to do otherwise.

This assumption of PAP shows why necessary universalism cannot be salvaged by insisting that there are conditions under which a choice for anything but Heaven would be impossible. Consider the following version of such an argument by Thomas Talbott:

> The picture I get is something like this. Though a sinner, Belial, has learned, perhaps through bitter experience, that evil is always destructive, always contrary to his own interest as well as to the interest of others; and though he sees clearly that God is the ultimate source of all happiness and that disobedience can produce only greater and greater misery in his own life as well as in the life of others, Belial freely chooses eternal misery (or perhaps eternal oblivion) for himself nonetheless. The question that immediately arises here is: What could possible qualify as a motive for such a choice? As long as any ignorance, or deception, or bondage to

desire remains, it is open to God to transform a sinner without interfering with human freedom; but once all ignorance and deception and bondage to desire is removed, so that a person is truly "free" to choose, there can no longer be any motive for choosing eternal misery for oneself. (Talbott 1990, p. 26)

Talbott maintains that God can transform a person so that they will no longer have any motive for choosing otherwise than in the way necessary for presence in Heaven. There are two difficulties with this argument, one having to do with the cognitive transformation posited and the other concerning the relationship between motives and choices.

Talbott assumes that God can correct cognitive errors in Belial, getting him to the point of seeing the truth of certain claims that the wicked often ignore or prefer to avoid. It is not clear, however, that God can do so consistent with assumptions about human freedom. Though it is clear that doxastic voluntarism is false, the view that we can simply choose what to believe in any given case, it is far from clear that doxastic involuntarism is true. On this view, the operations of cognition and the operations of the will are never intertwined, so it would never be an intrusion on the operations of the will for God to correct Belial's, or anyone else's, cognitive mistakes. Such a view, however, is not clearly true. There is, at least in certain cases, a sense of optionality regarding what opinion to form or cognitive attitude to adopt. For one thing, evidence is sometimes only vaguely good evidence for a certain claim, giving rise to a feeling of optionality about whether to believe. Moreover, any empirical testing situation triggers the Quine/Duhem thesis that there are always options regarding what to make of recalcitrant experience, and we often have a feeling of optionality regarding what doxastic response to make in such cases. Moreover, the feeling of optionality is even more present concerning large philosophical issues, including issues about what overall perspective on reality to hold. For example, suppose one is a convinced physicalist, denying the existence of God. Must this view change upon experiencing the afterlife? Nothing about such an experience compels any such alteration. For one thing, the affective side of such an individual, including the operation of the will, might overwhelm the operations of the intellect to prevent any such major revision in the cognitive sphere, but even on the assumption of a perfectly rational response to such recalcitrant experience, enough changes elsewhere in the noetic structure could accommodate the experience without abandoning physicalism and the accompanying atheism. If such optionality has even the slightest tinge of the will involved, then the assumption that God can correct cognitive errors without threatening human freedom is mistaken and Talbott's argument fails. While I have no definitive argument that the will is implicated by the optionality in question or by the sense of optionality present in some doxastic instances, I also know of no good argument to the conclusion that doxastic involuntarism is true. In the absence of such an argument, the assumption of the argument in the quoted passage above that divine intrusion into a cognitive perspective is unproblematic is uncertain enough to block the force of the argument.

There is a worse problem, however—a problem concerning the relationship between motives and choices. Talbott's argument can work only if the absence of a motive for resistance to God is logically sufficient for whatever is necessary for presence in Heaven, for without such a claim, the focus on motives in the quoted passage above would be irrelevant to the conclusion that universalism is necessarily true. But if the absence of such a motive is sufficient in this way, then nothing involving freedom can be necessary for presence in Heaven (since the presence of such a motive would be incompatible with PAP). Yet, Talbott doesn't deny the need for freedom here. Instead, he intends to argue that we can't make sense of a free choice against God in certain circumstances. Such an argument simply cannot succeed without denying PAP. The argument will have to maintain that if there is no motive and hence no sense to be made of a choice, then that choice is impossible. But such a result undermines even the most internal versions of PAP, and those versions are the only ones plausibly maintained in the face of Frankfurtian counterexamples, so Talbott's argument is successful only to the extent that the kind of freedom in question is not libertarian freedom understood in terms of some internal version of PAP. Hence, it cannot be viewed as part of an adequate response to McTaggart's Dilemma. As noted already, however, we cannot give a full response to the dilemma in question without assuming that PAP is a governing principle regarding concerning the type of freedom in question.

Given these assumptions, the argument against necessary universalism goes like this. Presence in Heaven involves the free submission of the will to that of one's creator, but in any display of freedom, there is the capacity to choose, or try to choose, otherwise. Hence, it is impossible that it be necessary that one freely submit in the way required. Hence it is not possible that it be necessary that everyone ends up in Heaven.

This argument is valid, and it appeals only to two claims, one involving PAP and the other tying presence in Heaven to a something freely chosen. We have already seen why there is no future in the present context in denying PAP, but there are two other ways to consider to try to avoid this argument. There is the premise that ties presence in Heaven to free responses, and there is also an assumption about the nature of necessity involved in getting to the conclusion that necessary universalism is false.

The latter issue concerning the nature of necessity involved in the free will argument against necessary universalism can be handled quickly. Recall that the problem for contingent universalism is the modal masking of McTaggart's Dilemma, and given this problem, the only hope for addressing that dilemma is to appeal to a notion of necessity that covers all of modal space. Such a notion is plausibly held to be governed by S5, the notion Plantinga characterizes as "broadly logical necessity" (Plantinga 1978). The particular implication of note in the present context is that such necessity does not change across time: anything possible and anything necessary, in this sense of the terms, is so always and everywhere. So, even if there is some other notion of possibility on which one can lose the power to resist the Divine solicitation, there must be this weaker notion on which such a possibility of resistance remains, on pain of denying PAP. Yet, if the possibility of resistance remains, then necessary universalism, in this sense of necessity, is false.

That, in a nutsHell, is the problem of free will for necessary universalism. Necessary universalism, if true, would solve McTaggart's Dilemma, but in the sense of necessity just outlined, it cannot provide a successful response to this dilemma while at the same time accepting a libertarian account of freedom governed by PAP (clarified using this broadly logical notion of necessity that is also used to characterize the notion of necessity involved in claiming that the salvation of all is necessary) and an account of presence in Heaven that makes free choices play an essential role in it. Since we have already argued that the assumption of libertarian freedom governed by PAP is essential to a full response to the dilemma, the only path left open for the necessary universalist is the path of denying that presence in Heaven requires a role for free choice.

In the next section, I will consider this position—the position that questions the central assumption of freedom in accounting for presence in Heaven. For reasons that will become clear later, I term this position "ersatz universalism." I will argue that this position offers little hope in avoiding McTaggart's Dilemma, and thus will turn in the following section to the question of whether there is an intermediate universalist position between contingent and necessary universalism that might fare better. First, though, we turn to ersatz universalism.

3.4 Ersatz Universalism

The ersatz universalist grants that necessary universalism cannot answer the free will argument, but insists that necessary universalism can be defended nonetheless. The defense proceeds by first granting the value of freedom, but denying that it is so valuable that it can sustain the possibility of a person ending up in Hell. The idea, then, is that God honors freedom and solicits our cooperation in securing our presence in Heaven, but if such an approach fails there is always the option of coerced presence in Heaven.

Consider Talbott's explanation of a view of this sort:

> . . .[E]verlasting separation is the kind of evil that a loving God would prevent even if it meant interfering with human freedom in certain ways. Consider the two kinds of conditions under which we human beings feel justified in interfering with the freedom of others. We feel justified, first of all, in preventing one person from doing irreparable harm, or what may appear to us as irreparable harm, to another . . . We also feel justified in preventing others from doing irreparable harm to themselves; a loving father may . . . physically overpower his daughter in an effort to prevent her from committing suicide. . . So . . . a loving God . . . could never permit one person to destroy the very possibility of future happiness in another; and . . . he could never permit his loved ones to destroy the very possibility of future happiness in themselves. (Talbott 1990, p. 27)

According to Talbott, we are allowed free rein regarding our eternal destiny only up to a certain point. That point is the point at which further exercise of our freedom will result in irreparable harm to ourselves or to others. The relevant option in the present context is that of doing irreparable harm to ourselves. The ersatz universalist claims, with Talbott, that there are situations where the impressive value of freedom can legitimately be overridden by other factors, and that one's afterlife destiny is a situation of precisely this sort. If one freely chooses Heaven, all is well; but if one does not so choose, at some point the right thing to do, and the thing that God in fact does, is to override our freedom and secure our presence in Heaven. Freedom is important, the ersatz universalist claims, but it isn't *that* important.[7]

Before discussing ersatz view directly, I want to distinguish the view itself from Talbott's argument for it relying on the notion of irreparable harm. To tie this notion to the afterlife options of Heaven and Hell, some assumptions are needed about the nature of Hell. For consignment to Hell to involve irreparable harm, it must be a very bad thing and an inescapably bad thing. Thus, in order for this argument for a limitation on freedom to be accepted, one must already have adopted other elements of the strong view of Hell according to which escape from Hell is impossible. If we were to suppose, with second chance views, that escape from Hell is possible, then there would never be a time at which the envisioned intrusion into human freedom would be warranted, for whatever harm would be involved in the experience of being damned, that harm would be repairable by the change of heart and mind the experience of Hell was intended to produce.

The logical core of ersatz universalism, however, should not be understood to include any such assumption. If we are to reject the ersatz view, as I will argue we should, we should not reject it simply by claiming that though escape from Hell is metaphysically possible, it isn't possible in some weaker sense of 'possibility' (thereby allowing us to claim that the harm in question is never truly irreparable and thus that the point at which a restriction on freedom would be warranted is never in fact reached). So instead of focusing on the argument for ersatz universalism employing the notion of irreparable harm, I will focus on the view itself.

Ersatz universalists may characterize presence in Heaven in terms of acceptance of God's offer to join him in Heaven. There are other options as well, such as conceiving of Heaven as a geographical location and imagining salvation in

---

[7]I owe my understanding and characterizations of ersatz universalism to the discussions I have had on this topic with Keith DeRose over many years. Keith will, of course, object to the ersatz-ness characterization of his view, but he is the main exponent I have in mind of the view in question. It is unfortunate that Keith has only published his views online to this point: on his webpage in a contribution entitled "Universalism and the Bible" and through copies of his posts that originally appeared on the blog "Generous Orthodoxy Think Tank", a blog that no longer exists. In my opinion, his work here as elsewhere is superb and deserves a much wider audience than the present locations generate. Perhaps it would be appropriate for my remarks here to be a motive for him to change either his views or his publication practices!

terms of some Divine relocation package. Another alternative is to imagine presence in Heaven as involving two kinds of persons: those who want to be there and are happy about it, having so chosen; and those who are not and have not so chosen. But these other options make the view much less attractive, so I'll focus here on the notion of acceptance: some are in Heaven as a result of freely acceptance God's offer of salvation while others will be in Heaven as a result of a coerced acceptance of God's offer of salvation. Perhaps some will object that my use of the language of coercion is rhetorically prejudicial, but I don't see how it could be. The idea is that God directly and immediately secures one's acceptance and thus secures one's presence in Heaven, and such immediate and direct securing would clearly involve the use of power to guarantee compliance. But nothing in the discussion to follow will turn on the issue of whether one wishes to include or avoid the use of the term 'coercion' and its cognates.

The fundamental difficulty for this account is that it misconstrues the nature of presence in Heaven. Traditional Christian doctrine uses the language of Heaven and Hell to distinguish between those who will love God and enjoy him forever and those who will not. Now, perhaps enjoyment can be passive and imposed from the outside, but love cannot. To love another person requires an expression of agency, and such expressions of agency implicate the notion of freedom. The offer of salvation is, at bottom, the offer of intimacy with the Divine, involving reciprocal expressions of love. To imagine that the expressions in question can be controlled completely from one side of the relationship is to misconceive the nature of love. Love cannot be coerced, but must be freely given. The Biblical imagery of a lover wooing a beloved makes sense in this context, whereas the idea of compelled association is more appropriate to the relationship of master and slave, or even better, that of designer and machine.

Given this point, the account we ought to accept about the nature of presence in Heaven is one that involves the free union of self with the Divine. Anything less will not be involve the beatific vision itself, but something inferior to it. When we combine this result with the logical notice that there are only two afterlife possibilities, Heaven and Hell, we are left with the conclusion that forced results of any sort still leave one in Hell.

It is for this reason that I refer to this position as "ersatz universalism". There is a long history in Christian theology of attempting to mitigate the severity of the strong view of Hell by making the experience of Hell somehow less severe than some of the imaginative portrayals of Hell make it out to be. Thus, some adopt second chance views for this purpose and others opt for annihilationism, somehow thinking cessation of existence would be better than the misery of eternal conscious separation from God. In other cases, the pain of Hell is claimed to be only the pain of loss rather than the pain of sense, so that the suffering of the damned is less troublesome than it otherwise would have been. Whether these views succeed in being mitigations of the severity of the strong view is not the issue here. The issue is, instead, that they are developed for such a purpose, and once viewed in this way we can see that ersatz universalism is the same sort of view. Instead of Hell involving conscious eternal suffering of the worst sort imaginable, the ersatz universalism has God intervening into the will of the unredeemed, changing them in such a way that they can come as close as possible to the experience of Heaven, even though they can never quite get there. Even without the experience of Heaven, however, they can experience unimaginable happiness, joy, and bliss in spite of the fact that what they are experiencing is not Heaven but its logical contrast. They are in Hell, but it's just not that bad; they are not in Heaven, because the greatest good promised to the redeemed—the beatific vision itself—is unavailable to them.

For those more familiar and comfortable with the position of theological determinism, this argument will hold little persuasive power. For theological determinists hold that presence in Heaven is a matter of divine election and decree, completely independent of any libertarian activity of the human will. If one is attracted to such a position, then the account of Heaven presented above, involving a turning of heart and mind and will toward the source of all good and truth and beauty, will be perhaps one possible way of loving God and enjoying him forever, but not the only way. Recall that here, however, we are assuming a libertarian account of human freedom in order to provide a complete response to McTaggart's Dilemma. So, whatever the attractions of theological determinism, it is irrelevant here.

There is another way to ersatz universalism that I must caution against here. The debate about free will has led to the regrettable practice of referring to various positions in terms of philosophical terminology, so that some talk about libertarian free will and compatibilist free will, etc. This language suggests the possibility of their being two kinds of free will, and once one makes this mistake, one can then turn to another, asking which of the two is the more valuable kind of free will.

There are no different kinds of free will, however, at least not in the way needed here. There is just the ability to do otherwise, which is what human freedom consists in. The libertarian has a certain theory about what the ability to do otherwise involves, and the compatibilist has a different theory. The existence of a theory doesn't imply the existence of a kind. In this regard, the following remarks by Peter van Inwagen are worth taking to heart:

> Having said this about the word "able" I want to make what seems to me to be an important point, a point that is, in fact, of central importance if one wishes to think clearly about the freedom of the will: compatibilists and incompatibilists mean the same thing by "able". And what do both compatibilists and incompatibilists mean by "able"? Just this: what it means in English, what the word means. And, therefore, "free will", "incompatibilist free will", "compatibilist free will" and "libertarian free will" are four names for one and the same thing. If this thing is a property, they are four names for the property *is on some occasions able to do otherwise*. If this thing is a power or ability, they are four names for the power or ability to do otherwise than what one in fact does. (van Inwagen 2008a, p. 333)

Van Inwagen makes his point initially in terms of the meanings of the terms in question, whereas I have made the point in metaphysical terms. But both points are in order. One shouldn't let the language of libertarian free will and compatibilist free will confuse one into thinking that there are two different properties or powers or abilities in question so that we could inquire as to which kind of expression of free will is most valuable. There is only the ability to do otherwise, and the argument presented here claims that the union with God involved in the experience of the beatific vision is one that involves the acquiescence to the divine invitation with one's whole mind and will, for only in this way can one count as loving God with one's whole heart, soul, mind, and strength. If compatibilism were true, one could do so freely even though determined to do so. We are assuming, in the context of McTaggart's Dilemma, that libertarianism is true, so there is no possibility here about two different expressions of freedom, one having more value than the other.

Nor is there any comfort for ersatz universalism in positing different levels of Heavenly bliss among the redeemed, with those who love God in the way described above as in places of greater reward than those who have been coerced into Heaven. While it may be true that the experience of Heaven is better for some than others, there is a non-negotiable requirement here that draws a qualitative distinction between Heaven and its contrast. That requirement is the requirement of accepting the divine solicitation and loving him completely. All else is contrast only.

Thus ersatz universalism is not really a version of universalism at all, just as fake diamonds are not diamonds and decoy ducks are not ducks. It offers no hope of yielding an adequate response to the free will argument against necessary universalism. In light of this failure, the best strategy for a universalist is to admit the obvious: contingent universalism is too weak to solve McTaggart's Dilemma and necessary universalism is too strong. If there is any hope for solving this dilemma by appeal to universalism, what will be needed is some intermediate position between contingent and necessary universalism. I turn in the next section to the question of whether there is such a middle position.

3.5   Can a Middle Ground be Found?

If one wishes to find a position stronger than merely contingent universalism, the first natural step to take is to look at counterfactuals for help. Instead of saying merely that none will be lost, a stronger claim turns subjunctive, maintaining that none *would* be lost. Such a view invites perplexity, however, since such a claim involves some implicit condition, and it is not clear what the condition might be. If the full claim is that none would be lost no matter what, we get a view that implies necessary universalism (since the phrase "no matter what" expresses a universal quantifier reaching every nook and cranny of modal space). So the question is what the implicit condition might be that yields a middle position.

One idea is to appeal to is something involving God's creative purposes. If the purpose of creation is for fellowship, and if God is sovereign over his creation, exercising providential control in all of its affairs, it begins to look unsurprising if he would arrange things so that none would be lost. Of course, it can't be *impossible* for some to be lost, but that is not the claim being made. The claim, instead, is that none would be lost, if creation itself is the product of a desire for fellowship by a sovereign being exercising full providential control. Possibilities of damnation exist, but perhaps in as a remote a sense as the possibility that we are being deceived by a powerful demon so that most all of our beliefs are false.

Let us call this position "counterfactual universalism." Given this view, we are entitled to claim not only that all will be saved, but that all would be saved if God is loving, sovereign, and exerts providential control over the destinies of humanity.

The problem is that such a strengthening isn't a strengthening enough. The same problem that plagues contingent universalism also undermines counterfactual universalism. The problem, it may be recalled, is that contingent universalism only modally masks the problem of Hell that underlies McTaggart's Dilemma. The problem, at bottom, is that, whatever the details regarding Hell, the design plan is God's and so we can always ask about the design plan and whether it would be wicked to have left (or put) such an option in place. Thus, we may ask, would it be wicked, as McTaggart claims, to consign something to Hell? If the worry is that on the strong view it would be wicked to do so, there is no philosophical consolation in pointing out that no one will in fact be consigned there. But, for the same reason, there is no philosophical consolation in noting that no one *would be* consigned there, so long as God is conceived to be sovereign and exerting control over the course of human affairs. We still have modal masking of the problem occurring; it is just that, to use the language of possible worlds, the range of worlds in which the masking occurs is more extensive for counterfactual universalism than for contingent universalism.

The same points hold when one tries to use probabilistic notions and whatever modal implications they may have to sustain a universalist response to McTaggart's Dilemma. For example, suppose one claim that there is no *chance* that anyone will end up in Hell. It is not clear what modal implications there are for such a view, and there are multiple interpretations of the probabilistic notion in question. So, in a variety of ways, such a position is in serious need of clarification. Regardless of how such clarifications proceed, however, we will still be left with the following problem. Standard probability theory leaves open the possibility that things happen that have no chance of happening, and so long as this option remains, the problem of Hell underlying McTaggart's Dilemma remains. One might opt for some non-standard approach to probability to close off this possibility, but if one does, then this "no chance universalism" will imply necessary universalism, and thereby fall to the free will problem for that view. So either way, no chance universalism cannot avoid McTaggart's Dilemma.

To avoid the problem of modally masking the problem that underlies Mc-Taggart's Dilemma, we will therefore have to look for a kind of necessity that we can attach to the universalist doctrine in order to be able to claim, in some legitimate way, that modal masking is not occurring any more.

The difficulty in following this path is that the typical notions of necessity that philosophers speak about that are weaker than that of logical or metaphysical necessity won't help at all. For example, in descending order of strength, we might talk about nomological necessity, or counterfactual necessity, or even weaker notions such as psychological necessity or the necessity that attaches to some actions in virtue of being in character rather than out of character for a person. None of these options rule out the possibility of creatures for whom damnation occurs in a way that would trigger McTaggart's Dilemma all over again, and thus even if all actual creatures can't be damned consistent with their character or psychology or even the laws of nature, we would yet have no adequate response to McTaggart's claim that such damnation would be wicked. Such notions of necessity thus have no resources to block McTaggart's Dilemma, even if they have the capacity to provide reassurance that no one is under any real risk of being damned.

Those familiar with the literature on modal metaphysics, especially in the area of philosophy of religion, will immediately think of another alternative here, however, and it is the notion of necessity introduced by Alvin Plantinga in the context of the problem of evil. Since the problem that underlies McTaggart's Dilemma is a special case of the problem of evil—to my mind, by far the hardest version of this problem—it would be natural to expect Plantinga's notion of necessity to provide some hope for universalism in its attempt to avoid this dilemma. Though Plantinga did not use this term in describing the view in question, the standard terminology is now to distinguish the class of logically or metaphysically possible worlds from the class of feasible worlds. The class of feasible worlds is composed of those worlds that it is logically or metaphysically possible for God to actualize, and Plantinga's famous argument claims that not every logically or metaphysically possible world is a world that God can actualize.[8]

I will call the position that claims that there is no world actualizable by God in which anyone ends up in Hell "feasible universalism." The claim of the feasible universalist is that, if it is impossible for God to actualize any world in which someone is damned, then we get all the virtues of necessary universalism in replying to McTaggart's Dilemma without the burden of having to deny a libertarian account of human freedom. For the distinction between a possible world and a feasible world is, in Plantinga's argument, dependent on the assumption of libertarianism.

In order to understand feasible universalism, then, we need to see how libertarian assumptions imply the distinction between feasible worlds and possible

---

[8]The first version of this argument occurs, to my knowledge, in Plantinga (1967), though he has presented it in a number of publications.

worlds. Plantinga's argument for this distinction is set in the context of an example about Curley, where the question is whether Curley would freely accept a $20,000 bribe if it were offered him. Plantinga's summary of the argument for the existence of worlds God cannot actualize is as follows:

> There is a possible world W where God strongly actualizes a totality T of states of affairs including Curley's being free with respect to taking the bribe, and where Curley takes the bribe. But there is another possible world W^* where God actualizes the very same states of affairs and where Curley rejects the bribe. Now suppose it is true as a matter of fact that if God had actualized T, Curley would have accepted the bribe: then God could not have actualized W^*. And if, on the other hand, Curley would have rejected the bribe, had God actualized T, then God could not have actualized W. So either way there are worlds God could not have actualized. (Plantinga 1978, pp. 180–181)

Plantinga argues that if it is true that Curley would accept the bribe if offered, then God cannot actualize the possible world in which Curley would reject the bribe if offered. Hence, according to Plantinga, there are possible worlds God could not actualize. If we define the notion of a feasible world as a world God can actualize, we get the result that the class of feasible worlds is a proper subclass of the class of possible worlds.

This argument is controversial in a number of respects. First, it presupposes the Molinist view that there are true counterfactuals about what individuals would freely do in a given set of circumstances, and it assumes the Law of Conditional Excluded Middle (LCEM) about these counterfactuals. According to LCEM, for any propositions p and q, either p counterfactually implies q or it implies $\sim q$. The above argument presupposes LCEM in contrast to the prevailing opinion (Lewis 1973). Later on, however, Plantinga abandons this assumption (1978, p. 182), so in the present discussion I will ignore the fact that the above argument presupposes LCEM. That still leaves the Molinist presupposition in the argument, and there has been considerable discussion of this position in the literature.[9] I will not add to that literature here, since we needn't undermine this argument to see that it won't help in the context of responding to McTaggart's Dilemma.

Recall that the hope here is to find a kind of necessity that is weaker than logical or metaphysical necessity so that the modal masking of the problem of Hell doesn't occur and yet which doesn't succumb to the free will argument against necessary universalism. Feasible universalism is specially designed to avoid the free will objection, since it grants that there are possible worlds in which some people choose in such a way that they end up in Hell. The claim, however, is that God can't actualize such a world; such worlds are possible but infeasible worlds.

We must ask, then, why the feasible universalist thinks that such worlds can't be actualized by God. In distinguishing feasible from infeasible possibili-

---

[9] Many of the central articles in the discussion are collected in Fischer (1989).

ties, Plantinga appeals to counterfactuals of freedom. If we use only these resources, the truth of feasible universalism is held hostage to winds of Molinist fortune: if certain counterfactuals of freedom are true, then feasible universalism is true (call these the "pleasing counterfactuals"); if other counterfactuals of freedom are true, then feasible universalism is false (call these the "disturbing counterfactuals"). In order to complete the response to McTaggart's Dilemma, the feasible universalist would thus need to explain why it is impossible for there to be individuals regarding whom disturbing counterfactuals are true.

But the feasible universalist has a premise up his sleeve to solve this problem. The trick is that God knows in advance of creating any person which counterfactuals are true and which are false, and *given God's modally stable character*, God couldn't create any person of whom the disturbing counterfactuals are true. Even stronger, given his character, God could only create persons of which the pleasing counterfactuals are true. Hence, not only is the class of feasible worlds a subclass of the class of possible worlds, the class of feasible worlds contains no member worlds in which any person is characterized by disturbing counterfactuals and is thus damned.

Here, however, suspicions of logical legerdemain are appropriate. Note that there are two crucial steps in distinguishing feasible universalism from necessary universalism. The first step relies on Plantinga's argument, the step that yields a distinction between feasible worlds and possible worlds. But this step alone isn't sufficient. In addition, we need some way of guaranteeing that in no feasible world is some person damned. Here, the feasible universalist appeals to God's character, which is presumed to be modally stable. Because of this stability, there is no world actualizable by God in which someone is damned.

But why does God's character restrict the class of feasible worlds in this way? For it to do so, it looks as if it must be that God's character logically precludes his sending anyone to Hell. To see why, suppose that God's character doesn't logically preclude damnation. Then there are some possible worlds in which some are damned and other worlds where none are damned. For feasible universalism to be true under this assumption, there would have to be a perfect correlation between non-damnation worlds and feasible worlds. It would have to be that every creatable individual was an individual regarding whom only pleasing counterfactuals are true. Such a coincidence would be wonderful for the feasible universalist, but for those wanting understanding it is a bit too mysterious and inexplicable. If our answer to McTaggart's Dilemma requires positing such a Miraculous Metaphysical Coincidence, we could have avoided honest toil much more simply just by saying that there's a way out of the dilemma, though we just can't say exactly what it is.

It remains true, however, that if all we want is a view that is logically consistent, appeal to this Miraculous Metaphysical Coincidence can be useful. Mere logical consistency, however, isn't enough to rid the problem of Hell of its evidentiary power against religious viewpoints that involve a doctrine of Hell, just as mere logical consistency isn't enough to eliminate the general problem of evil.

So it looks as if the path of true philosophy requires explaining the claims of feasible universalism in terms of the idea that God's character is logically incompatible with damnation. But if we saddle the feasible universalist with this claim, the position becomes logically incoherent. For the feasible universalist doesn't think that God exists only in feasible worlds, and doesn't think God fails to exist in all those possible but infeasible worlds where damnation occurs. The idea of Plantinga's argument was supposed to be that among worlds where God exists, there are two kinds of such worlds: those that God can actualize and those that God can't. And then this distinction between feasible and infeasible worlds was supposed to work in such a way that in no feasible world did anyone end up in Hell. Yet, to avoid the free will problem for necessary universalism, we needed to maintain that in some infeasible worlds, some end up in Hell. To avoid contradiction now, the feasible universalist has to add: but God doesn't exist in those worlds, since his character is incompatible with damnation. So the Miraculous Metaphysical Coincidence above is here replaced by a different one, where the class of worlds where damnation occurs is a class of worlds where there is no God. It need not be said, but I will say it anyway: this is not the way to defend traditional Christianity.

So if one of the two metaphysical coincidences is to be embraced in some mad and feverish philosophical attempt to hang onto feasible universalism in spite of how fantastic, bizarre, and kooky these claims of coincidence are, it had better be the first one that allows that God's character is compatible with damnation. If one endorses this version of feasible universalism, however, it faces a version of the original charge that undermined the power of contingent universalism to avoid McTaggart's Dilemma. The version of feasible universalism in question admits that God's character is compatible with sending someone to Hell forever, but McTaggart's Dilemma rests in part on the claim that damning someone is a very wicked thing to do. A universalist wishing to retain a traditional conception of God can't admit that God's character is compatible with doing something very wicked. And yet, the version of feasible universalism in question does precisely this. Hence, feasible universalism fails in either being unable to retain a traditional conception of God or by failing to do any better with McTaggart's Dilemma than contingent universalism did.

3.6   Conclusion

I conclude that universalism fails to solve the problem of Hell. Contingent universalism only modally masks the problem, and necessary universalism succumbs to the free will argument, and attempts to find some intermediate position between these two have failed as well. The argument about intermediate positions proceeded by ruling out possibilities, and it would be a mistake to claim that every imaginable intermediate position has been covered by the above discussion, and perhaps some might still hope to find an intermediate view that can be used to answer McTaggart's Dilemma. I think that such hope is misplaced, however, for I have presented a general challenge to any intermediate position. To the extent that such a position treats damnation as compatible with the existence of God, population studies about residency in Hell have no power to address the wickedness point central to McTaggart's Dilemma.

In this respect, the question of who and how many will be in Hell must be separated from the question of the nature of Hell. In order to respond to McTaggart's Dilemma, the question of the nature of Hell must be met head-on, and no discussion of who and how many will be in Hell can do that. The history of discussions of Hell is thus deeply confused, since whatever popularity universalism possesses can be traced to perceived moral difficulties with the strong view of Hell. McTaggart's Dilemma focuses these difficulties in a rhetorically useful way, for it shows exactly why universalism cannot be a response to that dilemma.

With this correction, the topic of who will be saved can be explored, unencumbered by the problem of Hell. In one way, breaking the perceived connection between the population of Hell and the nature of Hell makes the former topic more relevant to the type of curiosity that leads some to wonder whether St. Paul thought, at least during one period of his life, that the second coming of Jesus would occur during his lifetime. Of course, for those with even a tad of concern for the long-term welfare of their fellows, the question of the population of Hell is of practical concern as well. But it is of practical concern because of the possibility of loss of fulfillment and a kind of misery that can be avoided, not an unanswerable moral concern arising from metaphorical descriptions of the horrors of Hell. To arrive at such a point requires, of course, a solution to McTaggart's Dilemma, and nothing in this essay provides such a solution, though I have argued for one elsewhere.[10] Even without such an account of the nature of Hell in front of us, however, we are entitled to note the following. No one should ever be tempted toward universalism because of perceived difficulties with the strong view of Hell of the sort nicely encapsulated in McTaggart's Dilemma, and no one should opt for universalism by pointing out contrasts between universalism and perceived failures of the strong view involved in that dilemma. To do so is just a rehearsal of the historical confusion that universalism provides some comfort for those troubled by the problem of Hell. Instead of playing off moral difficulties of alternative accounts of the nature of Hell, the universalist should argue against alternatives that share a morally adequate conception of the nature of Hell.

e strong view involved in that dilemma.

---

[10]For interesting discussion of the disparity between the Biblical conception of God and the strong view of Hell, see Adams (1975).

PART II

DIVINE DELIBERATION AND ACTION

OPEN THEISM AND THE FUTURE

4.1 Introduction

Open Theists all deny that God has exhaustive foreknowledge of the future, but they differ in their accounts as to why this is so. They tend, however, to want to maintain the doctrine of omniscience in spite of the limitation in question. Some say that God is omniscient in spite of the limitation because the claims about the future that he does not know are not true in the present, but will only come to be true later, and omniscience doesn't require knowing anything that isn't true. Others say that all claims about the future are truth, but some of them are unknowable and God is omniscient in virtue of knowing all that can be known. These positions share a common theme, however, and it is this: the future is composed of two parts, one part open to omniscience and the other part not. The part of the future that is not open to omniscience is the undetermined part, with future free actions being the prime and motivating example of such.

Here I will term this aspect of Open Theism "the Asymmetry Thesis"—the thesis that the part of the future that is determined by present and past events is secure in truth value and falls within the scope of omniscience, whereas the parts of the future that remain undetermined by the present and past do not fall within the scope of omniscience and perhaps are not secure in truth value. The Asymmetry Thesis faces serious troubles, and here I intend to cast doubt on its plausibility. I will argue that, given Open Theist assumptions, there is no part of the future that can be known to be true, including the determined part of it. I will begin by explaining what one needs to say to defend the Thesis and then say why it fails.

4.2 Explaining and Defending the Asymmetry Thesis

Worries about the future, both the possibility of knowing it and the possibility that claims about it lack truth value, are rooted in the idea that for something to be true and knowable there must be something accessible to us or God that makes the claims in question true. This claim involves two aspects. The first aspect is that truths require a truthmaker. The second aspect is an accessibility claim, expressible as the idea that whatever the truthmakers are, they have to be knowable. Knowable truthmakers for the future would clearly be enough to open the future to being known, and only knowable truthmakers would be enough in the present context. For God is not only a knower, but an infallible one; he is not only omniscient but essentially so. So if he holds a belief about a certain matter on the basis of something else, then the basis itself better not leave open the possibility of the belief being mistaken. This point dovetails in a fine way with the literature on truthmakers, which are a subclass of entailers: where T is a truthmaker for p, the existence of T entails p.[1]

Whether there are such truthmakers for every truth is a matter of some controversy. For example, it is true that Obama is President, but neither his existence nor the existence of the property of being President entail that he is. Nor does the combination of the two, since Obama could have existed and not been President.

Similar issues arise for general truths, such as the truth that all ravens are black. Even if we could find a truthmaker for the truth that a given raven is black, the collection of such truthmakers for each black raven doesn't entail that all ravens are black. To get that entailment, one has to have the further information that there aren't any other ravens. But this additional claim is itself a general truth, leaving us in the position of not being able to provide truthmakers for general truths by appeal to particularities.[2]

In response to these difficulties, the truthmaker view has need of an ontology containing states of affairs such as *Obama's being President* and *All raven's being black*, so that truth can be explained in terms of the obtaining of these states of affairs. An alternative view here abandons the notion of truthmaking in favor of a slightly weaker view in terms of which truth is held to supervene on being.[3] On this idea, for any proposition that is true at one world but not at another, there is something that exists at one world but not the other or some fundamental property or relation that is instantiated at one world but not the other. Though there are questions that can be raised about this proposal as well, the idea it contains is at least as intuitive and attractive as the truthmaker idea itself.

For present purposes, however, I will continue to use the language of truthmaking, since it is a congenial terminology in which to discuss the Asymmetry Thesis. In addition, nothing in the discussion to follow triggers any of the issues that separate the truthmaker proposal from the more general idea that truth supervenes on being, so there will be nothing gained in the discussion here by using the more cumbersome notion of the supervenience of truth on being rather than the notion of truthmaking.

To defend the Asymmetry Thesis, the Open Theist needs to defend two claims. The first claim is that there are knowable truthmakers for the part of the future that falls within the scope of God's omniscience, and the second claim is that there are no knowable truthmakers for the part of the future that falls outside the scope of God's omniscience. The difference between the two parts of the future, for Open Theists, concerns the intrusion of freedom into the story of actuality and the indeterminism that results from this intrusion. The existence of a divide that was orthogonal to the issue of freedom and determinism

---

[1] "By the truthmaker axiom I mean the axiom that for every truth there is a truthmaker; by a truthmaker for A, I mean something whose very existence entails A." (Fox 1987, p. 186)

[2] For discussion of these issues, see Keller (2004), Lewis (2001).

[3] See, for example, Bigelow (1988), Lewis (1983), Crisp (2007).

would provide no comfort to the Open Theist, for it is not the mere fact of un-knowable aspects to the future but the existence of such aspects as a result of indeterminism that forms the core claim of Open Theism.

The simplest way to proceed in finding what an Open Theist must say here is to focus on the parts of the future that fall within the scope of omniscience, and then simply argue that the other parts lack the features in question. So what should an Open Theist say here? The first point to note is what an Open Theist cannot appeal to, which is states of affairs and their future obtaining. If the parts of the future that are true and knowable in virtue of the existence of states of affairs that currently exist and have the property of obtaining in the future, the Asymmetry Thesis will be incapable of defense. For, if there are such states of affairs with such properties, there is no reason whatsoever to think that the Asymmetry Thesis is true in virtue of some indeterminism that can be found. If the Asymmetry Thesis were true given this explanation of truthmakers for the future, it would have to be because some states of affairs haven't come into existence yet or can't have the property of obtaining in the future (perhaps because there isn't any such property). There are possible views of this sort. For example, Robert Adams has suggested that states of affairs involving individuals may not come into existence until the individuals in question come into existence (Adams 1986). Even if such a view were defensible,[4] it wouldn't help the Open Theist, since this way of dividing the future into parts with truthmakers and parts without is orthogonal to the division in terms of freedom and indeterminism that Open Theism needs (since it provides no basis for thinking that there aren't such states of affairs regarding the future free actions of presently existing individuals).

We can approach the issue of the needed view for Open Theism by noting the following. It is obvious that the only possible features that could function as knowable truthmakers with any hope of carving the future into regions as desired by Open Theists would be something about God or about the world. If it is something about God, we should expect the claim to be something about what God ordains to be true about the future. Today, perhaps, God ordains that a certain event in the future will occur, and this ordinance itself is the knowable truthmaker for the future truth. More generally, some truths follow logically from sets of ordinances, so if God ordains all the elements of the set, then these ordinances are knowable truthmakers for anything logically implied by the set in question.

While it is surely unproblematic to posit the kind of self-knowledge that would be needed for God to know what he ordains and what he does not ordain, it is not so easy to defend the idea that such ordinances are truthmakers. To be a truthmaker, the entity in question must entail the truth in question, so if God ordains that it will rain tomorrow, then it must follow logically that it will rain tomorrow, i.e, it must be impossible for the ordinance to presently exist

---

[4]I argue that it is not defensible in Kvanvig (1989a). Adams replies to these criticisms in Adams (1989).

and it not rain tomorrow. Traditional theists have a ready explanation of why such an entailment is present, for traditional theists hold that God is essentially immutable in character, that he cannot will one thing at one time and change his mind to will something else at the next. But Open Theists don't envision God in this way. On the Open Theist position, God's nature changes in response to the indeterministic unfolding of the history of the world he has created. So, whereas the ordinances of God, on traditional theism, have an immutable character to them, they have no such character according to Open Theism. Without such an immutable character, however, ordinances cannot function as truthmakers, since they do not entail the content of the ordinance. If God's will is not immutable, he could ordain today that it rain tomorrow and yet it not rain tomorrow because he changes his mind in the meantime.

The Open Theist might try to solve this problem by agreeing that some ordinances are not immutable, but claiming that others are immutable. Such a move is a philosophy shrouded in mystery. What makes the difference here? Does God say to himself, "I really mean it this time!" when ordaining an immutable ordinance? Does he have more resolve about some ordinances than others? Maybe the furrow in the brow upon ordaining imparts the necessary permanence here.

Rhetorical questions don't take the place of an argument, however, so we must probe deeper if we are to find this proposal unacceptable. If we think carefully about what such a proposal requires, I believe we can see why this proposal will fail. As noted already, there is no account of ordaining that by itself entails that things ordained about the future will in fact happen. This point is independent of what kind of theist one happens to be, whether a Classical Theist or an Open Theist. What is needed in order to secure the implication is some further property of God. Classical Theists have the resources to secure the implication by noting that God is immutable, so that it is impossible for him to ordain one thing yesterday and something else tomorrow.[5]

If God is mutable, then his ordinances fall into two possible groups: those that will be revoked and those that won't be revoked. But this division among ordinances doesn't provide the resources needed to make some ordinances into truthmakers. If O is an ordinance regarding proposition p, then even if O is an ordinance that won't be revoked, O still won't entail p. We get the entailment only with the added information that O won't be revoked, so O alone isn't a truthmaker of p. Such an account is buck-passing of a most objectionable sort, since we now explain the truth of some claims about the future by appeal to another truth about the future, a truth about the free choices of the Divine. If the existence of freedom is somehow behind the truth of the Asymmetry Thesis, such an appeal is surely untoward.

---

[5]We could, of course, define 'ordinance' in such a way that only an unalterable entity could count as an ordinance. Then the question would be whether a mutable being could have the ability to ordain. But the issues would be the same, with no advantage to either side from the understanding of ordinances used in the text.

Perhaps an Open Theist might claim that there is a special class of potential ordinances that can only be ordained irrevocably. We might try to generate some plausibility to the idea in this way. Suppose that to annihilate an object requires doing something that makes it go out of existence. Suppose further that "gappy" existence isn't possible: it isn't possible, that is, for a thing to exist for a span of time, cease to exist for a time, and then reappear. Suppose further that one cannot ordain at t that a certain thing happen at t without making that thing happen at t when one has the power to do so. Then God's ordaining the annihilation of a thing can only be ordained irrevocably, and there is a non-empty class of irrevocable ordinances.

But even if there are some irrevocable ordinances of this sort, they provide no basis for arguing that the ordinances of a mutable being could be irrevocable regarding events in the future, for the example only shows that there are irrevocable ordinances where the event is simultaneous with the event. Moreover, the supposition that the ordainer is mutable provides a *prima facie* reason for thinking that any such ordinances about the future can be revoked. If there are some ordinances that, by their very nature, cannot be revoked, we need an account of the nature of such ordinances that, in the way described in the above paragraph for these very special synchronic annihilation ordinances, generates the conclusion that some diachronic ordinances (ordinances where the time of the ordinance and the time of the event diverge) can't be revoked. Merely claiming that there is no conclusive argument for claiming that they can be revoked has no probative value to rebut the *prima facie* evidence that such ordinances are revokable on the basis of the fact that it is a mutable being doing the ordaining. Such evidence leaves open the epistemic possibility of a defense of the idea of irrevokable diachronic ordinances, but no theory can be defended solely by appeal to its epistemic possibility.

For those who are willing to take the argumentative task seriously, the only hope I can see for providing a rational account of how some ordinances are irrevokable is by appeal to God's moral character. Even though Open Theists deny that God is immutable, they do not go so far as to deny God's moral perfection. Part of God's moral perfection involves the inability to do wrong, and since ordaining that a certain event will occur falls into the same general moral category as promising that it will occur, an Open Theist might argue that all of God's ordinances have to be irrevokable to avoid the charge that he is behaving wrongly in the same way that occurs when someone breaks a promise. Thus, it might be claimed, even though God is not immutable, he is immutable enough that we can conclude that he won't ordain anything in anything but an irrevokable way.

This line of argument cannot succeed, however, since breaking a promising and revoking an ordinance are not always wrong. They are always wrong for beings who have perfect predictive powers, for nothing unanticipated or unexpected can occur for such beings to explain why the *prima facie* wrongness of breaking a promise or revoking an ordinance is permitted in a given case. But for individuals lacking such perfect predictive powers, things can happen that justify the breaking of a promise and the revoking of an ordinance. It is of the essence of Open Theism that God is just such an individual lacking perfect predictive powers, so even if it is impossible for God's moral character to change or for God to do something wrong, it remains possible for God as conceived by Open Theists to break a promise and to revoke an ordinance.

A more general point can be made as well. The argument above relies on the idea that any promise is capable of defeat by further learning except for infallible promisers. Though relevant, this appeal to fallibility doesn't get to the core of the issue, since for any promise a fallible being might make and yet for whom predicting all possible futures was easy, a complete possible future could itself be the object of the promise. For example, God could promise to do whatever it takes to make the sun rise tomorrow, and then all possible futures will be covered by the quantifier "whatever", and so if the sun doesn't rise, it would count as a breaking of a promise and no information gleaned between now and then could count as a surprise to such a being that would warrant not keeping the promise.

There could be other defeaters of the *prima facie* obligatoriness of keeping the promise, however. One kind of defeater for keeping a promise is the "I've changed my mind but will make things up to you so that you won't be wronged and won't feel wronged" defeaters. So God can change his mind, if mutable, and still retain perfect goodness by failing to keep the promise in question in such a way that everyone affected by the change is not wronged because better off (or at least as well off) and suffers no remnant of feeling wronged because satisfied by what God does instead. In the limiting case, no moral patients are affected by such a change of mind, and so the justification is trivially present. But even in the non-trivial cases, such a defeater will be available to a mutable but omnipotent being. In short, the combination of fallibility, mutability, and omnipotence is a lethal combination for the attempt to generate truthmakers from God's moral perfection and the moral nature of promising.

Time for honesty. One can use the above to generate a defense of the Asymmetry Thesis, since it is possible for there to be a promise not subject to the above sort of defeater. Suppose the promise is that something exists or happens tomorrow. In such a case, no moral patients would exist to make things up to were such a promise violated. So, the advertised claim is false: there is a way for an Open Theist to defend the Asymmetry Thesis.

But: false advertising abounds on both sides, in a way of no comfort at all to Open Theism. The advertised view is that knowledge of the future is compromised by freedom and indeterminacy. What the above shows is that no rescue attempt for this view can be launched from the idea that some of God's promises might be irrevocable. It is true that some of God's promises might be of such a nature, and that because of this, the Asymmetry Thesis might be true. But if the class of knowable truths is so exceedingly small that it involves only claims such as *something will exist or happen* and its ilk, the false advertising by Open Theism vastly outweighs the false advertising of the claim espoused to this point that no defense of the Asymmetry Thesis is forthcoming.

The point is that there is nothing but hollow victory of the most philosophically ignominious sort in this defense of the Asymmetry Thesis. Except for the domains of freedom and indeterminism, any adequate defense must come close, at the very least, to covering all the remainder. The proposal here covers hardly anything of substance, leaving the motivations for even limited doctrines of providence unsatisfied. So, even if the Asymmetry Thesis can be rescued in this way, it provides nothing that will help explain how God can make promises and predictions about the future of the sort chronicled in the documents of the major religions of the Abrahamic tradition.

It is important to emphasize here that this counterargument doesn't affect the point that some of God's ordinances are *permanent*, i.e., that they never in fact are revoked. Such permanence of ordinance, however, is not enough for them to count as truthmakers, since a truthmaker has to entail, by itself, the truth of the proposition in question and also be a claim that itself is not about the future. When we need to add the idea that the ordinance is permanent before the inference to the proposition in question is valid, that guarantees that the entailment isn't present for the ordinance itself and thus that it isn't a truthmaker for the proposition in question. Moreover, the claim that a given ordinance is permanent is clearly an illegitimate truthmaker, since it is obviously about the future. So neither the ordinance itself nor the idea that the ordinance is permanent can help here.

Perhaps the most bizarre suggestion to try on behalf of Open Theism would be to suggest that God is eternal rather than everlasting, and that it is in virtue of God's being outside of time that some parts of the future are knowable and some are not. No Open Theist has ever suggested such an implausible view, and besides the fact that Open Theists generally reject the doctrine of eternity, it is fairly easy to see why adding the doctrine here and appealing to it to solve the problem under discussion isn't going to work. For if the Asymmetry Thesis about the future is true in virtue of something having to do with the doctrine of eternity, we should expect the same asymmetrical implications for the past and present, since it is at the core of the doctrine of eternity to deny that somehow there is greater intimacy between God and some parts of time over other parts of time. But Open Theists are averse to limitations on God's knowledge of the past and present, perhaps partly for the quasi-Ockhamist reason that difficulties a theory faces should not be multiplied beyond necessity, so any appeal to the doctrine of eternity will overreach wildly. In addition, if an appeal to God's eternity works to secure God's knowledge of some of the future, when that part of the future is unknowable on the basis of things past and present, there is no reason to suppose that God's eternity won't make available the entirety of the future.

The proper conclusion to draw here is that, if there is an explanation of how the determined parts of the future are fixed and knowable whereas the undetermined parts are not, it will need to be found in the created order itself rather than in some fact about God's nature, character, or intentions (as conceived by the Open Theist). This result is not terribly surprising, however, since Open Theists typically do not appeal to God or his activity to explain the distinction. It is rather some feature of the world itself that does explanatory work. And the feature is not hard to find; it is contained in the very description of the distinction in question. Some parts of the future are causally determined by events that have already occurred and some parts of the future are not causally determined. The former can be known and may partake of truth value; the latter cannot.

So the second option for defending the Asymmetry Thesis is simply to find an account of the distinction in an appeal to laws, initial conditions, and deterministic relationships between earlier states and later states. Here the Open Theist may try to exploit the usual introductory formulations of determinism. Such formulations go as follows. If you know the complete state of a deterministic universe at any one point in time, and you know all the laws that govern transitions from one state to the next, you can easily infer what will happen at the next instant. And then you'll be able to repeat the process for the following instant, and for every instant in the future. Thus, if the universe is completely deterministic, it is a fairly simple logical matter to use knowledge of the laws and of any given state of the universe to come to know completely what will happen in the future.

Of course, once an indeterministic component is thrown into the mix, things get more complicated. Perhaps, for example, the warming and cooling of the earth would be a completely deterministic process if human beings were removed from creation, but that with human beings thrown in with their freedom to pollute (or not), the future patterns of warming and cooling can no longer be predicted with full confidence. In fact, the degree to which the intrusion of freedom into creation muddies the waters of predictability may be so extensive that there is very little of the future that is predictable, if predictability requires immunity from possible interaction by indeterministic processes. The laws of nature do not cover whether or to what extent the relationships described will be interrupted, and they do not themselves describe when interruption is even possible. The laws contain at least implicitly *ceteris paribus* clauses about intrusion from outside the physical systems they govern, and one such intrusion is that provided by free human individuals.

In order, then, to find any part of the future to be knowable, the Open Theist will have to have some further information about which subsystems of nature are immune to human intrusion. Perhaps there are some subsystems of nature that human beings cannot affect. For example, if we knew that free individuals are only found in our solar system, then we could point out that interference cannot occur outside the light cone for our solar system (assuming, of course, the truth of the physical theories that limit interaction in this way). Of course, the antecedent here is a whopper for us, but not for God. So even given the messiness that the intrusion of freedom produces, there is no reason to suppose that the messiness extends so far as to undermine the distinction between the predictable parts of the future and the unpredictable. Perhaps not as much of the future can be known as some have thought, but that is no argument against the Open Theist position that there are two parts of the future, one having truth values and being knowable, and the other lacking truth values and hence being unknowable.

So we have found what the Open Theist must say here. The explanation of the Asymmetry Thesis is found by appeal to the power of determinism to allow predictions of the future. By knowing the laws and what has already occurred, the rest is simple logic. Where it isn't is the land of epistemological dragons: not even God will wander there, for therein lies inescapable risk of error.

4.3 The Nature of Laws and the Problem of Miracles

There is a problem, however, for this account and defense of the Asymmetry Thesis. The problem is miracles. In the global warming example, we saw how the intrusion of free individuals into the system of nature can rob the laws of their predictive power. Human beings may or may not pollute, and there are no laws that make it perfectly predictable whether they will or won't, and hence none of the laws that would be useful for predicting global warming and cooling can be used for that purpose once the human element is introduced into the system. Instead, the laws must be conceived as having *ceteris paribus* clauses that are violated by the intrusion of the human element. The laws themselves are not violated, however. It is just that the laws for a physical subsystem must be thought of as laws for the system on condition that no intrusion from outside the system occurs. Since human beings have the power to intrude into this particular physical subsystem, the laws become impotent for full and accurate prediction so long as such intrusion is possible.

If this is so of the minor power to intrude that human beings possess, it is also true of the immense power an omnipotent being has to intrude into any physical system whatsoever. If we have correctly characterized the situation of global warming in relation to intrusion by free human beings, then we will need to conclude that a similar problem undermines any attempt to predict the future because of the possibility of free intrusion into the universe in the form of miracles.

This result arises immediately on a very intuitive account of the laws of nature. On this account, a law of nature is a true conditional of some sort that contains a *ceteris paribus* clause in its antecedent to cover intrusions from outside the system governed by the law. For example, the laws of psychology involve an assumption that more fundamental biological features remain constant, so that the laws concerning human behavior aren't undermined by the fact that a bullet to the head keeps people from behaving in the way our best psychological theory predicts (assuming we had a good one, that is). The same is true about biology and the underlying chemistry, and it is true about the relationship between chemistry and the underlying physics. Finally, in the same vein, the laws of physics aren't violated when God chooses to intervene miraculously into the physical system of the universe, but the law is rendered explanatorily otiose in virtue of an intrusion from outside the system that is covered by the *ceteris paribus* clause of the relevant law.

The more empiricistically inclined Humeans among us will object, no doubt, to this understanding of laws of nature and the related notion of a miracle. On such a Humean approach, laws of nature are generalizations about the course of nature itself, and even if we can sort some generalizations for less basic sciences in a way that will be more useful to us by including *ceteris paribus* clauses, the basic laws of nature are nothing beyond the best system of regularities. As David Lewis puts it,

> Take all deductive systems whose theorems are true. Some are simpler, better systematized than others. Some are stronger, more informative, than others. These virtues compete: an uninformative system can be very simple, an unsystematized compendium of miscellaneous information can be very informative. The best system is the one that strikes as good a balance as truth will allow between simplicity and strength.... A regularity is a law iff it is a theorem of the best system. (Lewis 1994, p. 478)

Nothing is a regularity, of course, if it is not an exceptionless universal generalization, and the metaphysics that underlies this conception of laws is one on which the fundamental entities are particular, local facts and causation is nothing beyond a repeated pattern among types of particular, local facts that holds across all of spacetime. Lewis's "best system" account of laws is meant to address the problem that there are more regularities than laws, and so some device is needed to separate mere regularities from laws, and that is what the notion of a best system of regularities is intended to do. Laws are regularities that form the best trade-off between simplicity and strength.

On such a conception of laws, it is logically impossible for a miracle to be a violation of a law, for the laws contain no *ceteris paribus* clauses and it is incoherent to suppose that L is both a regularity across all of spacetime and yet has counterexamples to it induced by divine activity. Instead, miracles would need to be defined relative to the concept of a near-law, a regularity that holds almost always and everywhere, and to which a divine intervention is a counterexample. Of course, this necessary condition is far from a sufficient condition for being a miracle, but it is how the account must start.

Though nothing in what follows depends on the difficulties of turning this necessary condition for something's being a miracle into a sufficient condition, it is worth noting here that the problems for such a project are well nigh insurmountable. As noted already, being the violation of a near law is not sufficient for being a miracle, even if on the approach in question it is necessary. There are way too many near laws, leading to an easy reductio by pointing out that nearly every event in nature is a violation of some near law. In order to avoid a reductio from this point, a first step that some will want to take is to require that the near laws in relation to which the concept of a miracle is defined have to be near laws that are highly confirmed to be true. In this way, a miracle will need to be a very surprising event, whereas many violations of near laws are not surprising at all (think of highly correlated types of events such as being human and not having blue eyes, and the fact that some people count as violations of the related near law, the near law that no humans have blue eyes; or better yet, the near law that no humans are named J.L. Kvanvig, as close to a real Humean law as anything I know, even though I'm not at all surprised by my own name).

The kind of confirmation in question needs to be all-things-considered confirmation and not simply an overwhelming quantity of incremental confirmation. If we have an opaque and unopenable urn with one million marbles in it from which we've been sampling every second, with replacement, for the last ten thousand years, getting only white marbles except in one rare instance where we got a black marble, we don't want the selection of a black marble on the next draw to count as a miracle even though it is a violation of a generalization for which we have a great degree of incremental confirmation. We can avoid this result by noting that we have no all-things-considered confirmation for the generalization that there are only white marbles in the urn, since our background information entails that this claim is false.

This fact creates a difficulty for the near law conception of miracles, however. Suppose we start with confirmation at a time t for the claim that death is permanent. Suppose also that this isn't a law of nature, but only a near law. Suppose, then, that a miracle occurs at t^* (later than t) so that someone who was dead comes back to life. There is no longer any all-things-considered confirmation for the claim that death is permanent, so if there is another instance of someone who was dead coming back to life at t^{**} (later than t^*), this event cannot be a miracle in virtue of being a violation of the same near law. The only way for the same kinds of events to count as miracles is for later events to violate different near laws than earlier events. I believe there are ways to show that such generalizations can always be constructed by technical devices, but these devices provide no guarantee that the generalizations in question have ever entered into the minds of any person witnessing the events in question. Instead, the generalizations that will have entered our minds will be the original generalization that death is permanent and our immense surprise needs to be explained relative to that generalization and not some other one regarding which no exceptions have yet occurred. But if our surprise at a miracle is explained in terms of one generalization and the miraculousness of the event in terms of a different generalization, then once again we'll find ourselves admitting too many miracles into the natural world. If we are allowed technical devices to construct near laws for events, then nearly every event is a violation of some highly confirmed generalization. I'll give no argument for this claim, but just an illustration: the sun will rise tomorrow and won't do so miraculously even though it is highly confirmed for us that the sun has only risen on days prior to tomorrow. Now if we get to turn this event into a miracle by finding some other generalization relative to which the event in question is surprising, only a little philosophical ingenuity is needed to cause problems for the near law view of miracles. The weather prediction is that the sun will rise at 5:44 a.m. tomorrow. Such a prediction gives great fodder for surprise. If I've been unconscious since January and just awoke thinking that I've only been asleep overnight, I'll be immensely surprised by the time of the sunrise, since it is an inordinately early sunrise. But it is no miracle even though it is surprising (relative to one generalization) and a violation of a near law (relative to another generalization).

Moreover, even though the high confirmation requirement seems necessary in some cases, it seems unnecessary in other cases. A normal sequence of events would appear to be capable of being miraculous even though it doesn't surprise us and doesn't violate any regularities we are familiar with. Our knowledge of genetics is relatively recent in human history, but the regrettable effects of various genetic conditions are not recent. From all appearances, the longevity of a given person with a genetic condition that normally leads to early death may be unsurprising but undetectably miraculous. If we insist that it be a violation of a near law, there is no near law that we know of regarding which it is a violation. But it could be miraculous nonetheless.

Perhaps, though, we should think of the confirmation requirement in a slightly different way. We should think objectively in terms of the existence of evidence in the world, and note that this evidence confirms near laws as well as real laws. As cognizers, we fail to map these confirmation relationships in a number of ways. Sometimes we are unaware of the evidence in question, and other times we don't appreciate the force of the evidence. So when we say that something might be a miracle, that doesn't refute the confirmation requirement since the evidence might exist unawares and its force unappreciated. In both cases, however, the high degree of confirmation still exists for the near law.

Moreover, the reasons for wanting a high degree of confirmation to exist remain. Consider the following dilemma. Either it is possible for there to be a near law that is not highly confirmed, or it isn't possible. If it isn't possible, then the high confirmation requirement is automatically satisfied. So suppose it is possible and call one such near law "NL". We suppose that NL is false (since all near laws are), but that it has the power to imply counterfactuals, generate predictions, and undergird explanations in the way real laws do. We also have to suppose, however, that there are no patterns of events in nature that would make reasonable believing NL if they were discovered, since we are understanding confirmation here in the very objective way described in the last paragraph. Let M be an event that contradicts NL. Then M is a miracle, but would never be recognized as such if the only evidence considered is the basic evidence that noticed patterns in nature provide. But the status a regularity has of being a law or a near law must supervene on patterns of events in nature, since without such a supervenience claim, a regularity could be a near law even if hopelessly incompatible with the patterns in nature. For example, we don't want an account of near laws that lets it be a near law that everyone from North Dakota is over ten feet tall. But if we deny the confirmation requirement, interpreted objectively, we are stuck with such a possibility. So it appears that rightly interpreted, the high confirmation requirement can still be defended as essential to the near law account of miracles.

Specifying the confirmation requirement will take careful work, however. For the objective patterns in nature, considered as a whole, disconfirm every near law. So what must be said that is some proper subpattern exists which has confirming power with respect to a near law. Such a subpattern will need to be extensive enough that it generates a high degree of confirmation for the near law, so merely having a few instances of a false regularity won't be enough to show that a false regularity is a near law. The subpattern will have to be broad and extensive to have generate the required confirmation.

Consider in this context one actual miracle and one possible one. The actual miracle is creation itself; the possible one is the annihilation of the cosmos. For such events to be miracles, we would need to identify near laws that are highly confirmed and which are violated by these events. Moreover, the confirmation must arise objectively from subpatterns in nature, and this fact raises difficulties. First, if the laws supervene on the mosaic of local facts, it is hard to see how annihilation of the cosmos would differ from the non-miraculous cessation of the cosmos, so it is hard to see how such annihilations could be miraculous. Moreover, creation itself would require appeal to future regularities in order to be miraculous, and once again it is hard to see how creation itself would be a miracle whereas the unexplained origin of the total mosaic itself would not be.

The fundamental problems for such an account of laws and miracles, however, are not on the side of miracles but on the reductive relationship posited between the mosaic of local particular fact and the laws in question. We can begin to note where the problems will lie by noting that such a metaphysic makes it impossible to retain the truthmaker account being employed here, since the basic facts in question do not constitute truthmakers for the regularities in question, because the particular, local facts do not entail the generalizations (one must also have the information that there are no further facts that satisfy the antecedent in question before the generalization follows). It still may be true, however, that truth supervenes on being, in the sense that any difference at the level of truth between two worlds requires a difference at the level of local particular fact (i.e., a difference in basic objects or in the fundamental properties or relations that they display).

As noted earlier, the differences between the truthmaker account and the account on which truth supervenes on being have been ignored to this point since the language of the truthmaker account is quite intuitive and the differences have made no difference to the course of our discussion up to this point. But here they do. On a non-Humean account with a traditional understanding of God as being immutable in his decisions, we can talk in terms of truthmakers present at the original creation for everything that happens throughout the entire history of a deterministic cosmos. The laws are themselves fundamental facts about the cosmos rather than a kind of generalization having only derivative status from the more basic particular facts, and thus can be appealed to in an unproblematic way as truthmakers for everything subsequent (so long as we also know the immutable intentions of God concerning when to intervene into the created order and when not to). But if the laws are derivative entities that depend on God's creative choices regarding local facts, nothing of the sort can be said. There is only the actualization of "one damn fact after another," and the best system of regularities is elicited from these more fundamental creative acts rather than the local facts being generated by fundamental laws and initial conditions. In choosing to create, given this Humean metaphysic of the created order, God would have no choice except to select particular facts to actualize, and then calculate the nature of the laws from whatever sequence of particular facts is selected.

Once we adopt such an understanding of creation with respect to worlds assumed to be deterministic (so that God only needs to metaphysically determine the entire constellation of particular facts to create the cosmos), the next question that must be answered is how to conceive of creation under indeterminism. To retain the Humean flavor, the introduction of chance into the picture must still honor the idea that everything is fixed by the arrangement of local qualities and objects in spacetime, where this local requirement forbids appeal to such items as global features of the world, modal properties, and irreducible probabilistic properties as well. The attempt to retain such a Humean flavor, however, wreaks havoc with the Open Theist's attempt to divide the future into knowable and unknowable regions, where the latter is the domain in which chance plays a role. For on the Humean picture, what the chances are is a function of the totality of spacetime, and on any account of creation God creates by actualizing whatever is metaphysically basic. Once the metaphysically basic is actualized, however, the laws and chances are fixed on the Humean picture, but in a way that is irrelevant to God's ability or need to predict the future in order to know what will happen. For he has already, on this picture, fixed the entire mosaic of local qualities in spacetime—a mosaic that fixes both laws and chances. By knowing what he creates, however, he bypasses the need for any appeal to laws and chances to calculate what will happen in the future.

Nor is there any refuge in the idea of God's creative activity spanning all of the time involved in the spacetime of the cosmos, so that he too must predict what will happen next on the basis of what has happened to this point. A picture of diachronic creation in which God needs recourse to the created past and present to predict what he will do next is an unbecoming subjection of the Creator to the created order, positing some inability in the Divine Mind to know itself except through knowledge of past behavior. Moreover, if there is such a problem of prediction, the problem infects absolutely every nook and cranny regarding the future, and not just the undetermined parts of it, thereby undermining the Asymmetry Thesis.

The problem here is relatively simple to appreciate once we realize the implications of any reductive account of chance, according to which chance can be reduced to local particular facts. Our ordinary notion of chance allows that precisely the same total world history can result from different total chance patterns.

The precise, total history is, after all, a matter of chance, and different values for chance still leave some chance of same total outcome. It is this idea that lies at the core of the problem of undermining futures for David Lewis's attempt to describe the notion of chance in a way that is compatible with his Humean supervenience claim, for given a history of the world up until a certain time, where the laws both chancy and otherwise are L for that world, there is a chance of a future for that world that entails that the laws are not L.[6] Thus, on a reductive account of chance and laws, information about the future renders all predictability fallible, even when the basis of the prediction includes the laws themselves. To the extent that God's knowledge is incapable of error, reductive accounts of laws and chance are incompatible with any divine foreknowledge whatsoever, and hence cannot be used in defense of the asymmetry thesis. Avoiding such skeptical conclusions about the possibility of divine foreknowledge requires focusing on the supervenience base itself as the direct object of the divine creative activity, but then if God's knowing his own creative intentions allows divine knowledge of some of the future it also allows knowledge of all of the future, since all of it is the direct object of his divine creative activity.

These points can be summarized more succinctly by noting the following. The Humean picture according to which fundamental reality is simply the mosaic of local fact changes the terms of the debate regarding not only the nature of laws of nature but also the free will/determinism debate. On the Humean picture, laws of nature cannot play a metaphysically explanatory role regarding what comes next, since what comes next helps explain which generalizations are laws and which are not. Moreover, whether chance plays a fundamental role in creation is a matter, on this Humean metaphysic, of the best system as well, and the assessment of which system is best is one that can be made only after the fact, for there is always a chance of something happening that will make what is in fact a law into a non-law: that is, at its core, the problem of undermining futures for such a Humeanism. If all of this is correct, however, the metaphysical basis on which the Open Theist relies in carving the future into the parts that are determined and those that are not is undermined. It is only after the fact that the information would be available that reveals which parts of the future are chance-infected and which are not. As a result, the division into determined and chancy provides a distinction of no use in explaining what can be known in advance and what can't. The features required for such knowledge are in place only further down the road of time and history, and thus provide no resources for sustaining the Asymmetry Thesis.

In sum, a reductive Humean account of laws and chances yields nothing of probative value for the Open Theist attempting to defend the Asymmetry Thesis. To find such implications, the Open Theist needs to embrace an indeterminism based on powers and potentialities in things themselves. In such a case, precisely

---

[6]The literature on the problem of undermining futures has grown quite large. Here is a representative sample: Arntzenius and Hall (2003), Bigelow *et al.* (1993), Hall (1994), Lewis (1980), Schaffer (2003), Ward (2002).

the same total history can result from different types and arrangements of powers and potentialities, and this fact alone undermines any Humean supervenience claim about such powers and potentialities. Moreover, by appeal to such powers and potentialities in things themselves, we can define the collection of laws and chances for a world that similarly resists reduction to the mosaic of local facts. By generating the total mosaic through the direct dispersement of such powers and potentialities to things themselves, some hope arises for the Open Theist that a defense of the Asymmetry Thesis can be found, for such an account puts God in the position of needing to predict, from the character of such potentialities and powers, what the future will be like. Should these potentialities and powers be chancy through and through, then it appears that there will be no infallible guide to the way in which the total mosaic of local fact will turn out. Thus, on this conception, it appears that there will be parts of the future that are not knowable to a being who can only know by knowing infallibly.

Once the Open Theist goes this far from the Humean supervenience claim regarding laws and chances, however, the notion of miracle that fits best with this anti-Humean view is the one described earlier in which the laws contain *ceteris paribus* clauses. If God creates things with potentialities and powers, he has the power to override the display of these powers to his own ends, and when he does so, the result is a miracle. To claim that miracles of this sort cannot occur would require an argument that the only way a potentiality or power could be instantiated in an individual would be in a way which could not be overridden, and it would be truly amazing to find such an argument since we are all familiar with powers and potentialities that are overridden: think of, for example, arm-wrestling competitions, and what one must say about the one whose power to move things was defeated on that occasion.

There is a way to misunderstand this point that bears avoiding. The claim here is not intended to be an example of ordinary language philosophy in which I am clarifying the meanings of terms in ordinary language. I do not believe that what I'm saying about laws and miracles diverges to any great extent from how these terms are used in ordinary language, but the points I am making here do not depend on appeals to ordinary language and the meanings encoded in it. What is crucial to my case is that there is a kind of action that an omnipotent being could perform that involves overriding the powers and potentialities of the things he has created so as to secure a given intended result that was not guaranteed by the operation of the powers and potentialities themselves. I will here term such a divine intervention a "miracle," but in so doing I am not claiming and do not need to claim to be honoring standard usage for the term.

I will also refer to such miraculous interventions in terms of *ceteris paribus* clause of what I will term "laws", though again I make no claim to be using the term in a way that is not partially stipulative. What I am claiming is that powers and potentialities involve normal operations that can be described in terms of generalizations, and it is these generalizations (or a subclass of them) that I will term "laws." These generalizations, subject as they are to divine intervention if not intervention by more basic features of the created order, must contain *ceteris paribus* clauses in order to be true, and given my perhaps slightly stipulative use of the term "law", it follows that we can describe miracles in terms of an overriding of the *ceteris paribus* clause of laws of nature. I repeat, however, that I make no pretense to claiming that the terms in question in ordinary language are properly clarified in such terms.

So, the miracles I'm interested in here are overridings of *ceteris paribus* clauses of laws of nature. Such an overriding renders the law impotent for predictive and explanatory purposes without additional information about what overridings will in fact occur. The law is still a law. When its antecedent is true, including the *ceteris paribus* requirement that no intrusion from outside the system will occur, then the law is perfectly useful for prediction and explanation. But when God performs a miracle, the law sits idly by, useless for any such purpose.

The possibility of such miracles, however, has important implications for the attempt by the Open Theist to defend the Asymmetry Thesis on the basis of an appeal to powers and potentialities and the correlative notion of laws containing such *ceteris paribus* clauses. Above we noted how the appeal to such a conception of creation raises problems for infallible knowledge of the undetermined parts of the future, but the Asymmetry Thesis is not the general skeptical thesis that infallible knowledge of the future is not possible. In addition to arguing that the undetermined parts of the future cannot be known infallibly, a defense of the Asymmetry Thesis must also contain an argument that the determined parts of the future can be known infallibly. In order to find a knowable part of the future, God would have to be able to know the laws and what has already happened, but he would also have to be able to know when the *ceteris paribus* clauses will be overridden and when they will not. The Classical Theist can explain such knowledge, because if we assume that such miracles are performable only by God, then God can know when *ceteris paribus* clauses will be violated simply by knowing his own intentions. But Classical Theists get to carry forward in time any information about God's present intentions through the doctrine of immutability. Open Theists reject this doctrine, and hence have no vehicle with which to ensure that God's intentions tomorrow will be the same as they are today. So, given Open Theism, it is not predictable even for God when *ceteris paribus* clauses will be violated, and hence there is no part of the future that is predictable, even when the part of the future in question is causally determined by the things that have already occurred.

Let us apply this worry to a particular kind of argument that might be given for how God can know the determined part of the future. One might argue as follows. Certain aspects of the future are now causally inevitable. But if they are causally inevitable, then God can know that these aspects will obtain by knowing the conditions that make these aspects causally inevitable.

This argument fails because the operator "it is causally inevitable that" offers no metaphysical guarantee of a future when the notion of causal inevitability is understood to supervene on the powers and potentialities under discussion here.

It doesn't follow from the fact that p is causally inevitable in this sense that p is, or will be, true. What may follow is that there is nothing that you or I or anyone or anything else in the created order can do to prevent p's being true. Only with the additional information that the *ceteris paribus* clauses involved in the generalizations about the causal powers and potentialities will not be overridden does the conclusion follow.

Some may worry about these claims, thinking they conflict with the primary argument for the libertarian conception of freedom, Peter van Inwagen's Consequence Argument.[7] If such conflict exists, that's not a reason by itself to reject the argument, but in fact, no such conflict is implied. The argument for libertarianism employs the idea that given that certain features of the world are unavoidable for me resulting in a future that is unavoidable for me as well. The mere fact that the future is not logically implied by the laws plus the initial conditions doesn't by itself undermine this claim, and it is not hard to see that the failure of implication doesn't affect this part of the Consequence Argument. The future might be inevitable for me even if not knowable infallibly even to God, since the sorts of things one has to have control over in order to block the force of the causal factors already in place might be things that I have no control over at all. All that is blocked here is arguing for the inevitability of the future on the basis of an argument that the laws plus the initial conditions logically imply the future.

We can summarize the above argument in the following way. The problem of miracles makes it impossible for the Open Theist to find any part of the future which is knowable if there is any part of the future that is unknowable. The apparent refuge found in the distinction between the determined parts of the future and the undetermined parts is no refuge at all, given the possibility of miracles. The only hope for the Open Theist on this point is to claim that God has the power to decide something freely that then metaphysically binds him forever. The question for the Open Theist, however, is how this could be so. For the Open Theist conceives of God to be mutable, and thus cannot find a truthmaker for any claim about the God will do in the future any more than God can locate a truthmaker for what I will do in the future (given the account of truthmakers and the Open Theist restrictions on information available to God to use in trying to predict what I will do).

4.4   Conclusion

So the result is that the Open Theist should abandon the Asymmetry Thesis. Doing so results, however, in unbelievably severe restrictions on the doctrine of

---

[7]Van Inwagen holds that the argument for free will and the argument against classical omniscience are analogous. He says, "The . . . argument for the incompatibility of divine omniscience and creaturely free will (it is modeled on certain well-known arguments for the incompatibility of determinism and free will) seems to me to be irrefutable" (van Inwagen 2008a, p. 2). The free will argument employs the idea that given that certain features of the world are unavoidable for me, and they make the future inevitable for me, the future is unavoidable for me as well.

Providence and the scope of prophecy. Not even if God decides that Peter must deny Christ is that an adequate basis for a prophetic utterance that Peter will do so, since Peter's future actions, even if causally determined or ordained by God with the greatest divine resolve possible, aren't knowable to God at the time of the prophecy.

Open Theism could be revised further to avoid denying the Asymmetry Thesis, for it is central to the above argument that God only knows what he knows infallibly. If we loosen the requirements on divine foreknowledge so that being capable of being mistaken is compatible with divine foreknowledge in the same way that it is compatible with ordinary human knowledge, then the argument against the Asymmetry Thesis is no longer compelling. At the same time, however, there is little basis for the idea that we can't know what free individuals will do in the future, and so little basis left for the skepticism about the undetermined parts of the future that are central to the Asymmetry Thesis. Though these issues take us well beyond the purpose of this essay, it is implausible to suppose that I can't know that my daughter will be happy when I give her a new car tomorrow, and it would be an embarrassment of the deepest sort to claim that God is maximally excellent in cognition and yet fails to know some things about the future that I know.

My intention, however, is not to explore the details of revising Open Theism in light of the problem raised here. Instead, my goal has been to show that the changes wrought in a coherent conception of the divine by Open Theist assumptions are much more dramatic and deep than Open Theists have appreciated to this point. In particular, without altering the traditional understanding of divine cognitive perfection, which requires that God knows infallibly everything that he knows, there is no defense available of the view that there are some parts of the future that are knowable to God even if some other parts are not.

uch more dramatic and deep than Open Theists have appreciated to this point. In particular, without altering the traditional understanding of divine cognitive perfection, which requires that God knows infallibly everything that he knows, there is no defense ava

5

A TALE OF TWO CRONIES

Moll and Ott share a religious vision that includes thinking of creation of the inanimate parts of creation in terms of God's imparting certain causal powers to things. So, for example, limestone is softer than granite, and according to Moll and Ott the reason is that the two have different causal powers. If water runs over limestone, it wears away much faster than when water runs over granite. Water thus also has causal powers, here the power to wear away rock (though both agree that such a commonsense account of the causal power in question will likely give way to a much more sophisticated scientific description when the power in question is subjected to scientific inquiry). From these causal powers arise whatever laws of nature govern such entities, and the causal powers thus support counterfactual claims as well. In a deterministic world with nothing but inanimate things, God can create by creating things with causal powers. These powers perhaps even correlate perfectly with the truth of various conditionals, conditionals about what will happen given the original conditions and conditionals about what would happen had things been slightly different from what they in fact are.

Moll and Ott's happy moment of sharing is interrupted by Occ. Occ insists that the story is rather silly. Occ says that God created the things in question together with their characteristic behavior patterns. Occ insists that we not talk of creating things that have power until and unless we can show some need for such talk and we can show that such a creation is even possible. Occ claims that the view shared by Moll and Ott suffers on both counts. Occ notes first that all the explanatory work regarding the unfolding of creation is being done by the conditionals themselves which are claimed to be perfectly correlated with the causal powers. If so, Occ claims, there is no need for the causal powers at all, unless they come for free in virtue of being reducible to the conditionals. If they are reducible in this way, however, they don't really make anything happen. God makes it all happen with his almighty power—a power no one dreams of reducing to conditionals of one sort or another. *That* is real power, Occ insists; whatever is reducible to conditionals is just ersatz power—power in name only. So why bother with it when you want to engage in metaphysics? Perhaps when one is doing science, one might wish to resort to such language, but even there things are far from clear.[1] Talk of causal powers in nature is thus superfluous; it

---

[1] Consider, for example, Bertrand Russell's famous attack on the law of causality in Russell (1912).

is talk of a mere shadow, an epiphenomenon, of the real power to make things happen, and misleading to mention because of it.

Moreover, Occ continues, there is a problem with your theory, since you've got both causation and entailment in the same story. On your story, God creates by performing an action that entails the entire history of the cosmos: he makes the things that exist and the rules of the unfolding in the form of conditionals, and the rest is history. But entailment co-opts causation, doesn't it? If one event entails another, say, someone's being a bachelor entailing that they are male, then neither event is a cause of the other. The presence of entailment co-opts the situation in question, so that no power can be displayed by the first thing to bring about the second when conditions are in place that entail it. So, for any event in the course of the history of this cosmos, God's initial creative action entails that this event occurs. So there is no causality in nature and no causal powers distributed by God to the things he creates.

Moll and Ott balk at Occ's arguments, but Occ asks for patience to listen to a reminder. He asks not to be reprimanded on grounds having to do with freedom and other indeterminacies in nature. He points out that he already knows that Moll and Ott aren't determinists, but he asks that they simply assume determinism when thinking about what he's saying. What to say about indeterminacies can be addressed later, but for now, given determinism, they should agree that all power is God's power.

Moll and Ott wave the point away, saying they aren't convinced and for reasons that have nothing to do with their perspective on human freedom. They note that the entailment claim Occ makes is unassailable: there is an action God performs that entails the entire course of history for the inanimate, deterministic parts of our world. After all, a strong doctrine of providence is supposed to be easy to state, given the assumption of determinism, and the existence of such an action is what is required for a defense of such. But, they say, the existence of this action doesn't prevent the dispensing of causal powers, but rather involves it. The action in question entails the future because it involves the sharing of power with created things. It is thus not in competition with the presence of deterministic causal powers in things, but rather in cooperation with them. God could have created a world, perhaps, in a way that involved no sharing of power at all, but he could equally have created a deterministic world in which the entire future is entailed in part because he imparts deterministic causal powers to things.

They note also that Occ has noticed an important aspect of their view, that the impartation of causal powers here is rather fine-grained. It is fine-grained enough that the causal power of the water has the precise implications for true conditionals that it does, and fine-grained enough that the causal powers of limestone and granite have the precise implications for true conditionals that they do. It is not as if the imputation of power is one thing, distinct from the implications that displays of the power in question have. The correct story is that the imparted powers are crafted specifically to have the implications when displayed that they in fact have.

Even so, they insist, it is one thing for God to actualize a total world history by imparting such powers, and another thing for him to actualize a total world history by imparting no such powers to things, even if the two histories are, at some level of description, identical. The causal powers have precisely the implications they have because of aspects of the creative action of God—the action that entails the entire history of the world. But they are no less real powers because of the entailment. They are no less real because the act of God that entails the entire history also entails the existence of the powers in question.

Occ whines. God performs an action and creation flowers; given the action, the result follows logically. There is no work to be done beyond the work God has already done! Nothing more is needed. You grant that a world in which God makes everything happen just as it does in the deterministic world, with no help from causal powers of any sort, is possible. But you insist that the same sequence of events can be accomplished by the impartation of causal powers. In both cases, there is an action of God in terms of the creation of things and the conditionals that characterize them that entails the identical Humean history of particular local fact. But then causal powers are irrelevant unless they come for free. All the work in the unfolding of history is being done by the conditionals, and those conditionals are either metaphysically independent of the causal powers in question or the causal powers are reducible to the conditionals. You have to say this because you want the entailment from God's action to the unfolding of history so that a doctrine of divine providence follows. The central element in all this is the conditionals, not the causal powers. It is the conditionals that carry all the explanatory weight, and the action of God that entails the unfolding of history is the action specifiable in terms of these conditionals, whether, as you say, causal power is involved or not. So causation comes for free or does no explanatory work in the story, since once we specify the action of God in question, there is no difference to be made in the unfolding of history by anything else. The entailment trumps any such difference makers. There, I've had my say, Occ says, and sits down.

Moll responds. You're right that from the point of view of providence, it is all about the conditionals. But there are still two ways to get them. One is to make them true directly, and the other is to make them true by imparting causal powers to things. There's no need here to reduce the causal powers to the conditionals; after all, the history of attempts to give such reductions is uniformly littered with failures. What matters isn't reduction, but supervenience, conceived as one-way entailment. Same causal powers gives you same conditionals, and that's all that is needed here.

But there is something important in what you say about the relationship between causation and entailment. You think of God as performing an action specifiable in terms of the conditionals in question and thus entailing all of history (for our imaginary deterministic and inanimate world). Ott and I think of God as performing an action that entails the distribution of causal powers that entail the conditionals in question and thus all of its history. For God to perform the action we are thinking of, he also performs the action you are thinking of. So there is an action God performs that entails the unfolding of history without mentioning causal powers at all. Hence, your point is well-taken: we must deny that entailments trump causation. But we knew all that already, since we can specify causal powers in terms of their characteristic effects and thus generate entailments between events in terms of such specifications of the causal powers of the things involved in the events. Difference-making thus operates in an arena distinct from the arena in which entailments appear. So, you're right, Occ: we insist that causation can exist between events even when there is a description of each event so that an entailment can be found between the two as well. But that's not a problem, that's our theory!

Ott joins in. That may seem to be an awkward position to be in, but suppose we think of it this way. In some cases, entailments prevent the presence of causation, such as in the case of the event of some person being a bachelor and that person being a male. In other cases, such as the relationship between God's creative activity and the cosmos that results, entailments are compatible with the presence of causation. We have to find a way to split the cases, as the lawyers say. Maybe the difference is that entailments between events in the created order rule out causation. I don't know. But such an account has one virtue in its favor, since we want God's activity to necessitate its result and still be a display of God's power. For it to be such a display of power, it must be causal in some sort of way, for it *makes things happen.* If that's not causal, I don't know what is. So perhaps this way of splitting the cases will do.

Moll nods cautiously, though with a significant bit of intellectual discomfort. She is certain that causal powers in nature is not an incoherent idea, but she is also pretty convinced that logical relations are not causal relations. But of course they can be, since if God makes things happen just by willing them to be so, there is no possibility of the latter occurring without the former. She is finally convinced. That's it, Ott must be right: entailments that derive from God's activity don't threaten the existence of causal relations in nature.

Both Moll and Ott realize that Occ can turn to skeptical arguments against their view, but they take comfort in the fact that skepticism is a hard problem for any view. Occ realizes the power of skepticism here as well, but decides to respect the metaphysical context of the discussion and not raise epistemological problems at this point. So he says to Moll and Ott, yes, I see that you can save your view in that way. And I guess I have to agree that entailments aren't incompatible with causal relations in the case of divine activity. The difference is that you two have to bracket entailments from God's activity when looking for power in the world, for displays of causal power are things that make a difference to the course of history. That's a rough idea that needs refining to account for things like overdetermination, preemption, pseudo-preemption, double preemption, and

all the other fascinating obstacles to a proper understanding of causation.[2] I
won't bother to refine the idea here, because you've already granted the point I
need, which is that if we hold fixed God's actions, everything in our imaginary
deterministic and inanimate world follows, and there is no room for causal powers
to make a difference at all. I, on the other hand, don't have to engage in such
bracketing chicanery. I realize you can save your view from contradiction by this
device, but it is strained.

Ott objects. We're not bracketing God's activity, we're just bracketing certain
descriptions of it—the descriptions that entail the entire course of history. In the
two worlds with the same total mosaic of local fact, God's activity is different in
the two cases: in one case he imparts causal powers and in the other he doesn't.
In both cases, these different acts of God can be described in the same way,
and the description is what entails the entire history in question. Bracketing the
description is not bracketing the action, just as refusing to allow a description
of a cause in terms of its effect isn't bracketing the cause.

Yes you pronounce it *poe-tay-toe* and I say *poe-tah-toe*, Occ retorts. You think
all you need is to separate the real activity in terms of causal powers from the
description in terms of conditionals. That's no argument, though, that's just your
theory. I say the real activity is in terms of conditionals, and the description is in
terms of causal powers. But you also say that the causal powers in question are
individuated in a very fine-grained way—so fine-grained that they implicate the
precise conditionals which supervene on them. So you cheat when you distinguish
the activity of God specifiable in terms of imparting causal powers from a mere
description in terms of making conditionals true. In the case of describing a cause
in terms of its effect, it is plausible to ask for an intrinsic characterization of the
cause in place of such an extrinsic one. But when describing God's activity,
you've already committed yourself to the presence of the conditionals in the
intrinsic characterization of the activity. Without it, you haven't got the causal
powers fine-grained enough for the remainder of history to unfold from the initial
creative act of God. So what you have to have in the characterization of God's
activity is the conditionals. The rest is gravy.

Yes, Ott says, you can legitimately push us here, and we may have to resort
to the idea of characterizing an event or act in terms of its most fine-grained
description to draw the distinction we need.

As soon as he said it, though, he realized the mistake. Occ starts to say
something, but Ott stops him: Oops, that won't work, will it? In the case of
God's activity, the most fine-grained description entails all of history. Hmmm. . .

Moll comes to Ott's rescue here. Occ, you're right, she says. We are going to
have to say something a bit uncomfortable about the relationship between the
divine creative activity and causal powers in nature. We are going to have to
say one thing about the relationship between entailment and causation in the
created order itself, and another thing about the relationship between entailment

---

[2]For an excellent group of articles on these complexities, see Collins *et al.* (2004).

and causation in order to avoid God's power from engulfing and eliminating the possibility of causal powers in the created order. That's OK, though, since God's activity both causes and entails one and the same effect, so everybody has to allow some overlap here when including the supernatural realm in the discussion. So it's a bit of a problem to have to say that causation can happen in nature even in the presence of entailment from supernature, but not enough of a problem to compel adopting your perspective.

Ott is nodding enthusiastically. That's what I think I was trying to get at when I suggested earlier that we carve off intramundane claims about the relationship between causation and entailment from those involving God's activity. We should expect some incompatibility between the two when dealing with intramundane matters, but not when God is brought into the picture. We can then get a strong doctrine of providence for deterministic worlds without having to endorse the view that God cannot impart powers to his creation.

Occ says something under his breath about theft and honest toil, but decides to pursue a different line of thought. He'll let that point go for now, since, he says, I notice some implications here for something you two disagree about. Neither one of you thinks that our world is either composed solely of inanimate things or that it is a deterministic world. Both of you think there is such a thing as libertarian freedom. And what you have just said makes Moll's position easier to defend, doesn't it Ott?

Moll and Ott are puzzled. They agree on some things and disagree on others, but aren't sure to which disagreement Occ refers. Moll is courageous, though, and speaks up. Let me see, she says. You refer to libertarian freedom, and to a disagreement we have about its effects. So let's set up the case by adding to our description of the world some animate and free creatures, endowed by their Creator with libertarian causal power. The causal power in question is libertarian because it concerns actions—human actions, we may assume, that are free, and libertarianism is the correct theory of free human action. For simplicity, let's assume that the characteristic feature of this theory is that it endorses some version of the Principle of Alternative Possibilities (PAP), according to which a person has libertarian causal power (or freedom) only if that person could have done otherwise (in some sense). I know there is a bevy of proposals about the exact sense of "could have done otherwise", but let's not get into that unless we have to.

So back to the question of what disagreement Ott and I have. Ott doesn't want these powers to be fine-grained, while I do. I want to endorse the view that in creating, God exercises full providential control over every detail of history. Ott doesn't. He wants a responsive God—a God who creates, and then acts further in response to how things unfold. How things unfold, on his view, is neither controlled by God nor fully predictable. I, on the other hand, want libertarian causal powers to be fine-grained, as fine-grained as deterministic causal powers are: they are fine-grained enough that they come with conditionals attached about what the individual with that power will do and would do. Is that the disagreement you have in mind, Occ?

Occ nods agreement that this is the dispute he has in mind. Occ turns to Ott and says, so what don't you like about Moll's view? I'm betting that when you answer, you'll say something that takes us back to the dispute between you two and me.

Ott says, well, I don't think such fine-grained libertarian causal powers are possible. If God imparts such causal powers, then he has done something that entails that the free individuals in question behave as they do, and hence they are not free.

See, Occ exclaims, I told you so! A moment ago, you two agreed that you have to bracket God's entailing activity when discerning whether and which causal powers exist in the created order, and now you appeal to God's entailing activity to claim that Moll's view is incoherent! I think you are right: her view should be rejected. She shouldn't be allowed to bracket God's entailing activity here, just as it shouldn't have been bracketed when discussing the possibility of causal powers in nature. Gee, that would get us my view, wouldn't it? I like it!

Ott resists, though. Having once practiced the art of splitting cases, he tries to apply the skill again. He claims that the entailment isn't an issue when it comes to deterministic causal powers, but it is an issue when it comes to libertarian causal powers. For libertarian causal powers are governed by PAP, and thus require a kind of openness of the future that deterministic causal powers do not. So prior conditions that entail an action eliminate the possibility of freedom.

Moll asks if she may take a role in defending her own view, and threatens an accusation of sexism against the narrator if denied. She points out that some of her persuasion accept Ott's reasoning, and so deny that God's creative activity entails the entire unfolding of the cosmos. They hold, instead, that some additional premises are needed to yield the complete story of the universe—truths unlike the modal truths of mathematics and logic that are metaphysically necessary. These additional truths, though known by God, are not part of his creative activity.

But I think I see Occ's point: they lost heart too easily. Ott and I have already agreed that entailments from God's activity don't undermine the claim that there are powers in the created order that make a difference to its unfolding. I add that some of these causal powers are libertarian causal powers and some are deterministic causal powers. Ott claims that the entailment in question isn't relevant to the latter type of causal powers but it is relevant to the former. I've never seen why, myself, though we've never quite discussed the matter in these terms. But Occ's presence here makes all the difference, doesn't it? It shows that the worry about entailment is general enough that if we want to resist its relevance for deterministic causal powers, we should do so as well for libertarian causal powers. God is free to endow creatures with as fine-grained libertarian causal powers as he wishes, and in the view that Occ and I share, he will do so in such a way as to exercise strong providential control over his creation. Perhaps you, Ott, can split the cases in a way that allows his own denial of providence to avoid refutation here, but splitting the cases in such a way as to save your own view doesn't yield any problem for my view. When we split the cases against you, Occ, we didn't pretend that we now had a refutation of your view: we were just trying to keep your argument from undermining ours. Just so here, Ott: you can split the cases to preserve your own view, but in doing so, you don't create any problem for mine. So I repeat my own view: you and I share the view that entailments from divine activity need not undermine the presence in the created order of powers to make a difference, and I add that this goes for completely fine-grained powers of both deterministic and libertarian sorts.

Ott asks for a moment to think, since he finds this all very confusing. He thought he had a good objection, but it now seems to have disappeared. He wants to say that if the entailment holds, then PAP has to be false, since given God's action A, it is impossible for the individual in question to have done otherwise. But he knows this mistake well: it is the mistake of confusing the necessity of the consequent and the necessity of the consequence. God's action A doesn't entail that Fred can't do otherwise. It only entails that he won't.

But even a mistake can help one see the light, and Ott has the experience of a light going on. He says, Look, with deterministic causal powers, if we know the exact nature of the power, we automatically get the conditionals needed for perfect predictability. But that isn't so with libertarian causal powers, for if it were, PAP would be false and the distinction between libertarian and deterministic causal powers would disappear, wouldn't it?

Well, Moll says, the distinction won't disappear unless you can infer back from the conditionals to the powers themselves. So long as all we have is supervenience, as we agreed above, then there is no problem of a lost distinction here. Moreover, we really don't want more than supervenience, because we want to be able to explain how, for deterministic worlds, different laws of nature (elicitable, we presume, from the causal powers in nature) could yield the same Humean history. So there is no problem of a lost distinction here.

Ott grants the point, but inquires about the former point. He says, even if the conditionals connected to some causal powers are conditionals of freedom, these conditionals imply their ordinary cousins that make no mention of freedom. So I think there is still a problem here, since it should be possible to have the same libertarian power generate two different futures, whereas that isn't possible for deterministic causal powers. After all, isn't that just what PAP tells us? So if the conditionals in question are implied by the power in question, as supervenience claims, then we still get a violation of PAP.

Moll now sees the point, and points out that she only endorsed the supervenience claim for deterministic causal powers. Ott, you are right, she says, the power itself doesn't imply the conditionals when the power is a libertarian causal power. Only when it is a deterministic causal power can there be such an implication. Well, strictly speaking, not even then, she says, because such powers are always subject to divine intervention, in which case the conditional in question would not be true; but the complexities needed to handle the problem of divine intervention won't affect this issue, so let's just bracket the issue of divine intervention and assume that deterministic causal powers imply the conditionals that make for predictability in the unfolding of history. No such implication is present for libertarian causal powers, so to get predictability, God must attach to each such power a complete set of conditionals of freedom.

Ott is even more perplexed than ever. He understands the point Moll is making, but what perplexes him is the idea that has governed the conversation to this point, the idea about which entailments get bracketed when looking for causal powers and which don't. Ott reminds Moll that this point was crucial in their collective resistance to Occ's arguments, but then notes that Moll seems to be parting company on what gets bracketed here. In the case of an object with deterministic causal powers, if we bracket the conditionals implied by such powers, then we can't predict what will happen next. So it looks like we have to take such conditionals into account. But if we do the same with libertarian causal power, we get perfect predictability as well. We're supposed to be on the same side about what gets bracketed and what doesn't, he says, but if we don't bracket the associated conditionals for libertarian causal powers, PAP is undermined, isn't it?

Moll shakes her head. No, she says, we don't bracket the conditionals in either case. In the case of deterministic causal powers, the conditionals are included in a full specification of the power in question; in the case of a libertarian causal power, they aren't. Whether the conditionals are true is not the issue, since we've already noted that not everything true about the supernatural past can go unbracketed. It can't, if we still intend to avoid Occ's position.

Occ nods his head, all the while thinking to himself that once you start down the path of saving a view by making up distinctions, the conclusion is relatively uninteresting. Narrators get to exercise discretion about which insults by characters get ignored.

Moll continues. What we bracket is the entailing activity of God. Then deterministic causal powers make a difference to the unfolding of history because of the conditionals implied by these powers. And the libertarian causal powers make a difference as well, one that is not perfectly predictable based on the existence of the powers themselves, but only so in the context of God's overall, entailing activity. When predictability flows from a full specification of the power itself, we get a violation of PAP; when it doesn't, we don't. But the same key is being used as was used to open a way out of Occ's objection to causal power of any sort in the created order: bracket the entailing activity of God to show how God can share power with the created order itself.

So, Moll says, there is a view here that makes room for divine providence, even given the defining role that PAP plays regarding some of the causal powers in nature. God could have created a world in which none of the causal powers in question were associated with conditionals of any sort. But God could also create a world with non-deterministic causal powers that come in guises made up of conditionals that allow for predictability. These conditionals, together with the remainder of the divine creative activity, entail the future. But if entailment is allowed to run free as an objection to causal powers in nature, then Occ wins. Since we don't want that, we have to bracket entailments resulting from this activity. Once we do so, there is no objection left to the idea that God can impart libertarian causal powers in various guises in such a way that he displays full providential control over his creation.

Ott is stunned, standing speechless and stymied. He knows not what to say or think. He is convinced that there is still a problem here, but can't get a fix on it any more. Occ now takes Ott's side. He says that both he and Ott are perplexed by such metaphysical gerrymandering. He says the lesson of all this is to refuse to take the first step. Directing his remarks to Ott, he insists that the false move was to allow this talk of what gets bracketed and what doesn't to enter in at all. No such sophistical sleight of hand should have been tolerated. All power is God's power, and to try to think in terms of a metaphysical system that allows us to bracket the divine activity is confused. To try to think philosophically while ignoring the fundamental and indispensable role of God in the origin and continuation of the universe is both unwise and offensive—"unwise" because wisdom requires paying attention to fundamentals and there is nothing more fundamental that the dependence of everything on God, and "offensive" because it involves trying to conduct a part of life independently of an acknowledgment of God who is the source of all.

Occ's sentiments are exactly right, though perhaps not his conclusions. His heart is right, but Moll is my hero.

sdom requires paying attention to fundamentals and there is nothing more fundamental that the dependence of everything on God, "offensive" because it involves try

6

A DEAD-END FOR MOLINISM

6.1 Introduction

The core motivation for Molinism is a desire to preserve a libertarian account of human freedom while at the same time defending a strong view of divine providence, but in recent times it was introduced by Alvin Plantinga in order to rebut certain versions of the problem of evil. Viewed from this perspective concerning the problem of evil, the key ingredient of the view is the existence of counterfactuals of freedom—counterfactuals concerning what any free individual would freely do in a given set of circumstances. The truth of such counterfactuals of freedom was used by Plantinga to argue for a distinction between feasible and infeasible worlds, between possible worlds God has the power to actualize and those he does not (Plantinga 1978).

These same counterfactuals of freedom might also provide the core of a Molinist account directed at the fundamental motivation for the view—the motivation concerning the relationship between divine providence and human freedom. In this way, Molinism has come to be identified with the view that there are true counterfactuals of human freedom, when the notion of freedom in question is understood to be libertarian in nature. On this understanding, Molinism is defined in terms of core motivation and a core explanatory mechanism: the fundamental motivation is to preserve a strong doctrine of providence while retaining a libertarian conception of human freedom, and the basic explanatory mechanism intended to satisfy this motivation is the existence of true counterfactuals of human, or creaturely, freedom.

As noted by Thomas Flint (1998), it is crucial not only that there are true counterfactuals of libertarian freedom but that God's knowledge of them count as middle knowledge. Middle knowledge is contrasted with knowledge of necessary truths on the one hand and knowledge of truths that are the direct consequences of expressions of the divine will on the other hand. The former truths constitute God's natural knowledge, and the latter truths constitute God's free knowledge, according to the terminology of Luis de Molina (1988). In the account of creation thus proffered, God's knowledge of counterfactuals of freedom comes between his knowledge of necessities and expressions of his will that result in the actualization of some particular possible world, and for this reason is termed "middle knowledge."

Both of the above accounts correctly identify the core Molinist motivation, which is that an adequate account of God's relationship to his creation is one that preserves both full providential control and libertarian freedom. The core explanatory mechanism, viewed in terms of middle knowledge of counterfactuals of libertarian freedom, is the focus of this essay, the point of which is to cast doubt on the idea that such middle knowledge has the features required of it to reconcile providence and freedom. I will argue that the focus on counterfactuals and middle knowledge has taken us away from the track of explaining the compatibility of full providence and libertarian freedom, down a dead-end spur concerning counterfactuals and God's knowledge of them. Seeing that it is in fact a dead-end spur is something that comes only at the end of the discussion, however, so we must travel the rail awhile to see where it heads.

So we begin by assuming that the central claim of the Molinist is that there are true counterfactuals of freedom (where freedom is taken to be the sort characterized by libertarian accounts of it). In order to move from this commitment to a reconciliation of providence and freedom, we need an argument that such truths are contingent while retaining two special features. The first is that these counterfactuals are not true in virtue of some act of will on the part of God, for only by doing so do we end up with a view that posits middle knowledge of such counterfactuals. Second, we need an account of creation in terms of actualization of worlds that carves those worlds into feasible ones (those actualizable by God) and infeasible ones (those not actualizable by God). To do so, we need not only that counterfactuals of freedom have a truth value that is independent of God's will, but also an account of such counterfactuals that puts this pre-volitional truth value outside God's control. In sum, we get the standard Molinist picture by adopting the core Molinist motivation, which requires a strong doctrine of providence compatible with libertarian freedom, adding to it the idea that there are true counterfactuals of freedom, and insisting that these truths are pre-volitional and outside God's control. God's knowledge of these truths is thus middle knowledge, and the truths in question give the Molinist a basis for saying that whichever world God chooses to actualize, it will be a world over which he can exert full providential control.

I have argued elsewhere that this final step, in which the counterfactual truths in question are claimed to be outside God's control, is not trouble-free. I have argued, that is, that even if counterfactuals of freedom have to be true in a way that is independent of God's will, i.e., if they must be true pre-volitionally, it does not follow that they are outside of God's control (Kvanvig 1993, esp. Chapter 2). This point is important because of its connection to the argument developed by Plantinga that Leibniz was mistaken in thinking that God could actualize any possible world—a mistake Plantinga refers to as "Liebniz's Lapse" (Plantinga 1977, 1978). Though there is a technical notion of world actualization that can sustain Plantinga's charge against Leibniz, if it turns out that counterfactuals of freedom are pre-volitional but not outside God's control, there is an alternative technical notion of world actualization on which Plantinga's charge against Leibniz cannot be sustained.[1] The resolution of this dispute between such dueling

[1] I develop this point both in Kvanvig (1993, Chapter 2) and in a paper for the Central Division of the American Philosophical Association in April of 1984 on which Plantinga com-

techno-esoterica, I suggested, would be to change the focus of the discussion from counterfactuals of freedom and middle knowledge to the more fundamental issue of how to model God's creative activity in terms of deliberative conditionals.

Flint worries, however, that in arguing in this way, Molinism must be abandoned and that contradictions result. He labeled such a position "Maverick Molinism," and argued that the view is logically incoherent (Flint 1998). I replied on behalf of the Maverick in Kvanvig (2002), but Flint found the replies less than compelling, insisting that contradictions remain (Flint 2003).

Here I will pursue the discussion further. The goal here is to turn the discussion in what I consider to be a more fruitful and interesting direction. The fundamental issue, as I see it, is not the question of counterfactuals of creaturely freedom, but rather what a deliberative model of God's creative activity should look like. In order to motivate this more fundamental reappraisal of the doctrine of creation, we need to see more clearly what happens to Molinism on the standard assumptions noted above. The present essay thus plays the intermediary role of showing why we need to retrace our steps to a more fundamental starting point if we hope to find a theory of creation allowing both libertarian freedom and full providential control.

6.2   Molinism, Standard and Maverick

Molinism is the view designed to preserve both a libertarian conception of freedom and a strong view of divine providence. The standard version of it does so through the vehicle of counterfactuals of freedom—the doctrine according to which there are true counterfactuals concerning what any free individual would freely do in a given set of circumstances. God's providential activity adverts to these counterfactuals, employing them to calculate what God should do to secure the ends at which he aims. Maverick Molinism is a special version of this view, according to which, though counterfactuals of freedom have their truth-value logically prior to God's acts of will (they are thus pre-volitional), God could have so acted that these counterfactuals would have had a different truth value from that which they actually have (they are thus not outside of God's control). Standard Molinists hold that the truth value in question is both pre-volitional and beyond God's control, for without such a claim we lose the distinction between feasible and infeasible worlds. On Standard Molinism, if S is free to do A or refrain from doing A in circumstances C, then there is a world where C obtains and S does A, and a world where C obtains and S refrains from doing A. According to Molinism, there is a true counterfactual of freedom linking C to one of the two options—a counterfactual that is both contingent and not true because God made it true. On the standard view, this latter point implies that such counterfactuals are outside God's control, so that whichever one is true, one of the worlds is infeasible even though possible, since all God can directly

---

mented, and which was published as Kvanvig (1994).

do is strongly actualize C and leave the rest of the story of actualization up to the true counterfactuals of freedom.

The Maverick Molinist denies this last step, that the truth value of counterfactuals is outside God's control. Whether they are outside God's control isn't a question of whether God makes these counterfactuals true, but whether that truth value is invariant under any embedding. An embedding occurs when we move from a simple counterfactual of the form

$$\phi \mathbin{\Box\!\!\rightarrow} \psi$$

to a complex one having the form

$$\chi \mathbin{\Box\!\!\rightarrow} (\phi \mathbin{\Box\!\!\rightarrow} \psi).$$

For a counterfactual to be invariant under embeddings of this sort, we would need to claim that

Necessarily, for any χ, if $\phi \mathbin{\Box\!\!\rightarrow} \psi$, then $\chi \mathbin{\Box\!\!\rightarrow} (\phi \mathbin{\Box\!\!\rightarrow} \psi)$.

Such a principle regarding counterfactuals in general is certainly false: while it is true that if I were to drop this glass from the rooftop, it would shatter; it isn't true that if a safety net were in place, then if I were to drop this glass from the rooftop it would shatter. Moreover, this point would seem to extend to counterfactuals of freedom as well, so that it can be true that if S were in C, S would freely do A, and yet also be true, that if God were to actualize condition $C*$, then if S were in C, S would freely refrain from doing A. If W is a world in which C obtains and S does A, and W' is a world in which C obtains and S refrains from doing A, without invariance under embeddings, we no longer have any straightforward story as to why W is actualizable and W' is not. Without such a clear story, we no longer have any Molinist account of how providence can be maintained regardless of which creative choices God makes.

Against this position, Flint provides two quite different types of argument. One is a more informal argument, depending on particular examples, and the second is more formal. The second provides a deeper challenge to the Maverick, but before examining it, it is worth seeing why the informal concerns are not persuasive.

6.3 An Informal Argument Against Maverick Molinism

An intuitive example of a truth that is pre-volitional but not under my control concerns the presence of a snow at a particular spot in northern Indiana: its presence is not caused by any act of my will, but the snow would not have been there had I chosen to act in certain ways. No act of will played any direct causal role in the snow being at the particular spot in question.

Flint introduces the following concepts to be used in rebutting such examples: "a truth T is *pre-volitional* for a person S if and only if it's not the case that T is true in virtue of some act of S's will; and truth T is *resilient* for a person S if and only if S lacks counterfactual power over T" (Flint 2003, p. 93). Flint wishes to argue that even though there is a distinction to be drawn here, the distinction collapses under certain assumptions. He imagines that I have thought about the snow, realizing what was in my power to do, and choosing to refrain from removing the snow. He then says,

> Here, a full explanation of why the snow is there would have to take account of the various acts and processes going on in my mind. So the ground's being snow covered would obviously be both post-volitional and non-resilient. (Flint 2003, p. 96)

He then uses this idea to argue that no truth could be pre-volitional but non-resilient for God.

There is a perfectly straightforward and common notion of causality on which Flint's claims are misguided. A squirrel is sitting at the edge of the green when I hit my tee shot, which goes in the hole for a hole-in-one. An unbelievably fortunate result, but, I will insist, not a miracle. There is a causal process involving my swing, its trajectory and speed, the density of the ball, the character of the club, the wind patterns in place, as well as the texture of the grass and amount of moisture in the soil with reference to which the causal story of the hole-in-one can be told. The squirrel plays no role in this causal process, even if the squirrel considered leaping at the ball and then declined to do so. Neither does the thought life of Vladimir Putin, who that very morning considered hiring an assassin to kill me, but thought better of it. None of these "woulda-coulda-mighta-shoulda" events (to enhance the formal elegance of our discussion, let us call the events in question "WCMS events") plays a causal role at all. Events that might have, or could have, or should have, or would have interrupted the causal process are not themselves part of that process.

A common distinction from the literature on causation and explanation may help make this point. There is a distinction between overdetermination and pseudo-overdetermination. The former occurs when two events overdetermine a given response. Pseudo-overdetermination occurs when there are two events, one of which causes the given effect, but where the other event would have caused that effect had the first one not done so. The point to note here is that *pseudo-overdetermination is not a type of causal relationship*, even though overdetermination is, and even though pseudo-overdetermination is relevant to a full and complete understanding of any scenario in which the event in question occurs.

A similar point applies to our examples. In the snow example and the hole-in-one example, there are pseudo-preemptors of a causal process: I could have chosen to intervene to stop the snow from covering the spot, and the squirrel could have blocked the path to the whole. These features are pseudo-preemptors only, however, playing no role in the causal processes involved in the snow example and golf shot example.

This quite ordinary notion of causation honors the platitude that causes are things that make a difference to the course of affairs, though perhaps only in a probabilistic way, and the squirrel's deliberations don't make any actual difference and so aren't part of the causal story (even if relevant is some way to full and complete understanding or explanation). It is not that the deliberations of the squirrel are completely irrelevant, it is simply that what they are relevant to is something other than the causal sequence or causal process in question.

Flint may wish us to define the notion of pre-volitionality using some alternative notion of full and complete explanation in place of one involving causation, but nothing of philosophical substance is gained by mere redefinition. Flint's rejection of Maverick Molinism would then require an argument in favor of his alternative conception to the quite ordinary causal notion, on which my failure to protect a certain location from falling snow is not itself part of the causal process that leads to snow at a particular location in northern Indiana.

The fact is this: even if I deliberate fully and choose to refrain from preventing the presence of snow at a certain spot, my choice for inaction makes no change, probabilistic or otherwise, to the causal process leading to snow at that spot. Reading in the history of the literature on causation, given as it is to the idea that the concept of causation can be analyzed in terms of logical relationships of sufficiency, necessity, counterfactual connectedness, INUS conditions, and the like,[2] can incline one to the idea that anything that would have made things turn out different had it occurred is an event whose absence is a partial cause of the effect in question. One antidote to this inclination is to examine the variety of counterexamples to such attempted analyses. Another antidote is to attend to the platitude that a cause is something that makes a difference. To screen out such objectionable results is that the squirrel helped me get a hole-in-one, all that is needed is some straightforward sense of there being a way for things to go "on their own" independent of my (or the squirrel's) interference, and then there is room for the distinction between pre-volitionality and resilience so that even deliberate non-interference leaves the presence of snow pre-volitional with respect to me.

Once we appreciate this point, we can also appreciate the Maverick's insistence that pre-volitionality does not imply being outside of one's control. Note first that it is at the heart of standard Molinism to hold that there is a way for things to go "on their own" independent of God's interference in certain cases. Combine that with the quite ordinary notion of a direct result outlined above, and there is obvious room for a distinction even with respect to God between that which is pre-volitional and that which is resilient.

Thus, the informal argument against Maverick Molinism, depending on an evaluation of particular examples, fails to undermine this position. The more challenging attack, however, is a formal one, to which I now turn.

6.4 Formal Arguments Against Maverick Molinism

As noted already, Maverick Molinism relies on an argument denying invariance of truth value for counterfactual conditionals under embeddings, and the formal argument Flint raises attempts to show that this position implies a contradiction.

---

[2] A fairly complete introduction to the attempt to understand causation in terms of conditionals of various sorts can be obtained from Mackie (1974). For more recent attempts, see Hall *et al.* (2004).

His argument proceeds in three steps. The first step we may call "the vicious regress premise." If we suppose that the counterfactual $A \mathrel{\square\!\!\rightarrow} B$ is post-volitionally true, so that there are propositions C and D within God's power to bring about such that $C \mathrel{\square\!\!\rightarrow} (A \mathrel{\square\!\!\rightarrow} B)$ and $D \mathrel{\square\!\!\rightarrow} \sim(A \mathrel{\square\!\!\rightarrow} B)$, these latter two truths must be pre-volitional on pain of an infinite regress of things that God would have to do to make $A \mathrel{\square\!\!\rightarrow} B$ true. The second step endorses the Law of Conditional Excluded Middle, according to which, for any A and B, either A counterfactually implies B or A counterfactually implies $\sim B$. The final step of the argument is the reductio step. Where $A \mathrel{\square\!\!\rightarrow} B$ is a counterfactual of world actualization (so that A is maximal with respect to what God strongly actualizes and B specifies which world would result), consider the expanded counterfactuals $C \mathrel{\square\!\!\rightarrow} (A \mathrel{\square\!\!\rightarrow} B)$ and $C \mathrel{\square\!\!\rightarrow} \sim(A \mathrel{\square\!\!\rightarrow} B)$. By the LCEM hypothesis, one of these two must be true, regardless of the value for C. So suppose $C = A$. Then either $A \mathrel{\square\!\!\rightarrow} (A \mathrel{\square\!\!\rightarrow} B)$ or $A \mathrel{\square\!\!\rightarrow} \sim(A \mathrel{\square\!\!\rightarrow} B)$. Since the first is logically equivalent to $A \mathrel{\square\!\!\rightarrow} B$, the two could not differ regarding their status as pre-volitional or post-volitional. The vicious regress premise requires, however, that they do so differ. Hence, the only option is that $A \mathrel{\square\!\!\rightarrow} \sim(A \mathrel{\square\!\!\rightarrow} B)$. But this claim can't be true either. For $\sim(A \mathrel{\square\!\!\rightarrow} B)$ entails $(A \mathrel{\square\!\!\rightarrow} \sim B)$ (by LCEM), and so $A \mathrel{\square\!\!\rightarrow} \sim(A \mathrel{\square\!\!\rightarrow} B)$ is logically equivalent to $A \mathrel{\square\!\!\rightarrow} (A \mathrel{\square\!\!\rightarrow} \sim B)$, which is logically equivalent to $A \mathrel{\square\!\!\rightarrow} \sim B$. This latter claim must therefore be pre-volitional, and since it is equivalent to $\sim(A \mathrel{\square\!\!\rightarrow} B)$, this latter claim must be pre-volitional as well. So, both $A \mathrel{\square\!\!\rightarrow} B$ and $\sim(A \mathrel{\square\!\!\rightarrow} B)$ have to be pre-volitional, but that is contrary to the Maverick's hypothesis. Hence Maverick Molinism is not a coherent position, and the threat it presents to the distinction between feasible and possible worlds need not concern us.

I have three complaints about this attempt to undermine the coherence of Maverick Molinism. First, the argument is cast in terms of the notions of pre-volitionality and post-volitionality, but the Maverick doesn't dispute the standard Molinist position on the pre-volitionality of counterfactuals of freedom. The Maverick insists only that such counterfactuals are not outside of God's counterfactual control. This conflation is most obvious in Flint's initial characterization of the position:

> [S]ome who are otherwise favorably disposed toward Molinism might be tempted to challenge the alleged pre-volitional status of such truths. That is, they may want to say that a Molinist can hold that, whichever truth-value [such] a counterfactual . . . has, there nevertheless were things God had the power to do such that, had he done them, that counterfactual would have had the opposite truth-value. (Flint 2003, p. 65)

To challenge the pre-volitional status of such truths would be, of course, to deny that such truths are pre-volitional. But in the very next sentence, the issue is not pre-volitionality, but rather the question of whether God has counterfactual power over such truths. Maverick Molinism endorses the view that counterfactuals of freedom are pre-volitional, but denies that they are outside God's control.

So in the above argument, the language needs to be recast in terms of the issue of what is outside God's control rather than in terms of what is pre-volitional.

When recast, the reductio step would then attempt to show that, since $A \mathrel{\Box\!\!\!\rightarrow}$ $(A \mathrel{\Box\!\!\!\rightarrow} B)$ is logically equivalent to $A \mathrel{\Box\!\!\!\rightarrow} B$, both will have to be within God's control if the latter is. This result is problematic, however, only if the regress step can be used to show a difficulty here. The regress step initially attempted to show that a regress looms if the truths in question are post-volitional, since then no claim could be made true by an act of God's will without infinitely many prior things having been made true. Regardless of what one thinks about that regress argument, a similar one used here will be useless. For there is nothing that needs to be done for something to be within God's control, and to argue that a regress looms here is hopeless. All that follows is that if a given counterfactual is within God's control, so will infinitely many other counterfactuals be within his control. There is nothing vicious about such a result, however, no more so than noting that for 2+1 to equal 3, 2+2 will have to equal 4, and so on. So the regress step of the argument fails to show a problem, given the logical equivalence Flint notes.

Note as well that the argument assumes LCEM but without the needed defense of that law to make the argument compelling. The standard semantics for counterfactuals provides no obvious defense of the law that would be useful in the present context.[3] The defenses available for the law depend on denying bivalence for counterfactual conditionals (Stalnaker 1981, Cross 2009), and the loss of bivalence for such conditionals would undermine any Molinist attempt to preserve full providential control. For suppose God actualizes C, but this condition is not counterfactually linked either to S's doing A nor to its not being the case that S does A. Then there is no basis for God to know in advance what S would do if he actualizes C, and hence no basis for full providential control in such a case. Since the arguments on behalf of LCEM presume failure of bivalence, any argument against Maverick Molinism that presupposes without argument that one can have both LCEM and bivalence is an argument with a serious shortcoming.

Moreover, there is a step in the argument that we should balk at independently of either of these points. Notice that the vicious regress step attempts to show that a subjunctive cannot be post-volitional (more accurately, outside God's control) in virtue of there being some condition that God could actualize that would have resulted in the the falsity of the subjunctive, i.e., that $A \mathrel{\Box\!\!\!\rightarrow} B$ is true while it is also true that $C \mathrel{\Box\!\!\!\rightarrow} {\sim}(A \mathrel{\Box\!\!\!\rightarrow} B)$. Flint's argument overgeneralizes this point, arguing that when $C = A$, a problem ensues. But the Maverick need hold no brief on what happens when $C = A$, for all the Maverick claims is that there are values for A, B, and C where B specifies the performance of a free action, while both $A \mathrel{\Box\!\!\!\rightarrow} B$ and $C \mathrel{\Box\!\!\!\rightarrow} {\sim}(A \mathrel{\Box\!\!\!\rightarrow} B)$ are true. It is fully compatible with this point that there are also values for A and C where no such possibility exists, which would be the case when $A = C$ if Flint's argument were valid. Since the Maverick need hold no brief about what happens when $A = C$,

---

[3]See Stalnaker (1968) for an account that sustains LCEM, and Lewis (1973) for an account that does not.

the argument is not relevant to the Maverick's claim that because it is possible for both $A \:\square\!\!\rightarrow B$ and $C \:\square\!\!\rightarrow \sim(A \:\square\!\!\rightarrow B)$ to be true, there is a distinction between what is pre-volitional for God and what is beyond God's control.

An argument that might have been more useful here would be an argument to show that the logical rule of importation is valid for counterfactuals:

$$\chi \:\square\!\!\rightarrow (\phi \:\square\!\!\rightarrow \psi) \vdash \chi \& \phi \:\square\!\!\rightarrow \psi$$

If this rule is valid, and if the antecedents of counterfactuals of freedom are maximal in the sense that they include everything strongly actualizable by God for the given type of world in question, then one could argue that the attempted embedding is either redundant (where $C = A$) or impossible (where $C \neq A$).

In arguing that counterfactuals of freedom are not outside God's control, I gave examples that presuppose the failure of Importation for counterfactuals. One such example involves a choice between asparagus and beans for dinner:

> [I]t is contingently true that if I were offered a choice between asparagus and beans for dinner, I'd not choose beans. Things could have happened to alter my preferences, however. The proliferation of special pests that blunted the growth of beans but allowed asparagus to flourish would have led to much more asparagus consumption in my youth, and to a preference for the unusual taste of beans over that of asparagus. . . (Kvanvig 2002, pp. 354-5)

Given this scenario, the conditional "Choice Implies Asparagus" could have been made false by God merely by increasing the number of pests in the environment of my youth. Flint objects to the example, however, and the central claim in his complaint about the example is as follows:

> What we seem to be asking ourselves here is: If I had to make the choice between beans and asparagus in a world where the pests had been mean to the beans, would I still choose the asparagus? I.e., is $[(C\&A) \:\square\!\!\rightarrow \sim B]$ also true? (Flint 2003, p. 97)

Flint then argues that for my example to work, I need to derive $C \:\square\!\!\rightarrow (A \:\square\!\!\rightarrow \sim B)$ from $(C\&A) \:\square\!\!\rightarrow \sim B$, but that any such derivation will be flawed.

Flint is right that the derivation would be flawed, being an instance of Exportation for counterfactuals:

$$\chi \& \phi \:\square\!\!\rightarrow \psi \vdash \chi \:\square\!\!\rightarrow (\phi \:\square\!\!\rightarrow \psi)$$

Putting aside the question of Importation, it is clear that Exportation is invalid. It is true that if Obama were both a member of a Muslim faith community and a Christian faith community, he would be a member of a Muslim faith community. But it is false that if he were a member of a Muslim faith community, it would be true that if he were a member of a Christian faith community he would be a member of a Muslim faith community. The antecedent of this embedding condition is irrelevant to the truth value of the embedded conditional. The embedded conditional ("if Obama were Christian, he'd be Muslim") is clearly false, and whether or not he's Muslim, the truth value of this conditional is unaffected. Hence, Exportation on counterfactual conditionals is false.

So Flint is correct to note that $C \:\square\!\!\rightarrow (A \:\square\!\!\rightarrow \sim B)$ cannot be derived from

$(C\&A) \;\square\!\!\rightarrow \sim\!B$. Notice, however, that to interpret the example as requiring such an inference misreads the example in a way informed by Importation for counterfactuals. The example has no conjunctive antecedent, and yet Flint interprets it as an example in which we "seem to be asking ourselves" about a counterfactual with a conjunctive antecedent. Now, the example clearly is one concerning an embedding: the counterfactual "Choice Implies Asparagus" is embedded as the consequent of another counterfactual the antecedent of which is "More Pests". Of course, if Importation on counterfactuals is valid, Flint's reinterpretation of the example is legitimate, but if Importation fails, his complaint about the example requires misreading it.

The standard possible worlds semantics for counterfactuals doesn't give any straightforward defense of Importation. The semantics for $C \;\square\!\!\rightarrow (A \;\square\!\!\rightarrow B)$ involves first finding a suitably close C-world, and then from that C-world, finding an A-world suitably close to C-worlds, and finally checking to see whether B is true in that A-world. At no point does the semantics guarantee that this A-world is also, itself, a C-world, which is what would be required for Importation to hold.

This point is most obvious when A and C are inconsistent. Suppose, for example, that we assume that $A = \sim\!C$, and then suppose we ask about the truth value of $C \;\square\!\!\rightarrow (\sim\! C \;\square\!\!\rightarrow B)$. Flint's interpretive devices require us to treat this question as somehow asking about the truth value of $(C \;\&\sim C) \;\square\!\!\rightarrow \sim\!B$ and thereby considering the impossible situation in which both C and $\sim\!C$ are true. That would be a mistake. The latter claim is trivially true on the standard semantics. The former is not.

Note further that the Beans/Asparagus example could be constructed so that C and A are incompatible. Instead of asking, "Had mean insects been more prevalent, would I have preferred beans to asparagus if given the choice?", the case could have been constructed asking the following question instead: "Had mean insects been more prevalent in a situation in which no choice was ever offered between beans and asparagus, would it nonetheless have been true that had I been offered the choice, I would have preferred beans?" Flint's interpretive strategy, applied to this question, would require thinking about the impossible situation in which I was both offered the choice and not offered the choice.

The fundamental difficulty here, then, is this. If a defense of Importation for counterfactuals could be mounted, there would be a formal argument available to show that Maverick Molinism is incoherent. The difficulty here for Standard Molinists is that Importation isn't valid for counterfactuals, and thus Maverick Molinism remains unscathed by this attempt at formal refutation.

6.5   Conclusion

As a result of this discussion, the standard Molinist identification of pre-volitional truths for God and what is beyond God's control is unsubstantiated. The Maverick points out that the two are not equivalent, and arguments aimed at buttressing the standard Molinist identification fail. That leaves the threat the Maverick

poses intact, since standard Molinism aims to preserve a strong doctrine of providence through a distinction between feasible and infeasible worlds, where there
are some of both among the totality of possible worlds. The Maverick questions
the distinction, since there might be something God could do to make a false
counterfactual of freedom true.

Faced with this problem, there is a fall-back position to take, inspired by the
mistake Flint makes in treating the beans/asparagus example in terms that require the validity of Importation on counterfactuals. When discussing the coun-
terfactual $C \mathrel{\Box\!\!\rightarrow} (A \mathrel{\Box\!\!\rightarrow} \sim B)$, Flint supposed that what I was talking about
involved a choice situation in which both C and A are true, which would requir-
ing evaluating a different counterfactual, namely $(C\&A) \mathrel{\Box\!\!\rightarrow} \sim B$. As I pointed
out, it is a mistake to confuse these two counterfactuals, but there is a deeper
point to note here, and it is the way in which Flint's discussion turns naturally
to choice situations. What we are interested in here, and what is most relevant to
the context of theological reflection on the nature of God's providence, is not the
counterfactuals themselves but rather the choice situation in which the individual
in question is deliberating about what to do. This point resonates with the point
I had been making in characterizing the attempt to find an account of creation
that leaves providence intact: what is needed is a more fundamental investigation, focusing on conditionals of deliberation rather than on counterfactuals of
creaturely freedom. It is a quite natural assumption to think of conditionals of
deliberation in terms of counterfactuals, and hence it is quite natural to clarify a Molinist account of providence in terms of counterfactuals. I believe such
an identification is a mistake, though I will only pursue that point elsewhere.[4]
The conclusion we can draw at present, however, is that attempts to avoid the
need to engage in this more fundamental investigation by showing that there
is no coherent Maverick position have failed. The best remedy is to abandon
such resistance and pursue the more fundamental investigation to see what the
prospects are for an account of creation that makes room for libertarian freedom
while leaving the doctrine of providence intact.

o avoid the need to engage in this more fundamental investigation by showing
that there is no coherent Maverick position have failed. The best remedy is to
abandon such resistance and pursue the more fundamental investigation to see
what the prospects are for an account of creation that makes room for libertarian
freedom while leaving the doctrine of providence intact.

---

[4]See, e.g., "Creation, Deliberation, and Molinism" and "An Epistemic Theory of Creation,"
this volume.

CREATION, DELIBERATION, AND MOLINISM

7.1 Introduction

In philosophical theology, Molinism is "the beautiful game." It allows one to hold a libertarian account of human freedom while at the same time preserving a strong view of divine providence. This aspect of Molinism provides the fundamental motivation for Molinist doctrine. In usual presentations, the core explanatory mechanism designed to satisfy this motivation is the idea of counterfactuals of freedom that are outside God's control, but I have argued that this approach is mistaken (Kvanvig 2002). Abandoning this standard form of Molinism raises the issue of what explanatory mechanism, if any, can satisfy the fundamental Molinist motivation. The answer to this question will require an explication of the deliberational model of creation and an investigation of conditionals of deliberation that are suitable for use in such a deliberational model. The difficulties faced by the standard Molinist approach provide the needed justification for this more fundamental investigation in search of an adequate Molinist explanatory mechanism. In the process, I will be arguing that no extant version of Molinism, neither standard nor Maverick, can offer an adequate account of creation and providence, and thus that a different approach will need to be developed if the hope Molinism provides is to be sustained.

7.2 God's Creative Activity and Deliberative Conditionals

A fundamental investigation of God's activity in creation must begin with a specification of a model in terms of which to think about this activity. In order to theorize in a way that has any hope of producing understanding about God's providential relationship to the world, we must adopt a deliberative model of his creative activity. In stressing the point that this approach involves adopting a model, we can endorse the obvious point that an omniscient and omnipotent being has no need to deliberate at all about what to do or what to think. Deliberation, in ordinary parlance, involves a process that takes an individual from a state of indecision to another state in which deliberation is either abandoned or the issue resolved, but an omniscient and omnipotent being has no need of undergoing any such process, and any story of God's relationship to the world that posits such a process will be subject to legitimate criticism. We avoid this problem by explicitly noting that the deliberational aspect of the account we develop is an aspect of the model itself, rather than an aspect of reality. We use a deliberational approach to *model* the divine creative activity, not to *describe* it. In doing so, we hope to achieve some understanding of God's activity in creation, once we specify which aspects of the model are intended to represent and which are not. As just noted, one aspect of the model that is not intended to represent the truth of the matter is the feature of deliberation that involves moving from a state of indecision to a state of resolution. We take this feature to be a feature of the model only, understanding that the reality so modeled is subject to no such process.

Even though this feature of the model is not a feature of the reality modeled, there might be an analogous aspect in reality nonetheless. Standard Molinists describe God's creative activity in terms of three "logical" moments (corresponding to the concepts of natural, middle, and free knowledge) (Flint 1998, especially Chapter 2). It would be a confusion, however, to take the Molinist to be endorsing some idea of temporal succession here. Instead, the Molinist is attempting to point out the way in which the reality modeled is analogous to, though not identical with, the relevant aspect of the model in question. The idea here is that the succession from indecision to resolution in the case of human deliberation is analogous to the way in which there are explanatory connections between some parts of God's knowledge and the creative act of will that constitutes creation. In this way, there is a logical arrangement to the reality of God's creative activity that is represented in our model in other ways. The key to avoiding confusion here is to be clear about the distinction between the model and what is modeled, and to allow the theory that results from endorsing the model to explain how the model in intended to reveal the reality it models.

Once we have adopted a deliberative model of creation, the central ingredient of the model will be conditionals of deliberation. To deliberate is to reason about what to do by appeal to connections between information that is treated as given or assumed and other claims that are implied or follow, in some sense, from what is given or assumed. This description of the tools of deliberation is just a pedantic description of a conditional: an "if–then" claim that provides fodder for a resolution of whatever indecision prompts the deliberation in question.

To those familiar with the literature on deliberative conditionals, the suggestion that a focus on such conditionals rather than on subjunctive conditionals themselves may seem perplexing, since the standard assumption is that deliberative conditionals are a species of counterfactual conditionals. Such an assumption is standard in usual presentations of Molinism as well, but I will avoid such an assumption here. The primary reason is that the standard assumption pays insufficient attention to the data of standard usage, and draws the distinction between various conditionals in syntactic terms involving the mood of a conditional. In a little while I'll deliberate about what to eat for lunch. In deliberating, I might use the subjunctive mood and I might not. Instead, I might use the indicative mood. I might reason thusly: if I eat a ham and cheese sandwich I won't be able to ride my bike for more than an hour, and I want to ride my bike earlier than that, so I'll have a fruit salad instead (because if I have a fruit salad, I will be able to ride immediately after lunch). I could have couched all this just as easily in the subjunctive mood: if I were to eat a ham and cheese sandwich, I wouldn't be able to ride, etc. Either way of reasoning is perfectly fine. But it is well-known that the semantics has to treat indicative conditionals differently than subjunctive conditionals. A standard example of this need concerns the assassination of JFK. Nearly all will agree that if Oswald didn't kill JFK then someone else did; only conspiracy theorists will claim that if Oswald hadn't killed JFK then someone else would have (Adams 1975).

For the moment, then, we will only assume that our deliberational model will involve conditionals, without any further assumption about the syntactic form that such conditionals take. The central fact to note about deliberation, however, is that it takes more than the truth of a conditional for it to be deliberationally useful.[1] In the central case we will be concerned with, an agent employs a deliberative conditional by making the antecedent true with the aim or intention or plan of making true the consequent. But even if a conditional is true, it may be deliberationally useless. We shall explore this idea more fully in what follows, but a couple of quick examples will make this point clear enough to warrant the exploration of it that follows. First, some true conditionals are deliberationally useless because they are not future-oriented. It may be true (I think it is) that if I had been taught by my thoroughly magnificent second grade teacher, Mrs. Buck, that George Washington wasn't the first President of the United States, he wouldn't have been. But this conditional is of no use to me if I want someone else to have been the first President. Note that this truth was true when I was in first grade if it is true now (though I would have had to express that truth using a conditional sentence with different tenses), but even then the conditional would be useless in service of any desire I might have that would require some change in the past. For one more example, even if both antecedent and consequent are about the future rather than the past, the conditional can still be true but deliberationally useless. The examples that motivate causal decision theory are of this sort (Joyce 1999). Suppose I have impeccable scientific confirmation that a certain genetic condition causes premature death, and also know that it is nearly certain that anyone choosing to write papers on Molinism has this genetic condition. I'm trying to decide whether to continue working on this paper. In such an imaginary situation, I can infer that if I continue to work on this paper, I'll suffer premature death (I hereby remind all the forces that be that this is a purely *imaginary* story, a reminder that, as we all know, blocks the tendency for such morbid examples to become self-fulfilling for those who construct them). But the conditional *If I continue to work on this paper, I'll die prematurely* is, even if true (and even if known to be true), deliberationally useless. It would be a mistake of practical reasoning to do a *modus tollens* here and stop working on this paper to further my plans to avoid early death.

The task, then, for a deliberational model of creation is to determine which conditionals can be used as conditionals of deliberation. While it is obvious that,

---

[1]My concerns about which type of conditional is appropriate for deliberation comes from (DeRose 2010). Much of my thinking here is a result of what I've learned from this paper.

in the context of this model, the conditionals must be true (unlike the context of human deliberation, infected as it is with the reality of human fallibility), we must not assume that the truth of a conditional is itself sufficient for usefulness.

7.3   Types of Deliberative Models

Let me begin with models that are obviously inadequate, though as we will see later, finding out exactly why they are inadequate will help us see our way through the thicket we will encounter later on. These models are Minimal Models, in the sense that they give as little information as possible in the conditionals employed in deliberation. Since we are looking for a model of creation that generates a strong doctrine of providence, according to which God creates in such a way as to exert control over and governance of even the minutest detail of creation, the consequent of each conditional needs to be a complete possible world. What makes a model minimal is what the antecedent contains, and as the name implies, a Minimal Model will allow the most minimal of antecedents to still function in a useful conditional of deliberation, so long as the resulting conditional is true. Relevant antecedents will be ones that specify some possible activity of God, and the types of Minimal Models are defined in terms of whether the minimal conditionals that they contain are material conditionals, indicative conditionals, or subjunctive conditionals.

7.3.1   *Models Using Material Conditionals*

The Material Minimal Model tells us that we can explain the divine creativity with reference only to what God knows, paying attention to the subclass of this knowledge that is in the form of material conditionals. The need for relevant information in the antecedent of a conditional arises from considering a weaker claim, one that allows conditionals with no information at all in the antecedent (i.e., a tautology). One such information-free antecedent would be "either God chooses to create or he doesn't". The model so developed then maintains that creation is the result of the truth of one such material conditional, where W is the actual world:

> Information-less Antecedent Conditional: If God chooses to create or he doesn't, W is actual.

It is clear, however, that any such account of God's creative activity is hopeless. Notice that the material conditional in question is logically equivalent to the claim that W is actual (since the antecedent is a logical truth). So the appeal to omniscience eliminates the practical aspect of the model altogether: we now explain creation by appeal only to God's knowledge of which world is actual rather than in terms of some deliberational process involving a preference for a particular outcome and a decision to achieve that outcome by making true the antecedent of some conditional. An adequate deliberational model will make God's complete omniscience depend explanatorily on his complete creative activity, and this model undermines this order of explanation. Its only explanatory resources for understanding how God determines what to do in creation appeal directly and immediately to his complete knowledge of which world is the actual world, and thus his creative activity would be explanatorily dependent on his total omniscience.

A Material Minimal Model, then, must involve conditionals with a relevant antecedent, one which specifies some action God might undertake:

> Material Minimal Model Conditional: If God does A, then W is actual.

Such conditionals are an advance over those with no information in the antecedent, since they conform to the point emphasized above that conditionals of deliberation specify entertained courses of action in their antecedents and results of such courses of action in their consequents.

Even so, the advance is insignificant. All such conditionals will be true when the consequent is the actual world, and any others that are true will have no claim to being deliberative conditionals used by God in creation (since their truth depends on God's refusing to follow the course of action specified in their antecedents). The use of such conditionals requires a sorting of them into those that are true and those that are false, and this sorting requires prior knowledge of which antecedents are true and which are false. This point is fundamentally a semantic one about the truth or falsity of a material conditional: such a conditional is semantically defined in terms of false antecedent or true consequent. Knowledge of the truth of such a conditional thus requires the semantically prior information of which antecedents are true, and which consequents are false (except in the degenerative case where the conditional in question is true for other reasons, such as when it is a tautology, e.g., *if God actualizes W, then W is actual*). The fundamental problem, then, with the Material Minimal Model is that it inverts the needed order between divine knowledge and divine action for our deliberational model. We need to find conditionals that can be used in deliberation without presupposing knowledge of their antecedents and without relying on knowledge of which world is the actual world.

This point deserves special emphasis here, for two related reasons. First, it is obvious on casual inspection that the Material Minimal Model and its subminimal precursor are inadequate models. Second, it is imperative to get the explanation of their inadequacy correct, since further development of a deliberational model depends on the criteria of adequacy built on top of failures of the simplest models. So the explanation that bears repeating here involves an interplay of fundamental points about meaning and semantics and the needed order of explanation in the deliberational model. The order of explanation for complete omniscience must proceed from conditionals of deliberation and the decision of which antecedent to actualize, to knowledge of which total possible world thereby results. In order for a collection of conditionals of deliberation to be prior in the order of explanation in this way, the account of the meaning of the conditional (its semantics) must leave open the possibility of knowing the truth of the conditional without having decided what to do and without knowing which possible world is actual.

This latter point depends on a connection between meaning and knowledge, and getting clear on the exact nature of the connection helps to elucidate what a deliberational model must look like to be an adequate model of God's creative activity. So, we must ask, what is the connection between the theory of meaning and the theory of knowledge?

The answer is "very little," if we are attempting to give a fully general account of the matter. We can come to know that a given claim is true without any recourse to the elements in virtue of which that claim has the meaning that it has. For example, we can learn the truth of the Pythagorean theorem by testimony from our teachers, with little or no explanation as to why the theorem is true. No such learning by testimony is relevant, however, to our present context. In the present context, we must imagine what is available to God prior to any creative act on his part, and here the connection between semantics and what God knows is more substantive. For certain types of claims, the proper semantics treats that claim as having a compositional structure, where an understanding and evaluation of the truth value of that claim is built upon an understanding and evaluation of the truth value of certain proper subparts of that claim. So, when considering the proposition that Jim is a loving husband of Joanne, the proper semantical treatment of that claim represents it as having a structure composed out of the claim that Jim loves Joanne and Jim is Joanne's husband. This semantical complexity yields a claim about epistemic priority in certain restricted cases—cases of the sort involved in the situation in our deliberative model involving God prior to creation. In that situation, we have no alternative but to explain God's knowledge of the semantically more complex by appeal to his knowledge of the proper subparts in question. Hence, if we wish to explain God's knowledge of a semantically complex proposition p, where p is compositional with respect to some further claims q and r, then knowledge of p is not in general possible without prior knowledge of q and r.

In the simplest case of compositional structure, any proposition will be a truth-functional combination of other propositions. In such a case, knowledge of the truth-value of the parts will be logically sufficient for knowledge of the truth-value of the whole. Such is the case with material conditionals. Given the connection between compositional semantical structure and the priority claim above, the Material Minimal Model violates a central condition of adequacy on any adequate deliberative model of creation. That condition of adequacy is that *God's complete omniscience of which world is the actual world must be posterior to his decision about which creative option to exercise.* On the Minimal Material Model, the deliberative process envisioned requires knowledge of the truth of the material conditionals in question, and since the truth-value of a material conditional is compositional in nature, the conditional in question being a truth-functional connective, the context in question requires knowledge of the parts in a way that is prior to knowledge of the whole. Since the consequents of these conditionals involves the actuality of an entire possible world, God would have to know which world is actual prior to any decision about which creative option to exercise. In fact, he'd also have to know which creative decision he will exercise prior to that very decision—a result that is paradoxical as well, though

I won't press that point here. It is sufficient for present purposes simply to know that God's complete omniscience on the Material Minimal Model is prior to his decision about which creative option to exercise.

What precisely is this notion of priority at work in this argument? First, the priority in question is in terms of things in the mind of God: it is priority in the relationships between what God knows and what God decides to do. Second, the order by which priority is identified in our model ends with God's complete omniscience, and this omniscience is preceded by his creative act of will, which will involve his decision regarding what to do. So we can identify the decision in question as part of the point in the model that immediately precedes his complete omniscience. God knows what his creative decision is because he has so decided; he does not so decide because of his knowledge of what he decides. The type of priority in question thus falls within the broad category of explanatory priority, restricted here to explanatory priority in the deliberative process itself. We thus have no need of some general account of explanatory priority that covers all possible cases of explanation, but only that notion of what is available in the process of deliberation at various stages of that process. The crucial point to note here is that on any adequate Molinist model, God's creative act of will is prior to his complete omniscience and prior to his knowledge of his own creative act of will, in the sense that he does not use either of these items of knowledge in the process of deciding what to do. Whatever knowledge he uses in making a decision, it must not be these.

I emphasize the limited nature of the notion of priority at work in this discussion to distance itself from Robert Adams' use of the notion of explanatory priority in an argument against standard Molinism (Adams 1991). Flint examines this argument, which employs a notion of priority that holds between truths such as counterfactuals of creaturely freedom and the choices and actions of a given individual (Flint 1998, Chapter 7). Flint presents a variety of possible interpretations of this general notion of explanatory priority, from an account in terms of causal power (whether it is within one's power to "cause it to be the case that [the claim in question] is false") to one in terms of counterfactual power to make the claim false (whether it is within one's power to act in such a way that the claim in question "would be false"), to one in terms of entailment (whether there is something one could do that would entail that the claim is false) (Flint 1998, pp. 164–175). Such proposals for the general notion of explanatory priority have little relevance in the present context, however. The notion of priority in place here concerns intentional elements involved in the deliberational model, not some general notion of priority that needs to cover all cases in which one item is explanatorily prior to another. Moreover, accounts of priority in terms of causal, counterfactual, or entailment power over the truth of various propositions are clearly alien to the notion of priority at work in our discussion. Our notion involves what God takes into account in arriving at a creative decision, and how his knowledge of his own decision and his complete omniscience is explained in terms of this decision rather than the other way around. These priority relations do not involve conceptually the notion of an ability to change or affect or control any of the items in the sequencing (though it is natural to suppose that God has such control and has it necessarily). Hence, issues about what kind of power or ability or control exists is irrelevant to the notion of priority required for the argument against the Material Minimal Model.

To review, on any model of God's creative activity, there is some knowledge which God uses to arrive at a decision about what to create. Upon so deciding, God knows what he will do and thus has complete omniscience as an explanatory consequence of this process of deliberation. When the model in question is the Material Minimal Model, conditionals that play a role in the deliberative process of the model are ones that semantically presuppose knowledge of which action God will perform and which world is the actual world prior to knowing which conditionals are true. It is for this reason that the Material Minimal Model must be rejected, since it inverts the order of explanation between God's complete omniscience and his knowledge of his own creative decision on the one hand and that creative decision itself on the other hand.

One way to put this point is that the conditionals in question are not *deliberative* conditionals. For them to be deliberative conditionals, it is not enough that they are true. In addition to being true, they must be knowable without first having to know God's creative decision and without first having to have complete omniscience. To speak in terms of the model itself, the process in the model should not explain God's creative decision in terms of a sequence that puts such knowledge at a prior point in the sequence to God's creative decision itself. Instead, the sequence should involve divine knowledge of some group of conditionals that give options regarding what to do and what outcomes will result, followed by a choice regarding as to which creative option to select, based on some preference regarding the outcomes specified in the consequents of these conditionals. No such order is present in the case of the Modified Material Minimal Model. Instead, the order is inverted in such a way that the model is no longer accurately characterized as a deliberative model. The model is not a deliberative one because the conditionals in question, even though true, are not deliberative conditionals because they cannot be used in deliberation.

This issue of the difference between deliberative conditionals and other conditionals is crucial for any attempt to construct a deliberative model of God's creative activity. In the context of ordinary deliberation, we would need to pay attention to the point that a conditional can be false and yet appropriate to use in deliberation, but in our context, no such concern will play a role. What is more pressing in our context is the difference between true conditionals that are appropriate for use in deliberation and those that are not. In the above discussion of the Material Minimal Model, we noted one difference between these two kinds of conditionals, for some true conditionals would require, in the context in question, using knowledge of the truth values of antecedent and consequent in order to know the truth value of the conditional itself.

There are more general lessons to learn here, however—lessons that can be elicited from Allan Gibbard's story of the riverboat gambler, Sly Pete (Gibbard 1980, pp. 226-234). For our purposes, we can imagine the scene as follows. Sly Pete cheats by having informers look at Gullible Gus's cards and signal to Sly Pete. The game is poker, and we are in the final hand of some tournament. Gullible Gus, now behind because of the cheating, puts all of his chips into the pot. Sly Pete has to decide whether to fold or continue the hand by adding chips to the pot and calling. To decide what to do, he looks for help from his cronies, Sigmund and Snoopy. As it turns out, both know of the cheating strategy, but only Sigmund is in a position to see Gus's hand this time. Snoopy cannot see Gus's hand, but can see Sly Pete's hand and understands Sigmund's signals. Sigmund looks at Gullible Gus's hand and sees a pair of 9s and a pair of 7s, and signals this information to Sly Pete. Snoopy sees the signal and also sees that Sly Pete is holding a full house, which beats two pair. So here's what Snoopy knows:

If Sly Pete plays, he will win.

Sly Pete, however, has had a lapse of concentration and missed Sigmund's signal. He won't make a move to either play or fold until he has more information than he presently has.

Now, imagine Sigmund turning to the crowd, and with a knowing wink, saying:

"If Sly Pete plays, he will win."

He says this because he knows of the set-up, and knows that Sly Pete is nobody's fool: he won't play without getting the information that allows him to win if he plays. The information from Sigmund's remark appears to be just the kind of information that Sly Pete needs to decide whether to play. But of course it isn't. He'd be nuts to conclude from what Sigmund says that he should play.

After a few seconds elapse, and bothered by Pete's indecision, Snoopy decides to help out by chiming in:

"Yep, Sig's right: if Sly Pete plays he will win."

This time the same conditional is deliberationally useful (in part because Sly Pete knows that Snoopy saw Sig's signal and can also see Sly's hand), but it is the same conditional in both cases. The difference is the informational basis of the conditional. In Sigmund's case, the evidential basis for the conditional makes it deliberationally useless.

Keith DeRose suggests that we can use the language of backtracking to explain the difference between true conditionals and deliberatively useful conditionals. He says (regarding a case involving the same players and set-up, but where the game being played involves picking one card from a sequentially numbered deck containing 101 cards),

> Compare the kind of grounds Snoopy has for the deliberationally useful (Oc) [the conditional as asserted by Snoopy] with Sigmund's grounds for the useless (O) [the conditional as asserted by Sigmund]. The reasoning that supports (Oc) for Snoopy involves his beliefs about how things are at and before the time at which the event reported in the antecedent of

(Oc) would occur. He then adds to these beliefs the supposition of the antecedent of the conditional he supposes that Pete will play and then reasons forward in time and in the causal order, asking what will happen if the antecedent of the conditional is made true, given how he thinks the world is and will be at times prior to and at the time of the antecedent. (Since he knows Pete holds the lower card, adding the supposition that Pete plays leads to the conclusion that Pete loses.) In contrast, Sigmund's knowledge of (O) is based on backtracking grounds. His reasoning, as it would be naturally expounded, involves something like the 'that would be because' locution, which, along with 'that will mean that', are good signs that backtracking reasoning is going on. His reasoning is something like this: 'If Pete plays, that will be because he has the higher card; and then, of course, he will win.' Note that Sigmund doesn't actually believe that Pete has the higher card. In fact, from Sigmund's point of view, the probability that Pete has the higher card is quite low. . . But after he provisionally supposes the antecedent of (O), he reasons backward in the temporal and causal order of things, and conditionally revises his view of what is happening before the time of the antecedent, and then reasons forward in time, using his conditionally revised view of the relevant state of affairs before the time of the antecedent, together with the supposition of the antecedent, to arrive at a conditional view of what will (probably) happen after the time of the antecedent. (DeRose 2010, pp. 25–26)

DeRose highlights certain features of backtracking reasoning, including the use of "that would be because" and "that will mean that" locutions. After provisionally assuming the antecedent, the backtracker "reasons backward. . . and conditionally revises his view" of what has happened before the time of the antecedent, and then reasons forward again.

This language is as useful in the case of Snoopy and Sigmund as it was in the genetic condition example I used earlier involving reasoning about whether to finish writing this paper. In the genetic condition case, I consider not finishing this paper to avoid a premature death. To decide not to finish, I would reason in a backtracking fashion: I would first look forward in time to finishing the paper, and then backtrack to the existence of a prior genetic condition, and then reason forward once more to a premature death.

I am describing such cases by saying that the conditionals in question, when they depend on such backtracking, are deliberationally useless even if true. What I mean by that is that for people in roughly our enlightened epistemic circumstances—those who know that this is not a useful way to figure out what to do—it is irrational to rely on such conditionals when deliberating. I do not mean that it is impossible for anyone ever to use such conditionals and make rational decisions as a result. I mean only that as a matter of fact, such reasoning is importantly suboptimal, and that for those of us who know this fact, it would be irrational to employ such conditionals in deliberation.

We can use this language of backtracking to clarify the objection above to the Material Minimal Model. When we imagined reasoning from God's perspective about what to do, we first began with a list of possible actions. In order to select between the host of possible actions available to him, God needs to employ conditionals of deliberation, and the first task is to determine which conditionals are true and which are false. As we model this activity with a process of calculating truth-values, things can go wrong in the sense that the process envisioned might involve an evidential basis for a conditional that prevents it from being usable as a conditional of deliberation. Here the language of backtracking is helpful. One way for the evidential basis to disbar a conditional from being a deliberative conditional is for the process of calculation to involve a backtracking calculation. In the case of Sly Pete, the backtracking calculation applies to Sigmund's claim that Pete will win if he plays: the evidential basis for this claim is general knowledge about the cheating set-up as well as particular knowledge that Pete is no one's fool. To use this background information to conclude that Pete will win if he plays will involve backtracking reasoning, as DeRose argues. The backtracking reasoning involved in the Sly Pete example involves known contingent information, and is thus different from the kind of information available in our deliberative model of divine creative activity, since there is no such contingent information available at the initial stage of the process so modeled. Since there is no such contingent information available to use in calculating the truth value of the conditionals in question, the only information available for the process in our deliberative model is semantic information. The special kind of backtracking that occurs in our model is thus semantic backtracking rather than the contingent, course-of-nature backtracking that occurs in the Sly Pete example, but both involve the kind of backtracking that prevents even true conditionals from being useful as deliberative conditionals. In the case of our deliberative model, the semantic information necessary for calculating the truth value of a material conditional is available at the initial stages of the process modeled, but in order to use this semantic theory to learn the truth value in question, objectionable backtracking must occur: we first imagine the being in the model moving forward in time to learn the truth value of antecedent and consequent, and then backtracking to the original deliberative situation to use the knowledge so acquired to calculate the truth value of each conditional and thus determine which to use in deliberating about what to do. Whether the backtracking is based on a semantic theory or the contingent setup of a cheating situation, as in the Sly Pete case, it is still objectionable backtracking, in the following sense: when knowledge of the conditionals in question involves such backtracking, the conditionals in question are not appropriately used as deliberative conditionals even if true.

7.3.2 *Models Using Indicative Conditionals*

This point about backtracking is equally compelling when we substitute other types of conditionals into a Minimal Model. In place of a Material Minimal Model, we might try an Indicative Minimal Model, where the conditionals in question are taken to be indicative conditionals rather than material conditionals. On some theories of indicative conditionals, such a proposal will make no sense at all. For example, Grice argues that indicative conditionals just are material conditionals (Grice 1968). On other theories of conditionals, there is no special Indicative Minimal Model as opposed to a Subjunctive Minimal Model, for on the theories of conditionals in question, any conditional that is syntactically in the indicative mood and "forward-looking" in virtue of having a future-tense verb in its consequent, is to be treated semantically the same as a subjunctive conditional (Gibbard 1980, Dudman 1984, 1988, Bennett 1988). (Bennett changed his mind, however, arguing later that the traditional view, on which semantics tracks syntax, is correct (Bennett 1995); defended as well in Jackson (1990).) To consider the possibility of an Indicative Minimal Model, we will ignore both of these positions here, since they eliminate the independent possibility of such a model.

There are two approaches one might take to indicative conditionals compatible with such a possibility. On the first approach, such conditionals express propositions with a special connective (that we may represent using the arrow: $\rightarrow$), which is neither the truth-functional connective of first-order logic (that we may represent with the horseshoe: $\supset$) nor the non-truth-functional connective involved in subjunctive conditionals (that we may represent with the box-arrow: $\Box\rightarrow$). On the second approach, such conditionals do not express conditional propositions at all, but rather express conditional probabilities (which we may represent as: $P(B/A)$).

Though the first approach seems the most obvious to pursue, the second follows a suggestion originally made by Frank Ramsey, who wrote, "If two people are arguing "If p, will q?" and are both in doubt as to p, they are adding p hypothetically to their stock of knowledge, and arguing on that basis about q; ... they are fixing their degrees of belief in q given p." (Ramsey 1990, p. 147). There are actually two suggestions here, but only the second is plausible. The first suggestion is a suppositional account of what it is to believe or assert a conditional sentence in terms of hypothetically adding the antecedent in question to a given stock of beliefs (or knowledge, as Ramsey puts the view), and seeing whether the new stock of beliefs favors or confirms the consequent of the conditional sentence. This particular suppositional account is not plausible, foundering on examples such as "if you are a covert KGB operative, you are so smart and clever that I will certainly never find it out." Once the antecedent is added to a stock of beliefs, the denial of the consequent is readily inferred. But Ramsey has a different suggestion. It is the suggestion that believing a conditional sentence is just a matter of fixing one's conditional degree of belief. In such a case, the view is best thought of in the following terms: the conditional sentence expresses a conditional probability rather than a conditional proposition, and is thus best represented in the form '$P(B/A)$', where P is a probability function and both A and B are propositions, rather than in the form '$A \rightarrow B$'. One might go further and adopt the view that probabilities are nothing but properly constrained degrees of belief, in which case one would hold that conditional sentences do not express propositions at all (where propositions are taken to be bearers of truth-value).[2] Here, however, I will make no such assumptions about the nature of probability unless required by the conditional probability view itself, since these assumptions simply add to the argumentative burden shouldered by the basic theory.

The conditional probability approach becomes more attractive when we see the difficulties that beset the alternative approach. The alternative approach claims that indicatives express conditional propositions, constituted by some component propositions as antecedent and consequent and a conditional connective linking these components, where our semantic theory will provide some truth condition for such a connective. The fundamental difficulty for this truth condition approach in the present context is the current state of the literature on indicative conditionals. It is well known that a complete theory of language will involve not only a semantic theory but other factors as well—factors that have been grouped under the label "pragmatics". A plausible view, for example, is that the semantics for the word 'or' are given by the standard truth-table for that connective, with an explanation of the exclusive sense of 'or' that is common in ordinary language explained in terms of pragmatics rather than semantics. A similar view is equally plausible about the word 'unless': the semantics treats this connective as meaning "if not". When I tell my daughter that she can't go to the party unless she cleans up her room, she will legitimately expect to be allowed to go after cleaning her room. This expectation is pragmatic rather than semantic, however, explicable in terms of the Gricean Maxim of Quantity, according to which one's contribution to a conversation should be as informative as necessary (Grice 1968). Thus, my daughter legitimately assumes that if there are other things she needed to do in order to go to the party, I would have mentioned them as well. What was communicated is thus something stronger than what can be gleaned from semantics alone.

This distinction between semantics and pragmatics is crucial to truth condition approaches to indicatives, since standard defenses of this approach try to explain what is distinctive about the indicative conditional in terms of pragmatic factors built on top of an assumed semantic theory for the material conditional or the subjunctive conditional. A standard example of the difference between indicatives and subjunctives is the Kennedy Assassination Case: it is obvious that if Oswald didn't shoot Kennedy, someone else did, but only conspiracy theorists would claim that if Oswald hadn't shot Kennedy, someone else would have. Standard defenses of the truth condition view in the literature attempt to explain such cases in terms of an underlying semantics for either material or subjunctive conditionals plus some special pragmatic feature at work in indicative conditionals. As noted already, Grice is famous for defending the view that the indicative conditional is just a special case of the material conditional, and more recently

---

[2]This view is articulated and developed in various places by Ernest W. Adams. See, e.g., Adams (1965, 1966, 1970, 1975).

the view has been defended by Frank Jackson as well.[3] The alternative view, on which the underlying semantics is the semantics for subjunctive conditionals, is defended by Robert Stalnaker (Stalnaker 1968). (It is worth noting that by the time of Stalnaker (1984), he had become more ambivalent about the truth condition view.) On Stalnaker's approach, there is a pragmatic constraint on which proposition is expressed—a constraint defined in terms of what hasn't been ruled out (what is a live possibility or an epistemic possibility) in the context in question. Stalnaker's semantics for subjunctive conditionals uses a selection function to pick out the nearest or most similar possible world, and for indicative conditionals this selection function is guided by the pragmatic constraint that this selection function applies only to worlds that are compatible with what hasn't been ruled out in the context in question.

In our special context, however, this pragmatic constraint does no work at all. In the initial stages of deliberative context prior to creation (in the model), all possibilities are live possibilities, and thus the selection function works in precisely the same way on indicative conditionals as it does on subjunctive conditionals, in the Stalnakerian framework. This point is a specific instance of a more general point, which is that the current state of the literature leaves the truth condition view of indicative conditionals offering nothing of use in the context of our attempt to construct a deliberative model of God's creative activity. The current state of the literature develops the truth condition view on top of a more basic semantic account of indicatives which identifies the semantics for indicatives in terms of the semantics for material conditionals or subjunctive conditionals. Thus, the truth condition view of indicative conditionals fares no better than either of these other views.

There remains the possibility, however, that the "no truth conditions" view of indicative conditionals might prove helpful. To begin, consider first the argument for calling the view the "no truth conditions" view. A version of the central argument for the view goes as follows (Edgington 1986, 1995). Any truth conditional view has to treat a conditional as entailing the material conditional: "if A, B" entails, if it entails anything, "$A \supset B$". It may be stronger than the material conditional, but it can't be weaker (if it were weaker, *modus ponens* would fail). But we can rule out both truth-functional and stronger-than-truth functional accounts by way of two questions: (1) "Assume that it is certain that $\sim(A \,\&\, \sim B)$, but not certain that $\sim A$; should you be certain that if A, B?" and (2) "If you think it likely that $\sim A$, might you still think it unlikely that if A, B?" Answering yes to question (1) is supposed to be the right answer according

[3]See Grice (1968), Jackson (1987). Grice appeals to the maxims of quality, quantity, relevance, and manner in explaining why there are some things one is justified in believing but which would be misleading to say. Jackson claims that indicatives obey a certain rule of assertibility, which he terms "robustness". In the work cited, robustness is understood in terms of a high degree of conditional belief, i.e., where $P(B)$ is a degree of belief in B and $P(B/A)$ is a degree of belief in B given A, robustness for the claim 'if A, B' requires that $P(B/A)$ is high.

to our best epistemology for degrees of belief because $A\&B$ is just as likely as A, given the background certainty in question. But a stronger-than-truth-functional approach lacks the resources to draw this conclusion: just knowing the information in question doesn't tell you what to think about "if A, B". Answering yes to question (2) is also supposed to be the correct answer, because $P(A \& \sim B)$ might be considerably higher than $P(A\&B)$, leaving "if A, B" quite unlikely. But a truth-functional reading can't yield this result, since the truth-functional conditional is entailed by the falsity of its antecedent (and if A entails B, the probability of B can't be lower than the probability of A).[4] So, since conditionals have truth conditions only if they are stronger than or at least as strong as the material conditional, and answers to the two questions rule out both possibilities, conditionals have no truth conditions.

What is the metaphysical upshot of the claim that indicative conditionals lack truth conditions? I believe the best way to understand this idea is by analogy with expressivist and attitudinalist views in ethics. According to such views, well-formed ethical sentences do not express propositions that bear a truth-value. Instead, the use of such sentences involves the expression of some pro-attitude toward some state of affairs. For example, a very simple approach of this sort holds that when a person asserts, "stealing from the rich and giving it to the poor is permissible," that person is expressing some positive attitude toward the state of affairs in which the rich are robbed for the benefit of the poor. In the context of indicative conditionals, the best way to articulate the "no truth conditions" view in combination with Ramsey's proposal is to hold that when an indicative sentence is written or spoken, the utterance or inscription does not express a proposition, but rather expresses an attitude of high degree of conditional belief.

One might have the sense here of being philosophically cheated: we want to know how to interpret indicative conditionals, and are told that we can't do so in terms of propositions and their truth conditions, but we can interpret them in terms of degrees of conditional belief. But haven't we just postponed the task of interpreting the conditional aspect here? It was, originally, in the sentence itself. We didn't know what to do with the conditionality in question. We are now told that the proper understanding of the conditionality of the sentence is in terms of the conditionality of degrees of belief. The feeling of perplexity about the nature of conditionality linguistically recorded in the indicative mood is not diminished by such buck-passing, is it?

One might attempt to evade this concern by insisting that there is a basic, unanalyzable mental state between two propositional contents A and B that just is conditional belief, whether coarse-grained belief itself, fine-grained degree of belief (which we might call "credences") or broader states that cover intervals of

---

[4]To avoid confusion, I should note here that the presentation of the argument is meant to be conversational. In particular, I avoid the perplexing practice standard in the literature on probability of using the notion of a likelihood as an inverse conditional probability, relying more on the ordinary language synonymy of the notions. Where careful evaluation of the argument is the goal, a more careful explication would be required.

credences (which we might call "confidence intervals", or "confidences"). What is crucial is not so much the states themselves, whether beliefs, credences, or confidences, but rather the fundamental, unanalyzable conditionality that some of these states display (see, e.g., Sturgeon (2002)).

One might be forgiven here for failing to be comforted. The analogy with attitudinalism in ethics is instructive in this regard. In that domain, we have a sentence that, if treated in terms of the standard semantical maneuvers, yields a proposition expressed that has features that are discomfiting to some. The proposition would involve features that don't fit well with a naturalistic conception of reality. So the attitudinalist has to adjust, and the adjustment has two aspects. The first aspect is the move from the cognitive to the non-cognitive realm, to explain the significance of such sentences from the usual cognitive side of our being to the affective side. The second aspect involves replacing the apparent normative proposition with a purely non-normative state of affairs at which the affective side of our being is directed. So instead of a normative proposition that is the object of belief and other cognitive states, we get a non-normative state of affairs that is the object of a pro-attitude.

The "no truth conditions" view is not able to mimic these features. Instead of moving from the cognitive to the non-cognitive side of our being when faced with the troubling sentences, the "no truth conditions" view stays on the cognitive side, espousing the view that the troubling indicative conditions really do have cognitive significance. That in itself is problematic enough, since it would appear that a distinctive feature of cognitive attitudes is that they have contents that are alethically evaluable. But the difficulties do not end here. Attitudinalist in ethics not only moved from the cognitive to the affective sphere, they also replaced the expected normative proposition that would typically be the content of some cognitive attitude with a non-normative state of affairs or proposition that is the object of some pro-attitude. But when the "no truth conditions" view is developed in the way described, we get nothing like this story. We fail to move out of the cognitive sphere, as one would expect, and we fail to replace the troubling conditionality of the sentence in question with some content of object of an attitude that lacks conditionality. In the ethics case, we move out of the cognitive sphere and away from the troubling normativity. In the "no truth conditions" case, we stay in the cognitive sphere and retain conditionality. So it is no wonder that one feels philosophically cheated, and that the feeling doesn't go away when we are told that the troubling conditionality of the sentence is explicable in terms of some unanalyzable conditionality involved in the cognitive attitude of degree of conditional belief.

But perhaps we are too demanding here. The "no truth conditions" theorist can insist that we are confusing judgments with conditional judgments. The former are relations between a mental state of a cognizer and a propositional content. The latter are not relations between a mental state of a believer and a conditional content of some sort. Rather, the conditionality is in the judgment or belief or degree of belief itself, which is a relation between a mental state of a cognizer and two different propositions which play different roles. One role is the role of the supposition, and the other thing is the thing judged under that supposition. So, it might be said, the troubling conditionality in the sentence under consideration is removed. It is removed from every possible content of mental state and is instead placed in the special nature of conditional mentality.

Even if we grudgingly grant the respectability of explaining the conditionality of an indicative conditional by appeal to the conditionality of judgment itself, this proposal will generate troubling theoretical complexity if it works only for indicative conditionals and not for other types of conditionals in natural language. For example, suppose we combine this "the conditionality is in the judging" view with a standard Lewis/Stalnaker approach to subjunctive conditionals (Stalnaker 1968, Lewis 1973). Subjunctive conditionals would then be conceived of as having truth conditions, with the conditionality of such sentences explicable in terms of similarity relations on worlds, whereas indicative conditionals would have no truth conditions, with the conditionality of such sentences explained in terms of the conditionality of judging itself. We know, of course, that there is some difference between indicative and subjunctive conditionality, but it would be a surprising philosophical fact of the first order if the difference were like this.

There is some hope for a unified "conditionality in judgment" view at least for a restricted range of conditionals. Recall the original Kennedy Assassination counterexample to identifying subjunctives and indicatives: it is clear that if Oswald didn't shoot Kennedy then someone else did, but it is likely false that if Oswald hadn't shot Kennedy then someone else would have. Call such counterexamples "Adams pairs."[5] There is a surprising fact about such counterexamples, a point Lycan notes (Lycan 2001, pp. 162-166). When we restrict our attention to conditionals that are directed toward the future and which do not involve backtracking features, Adams pairs cannot be found. Moreover, when using such conditionals for deliberation, as noted already, one is hard-pressed to find any interesting difference at all. When we reason, "If I buy this horse, I won't be able to make my mortgage payment, so I won't buy this horse," it wouldn't make any obvious or interesting difference to have reasoned subjunctively "If I were to buy this horse I wouldn't be able to to make my mortgage payment, so I won't buy this horse." If we refer to such conditionals usable in the context of deliberation as future-oriented conditionals, the point Lycan makes is that there are no Adams pairs for future-oriented conditionals. That suggests that for future-oriented conditionals, a unified treatment should be expected, and a "conditionality in judgment" approach seems as good an approach for the subjunctive future-oriented conditionals as for the indicative ones.

But this result doesn't generalize to all subjunctive conditionals. What to make of this point is a complicated matter. Maybe philosophical theory shouldn't

[5]To use Bill Lycan's felicitous phrase in honor of the originator of the counterexample, E. Adams. See Lycan (2001).

track grammatical categories, and so the division between subjunctive and indicative conditionals should take backseat to the division between future-oriented
and deliberatively useful conditionals and all the rest.

In our context, however, we can let these concerns pass. Our interest is in
what to make of this proposal for the attempt to construct a deliberative model
of God's creative activity. Assume, then, that indicative conditionals, when used
in deliberation, express high degrees of conditional belief. When used in ordinary
deliberation, the question of how high a degree of belief is needed is an important
and difficult one, but in the context of our model, the answer is simple. The degree
of conditional belief in question would have to be as high as possible, since our
model is intended to preserve the traditional understanding of divinity in terms
of universal and necessary omniscience. If some degree less than full certainty
were allowed, this understanding would be compromised. So in the context of our
project, we may assume that indicative conditionals used in deliberation express
conditional certainties.

Espousing such a view is one thing, and explaining what warrants such a
strong opinion is quite another, however. We imagine that God is certain that if
he performs action A, world W will be actual. Hence, he can use the conditional
sentence "if I do A, W will result" in deliberating about what to create. We
make no theoretical progress, however, without some account of what warrants
the opinion that licenses the deliberation in question, and here the attitudinalism
at the heart of the "no truth condition" view is a conversation-stopper. At least,
when we had conditionals with truth conditions, we had semantic information
available to God prior to deciding what to create that could be appealed to in
explaining how he could know which conditionals are worthy of use and which
aren't. But once we go attitudinal about conditionals, we lose that explanation.

There is a hint of where to look in the proposal itself. Recall that the argument for the "no truth condition" view appeals to our best epistemology for
degrees of belief. On that epistemology, rational degrees of belief must satisfy the
probability calculus. So suppose we take this hint seriously enough not only to
require probabilistic coherence but to regard it as sufficient for the kind of warrant in question. We thus maintain that God deliberates by employing exactly
those indicative conditionals which express conditional certainties that cohere
probabilistically with all other certainties for God.

Such an approach cannot succeed, however. To see why, recall one of the
classic objections to coherence theories of justification, the "alternative systems"
objection. Put in somewhat careless jargon, the complaint against coherentism
is that for any belief there is some system or other into which that belief can be
put and where the resulting system is coherent. As an objection to coherentism,
this remark is not especially troubling, since it is not clear that there are beliefs
that cannot, as opposed to are not, justified. More generally, it is a virtue of
coherentism to be able to explain how diversity of opinion can nonetheless be
fully justified. Viewed in this way, the point about alternative systems isn't an
objection to coherentism, but rather a virtue of it.

In the present context, however, the existence of alternative doxastic systems for God is devastating. Recall that our context is that point in the model prior to an creative activity by God. The certainties for God at the initial point in the model are necessary truths, and no truth dependent on his creative activity can be included in the doxastic system at this point in the model. Now add any group of conditional certainties you wish to this initial point. There will always be an alternative group that would fit equally well. For just one example, define a contradictory conditional certainty as follows: where $c(A/B)$ is the certainty that A given B, the contradictory conditional certainty is $c(\ A/B)$. Where G is the initial group of conditional certainties added to the initial certainties about necessary truths, let G' be a different group composed of all the contradictory conditional certainties for the members of G. Then G' will display whatever requirements of fit with the initial certainties concerning necessary truths displayed by G itself. As a result, we have two possible systems that are equally warranted from the point of view of the initial stage of our deliberative model, and thus the notion of warrant can't explain why God would endorse one group rather than the other.

I'm imposing a contrastive requirement here on the adequacy of our model, even though I think that epistemically normative notions are not in general subject to such a requirement. In the context of our model, however, such a requirement is appropriate (see Kvanvig (2011*b*)). We should not imagine that there are possibilities that have escaped God's attention, since one of the things he will be certain of is which groups of conditional certainties display probabilistic coherence and which don't. Hence, one of his certainties at the initial stage in the model will be claims to the effect that there is no good reason in terms of probabilistic coherence itself to favor one group of conditional certainties over other groups of conditional certainties. Moreover, if probabilistic coherence is the only reasonable basis available for selecting conditional certainties, then God will also be unconditionally certain that there is no reason to favor one group of conditional certainties over any of the probabilistically coherent competitor groups. Even for those who wish to leave some epistemic optionality in place, so that in some situations there can be two competitor views that would be equally rational or justified or warranted to believe, this situation shouldn't be tolerated. The trick for the epistemic optionalist is to find a middle ground between epistemic prodigality, as would be displayed by allowing arbitrary choices in the cognitive domain in the same way we do in cases of action such as the Buridan's ass situation,[6] and the alternative restrictivist view that there is one and only one attitude that fits any given body of evidence. The appropriate middle ground is one that doesn't tolerate alternatives to be equally acceptable when absolutely no explanation whatsoever can be given for going for one view rather than the other, as would be the case here. So, though the alternative systems objection to coherentism is not compelling, in the context of our model, the existence of

---

[6]For a defense and explication of this difference, see Kvanvig (2009*b*).

alternative collections of conditional certainties undermines the role any such collection could play in modeling deliberatively the creative activity of God.

The conclusion to draw, then, is that our current understanding of indicative conditionals provides no hope for escaping the problems encountered with the Material Minimal Model. An Indicative Minimal Model is, at best, no better than the Material Minimal Model, and if certain views of indicatives are adopted, may generate additional problems to those faced by the Material Minimal Model.

7.3.3 *Models Using Subjunctive Conditionals*

The only remaining possibility for a Minimal Model is thus the Subjunctive Minimal Model. On this model, we consider various possible actions of God and worlds that result from such via subjunctive conditionals (which I will sometimes call "counterfactuals of creation"), which have the following form:

Subjunctive Minimal Model: (God does A) $\square\!\rightarrow$ (W is actual).

In English: If God were to do A, W would be actual. The explanation of divine creative activity we get on the Subjunctive Minimal Model is that God picks a counterfactual of creation, evaluates the desirability of various outcomes, and by assessing the desirability of these outcomes, chooses which antecedent to actualize. The result is the actuality of the, or a, preferred world.

Even so, nobody should be happy with the Subjunctive Minimal Model. It is too minimal in terms of explanatory details to be helpful in terms of providing any significant understanding of creation and its rationale.

It is worth recalling at this point the complaint against the Material Minimal Model, for the same complaint can be lodged here. That complaint concerns illegitimate appeals to omniscience in an account of the divine creative activity. What a model needs to do is to contain conditionals for which there is a good explanation of how they count as deliberative conditionals. For this to be the case, we must first posit divine knowledge of some group of conditionals that give options regarding what to do and what outcomes will result. Then, in light of these conditionals, a choice is made, based on the desirability of the outcomes in question. No such order was present in the case of the Modified Material Minimal Model. Instead, an action is chosen to be performed, and knowledge of the needed conditionals was explained in a truth-functional manner concerning which world is in fact the actual world. The paradigmatic story of deliberation isn't present here—one in which an individual first knows what outcomes attach to which courses of action, and then a course of action is selected based on an evaluation of the desirability of the implied outcomes. Instead, the model works only to the extent that it first posits knowledge of certain features of the actual world that guarantee the truth of the conditional in question—features that are themselves contingent and thus part of what was supposed to be explained by the model in the first place. In the model, the reasoning that takes place doesn't proceed via calculation of outcomes based on antecedents made true. Instead, the deliberation proceeds via reasoning that selects between competing conditionals by appeal to knowledge of the consequent of the conditional.

Note the resemblance between such models and the earlier example of a genetic and statistical relationship between finishing this paper and premature death. In both cases, a description in terms of "backtracking" is appropriate. In the genetic example, we first reason forward in time by adding as an assumption that I continue to work on this paper, and then reason backward in time to the existence of a prior genetic condition and then forward once more to an imaginary premature death. With the Minimal Models in question, we first imagine God reasoning forward in time by adding the assumption that God does A, and then reasoning backward in time to determine which conditional is being used, and then are able to reason forward again to the actuality of the actual world only after the backtracking reasoning that involves knowledge of which world is the actual world. For notice that there is no story to be told about how God knows which conditional is the conditional being used that isn't already a story of which world is the actual world. The difference in backtracking is that in the genetic condition example, we are given the truth of the conditionals in question, and the backtracking occurs in terms of the features of the agent in question. In the creation example, what happens first is the imaginary decision by God to do a certain action, and second to resolve any uncertainty about which conditional is being used (since no conditional can be used unless it is true). Then backtracking occurs in terms of resolving any uncertainty about which conditional is in fact being used. In both cases, however, a resolution of uncertainty occurs by backtracking, and it is this feature that is objectionable in both cases.

Here, regarding the Subjunctive Minimal Model, the worry is the same. As with the Modified Minimal Models, a given action is selected, but not on the basis of the desirability of the outcomes in question. Such a basis would require already knowing which conditionals are true, but such knowledge, on the usual semantic model for subjunctives, requires information about which world is actual and which features of worlds are similarity-making features. Thus, just as with the Modified Material Minimal Model, the Subjunctive Minimal Model has to posit backtracking reasoning on the part of God to settle any uncertainty about which conditional is appropriate for use in deliberating about creation. It is the need for such backtracking reasoning in the model that explains why all the Minimal Models are defective.

One might think that this problem can be addressed by siding with Plantinga, holding that counterfactuals are constitutive of the similarity relation itself, rather than something inferred from some notion of similarity not including these counterfactuals (Plantinga 1978, p. 178). Such a maneuver is a non-starter in the present context, however. In developing a model, God needs to know which conditionals are true in a way that is explanatorily prior to his knowledge of what he will do and which world is actual. Even if the conditionals in question are constitutive of similarity, the explanatory backtracking problem remains, since making the conditionals constitutive of similarity doesn't block the need for knowing which world is actual in a way that is prior to knowing which subjunctives are true.

On this score, it is worth noting an assumption involved in standard Molinist accounts of creation and providence. Such accounts portray God's knowledge of subjunctive conditionals as logically prior to his decisions about what to create and what world will result. The point above is that the Molinist doesn't get to make this claim for free. What is required is an explanation of how such middle knowledge is possible, not the mere assertion that it exists. In this regard, the point above is simply that the standard semantics does not help in this task, and appealing to this semantics makes the problem insolvable.

When difficulties arise with possible explanations for some feature of a view, there is always the defense of last resort: make the feature in question fundamental to the theory and in need of no explanation whatsoever. Here, Molinists might try the same, insisting that the middle knowledge hypothesis is simply fundamental to the theory, and in no need of any explanation in terms of the semantics for subjunctive conditionals.

Such appeals should not move us toward a model using subjunctive conditionals, however, since the same explanatory evasion could have been used regarding the other models as well. Regarding the Material Minimal Model, we might insist that God's knowledge of such conditionals is not a function of his deployment of the truth-table semantics for such conditionals, and thus that the explanatory priority objection doesn't undermine the theory. If pressed concerning where God's knowledge of such conditionals comes from, we appeal to fundamentality, since explanations must end somewhere. Something similar could be said about the issues raised for the Indicative Minimal Model. So, if appeals to what is explanatorily fundamental in a given approach can save it from the problems noted above, such appeals reach too far, since they can be employed to save other approaches as well.

Moreover, while such a purely defensive strategy in defending the subjunctive approach might save the view from outright refutation, it remains true that the difficulties that prompt such a defensive move still have probative force against it.

Such difficulties explain well why it is so tempting to understanding God's creative activity in terms of deliberative conditionals takes these conditionals to be strict conditionals, ones in which the divine activity in the antecedent logically guarantees the actualization of the world named in the consequent. Regarding such conditionals, concerns about logical or epistemic possibilities that need to be resolved before determining which conditionals are appropriate for use are not present. First, there aren't competing logical possibilities, since the conditionals are necessarily true if true at all. Moreover, a deliberative model can't get off the ground at all if it doesn't assume that there is some information available from which to reason, and for a cognitively perfect being, we surely don't want any account of this information to fall outside the scope of what is logically possible. Perhaps there is an issue about the extent of logical information assumed in the model to be known by God, but it is hard to see any principled reason for claiming that some such knowledge by God is legitimate for the model to assume while other such knowledge is not. It would seem then that if we develop our model of the divine creative activity in terms of strict conditionals, we need not face the backtracking problem that affects models that use conditionals that are logically contingent and we have an initial knowledge base to appeal to, in terms of knowledge of necessary (and presumably *a priori*) truths from which to begin the process of deliberation.

Such a path is the path taken by all approaches except those that despair of providing a deliberative model of creation capable of sustaining a strong doctrine of providence. Even a version of Molinism can be developed that is a special case of an approach in terms of strict conditionals, and we can glean the needed background for evaluating this special case by first attending to versions of the Strict Conditional Model that are more deterministic in character.

7.3.4 *Models Using Strict Conditionals*

In order to move beyond Minimal Models, we'll need to impute a bit more structure to the antecedents of potential deliberative conditionals if the conditionals in question are going to have any hope of being strict conditionals. If we assume first that the only options available for possible worlds are ones that are deterministic in character, we have two options. One option is that of standard occasionalism, according to which there are no powers in nature itself but only in God himself. Such an account of creation exploits strict conditionals as a limiting case, one where antecedent and consequent are identical. I will say no more here about such an occasionalist option, other than to note in passing that most will want an account that allows God to impute powers and abilities to things themselves, in some way or other. To do so, our Strict Conditional Model will have to contain conditionals that have in their antecedents some reference to some aspect of the created order itself that is involved in the implication of the actuality of whatever world is referenced in the consequent. To make the implication strict, we will have to assume that whatever features are mentioned in the antecedent are sufficient to yield the complete world specified in the consequent; in short, we shall have to assume that possible worlds are causally, or nomologically, deterministic. Given such an assumption, it is tempting to describe God's deliberation in terms of selecting from various sets of possible laws of nature and various sets of initial conditions. For it is tempting to think that once we specify the laws of nature and the initial conditions, the rest follows as a matter of simple logic. That is, God's deliberation in such a case would proceed in terms of logically necessary conditionals such as:

> Strict Conditional Model: Necessarily, given laws of nature L and initial conditions I, W is actual.

It is worth noting that once the necessity operator is out front, it doesn't matter whether the governed conditional is put in the indicative mood or in the subjunctive mood. The difference between the two, whatever it is, is rendered irrelevant by the presence of the necessity operator out front. Given such necessary conditionals, God can see which worlds will result from which choices of laws and initial conditions, and can exercise control over which world is actual by such choices.

We should note that for this account of God's creative activity to work, we must be assuming that it is unproblematic for God to know which strict conditionals are true and which are false. The key to defending this assumption is to note that the strict conditionals in question are logically true, so that the cognitive abilities needed to discern their truth value are abilities for detecting *a priori* truths. If we imagine that there are *a posteriori* necessities, the mere fact that such a truth is necessary would not make the assumption that God knows this modal fact unproblematic. In the present context where we are modeling God's creative activity in terms of a model of deliberation independent of creation, we are entitled to assume only that everything *a priori* is detectable for purposes of deliberation. We must thus assume that the conditionals in question are not only strict, but also knowable *a priori*.

Such a picture of divine deliberation needs a bit of tweaking, however, even given deterministic assumptions and the assumption that the strict conditionals in question are knowable *a priori*. Complications arise because of the possibility of miracles. Nature constitutes a system which, if governed by laws, is governed by laws that involve *ceteris paribus* clauses protecting the law from being contradicted by intrusions from outside the natural system in question. We are familiar with the need for such clauses regarding laws in the special sciences: the laws of psychology aren't held hostage to the possibilities created by gunshot wounds to the head. Since we clearly don't want miracles to be violations of laws of nature, i.e., we don't want there to be true laws that have actual counterexamples to them, the standard approach is to view even the basic laws of nature as including *ceteris paribus* clauses concerning intervention from outside the system in question.

There is an alternative conception of miracles, but it isn't especially promising in our context. Some will want to think of miracles in terms of Humean laws of nature, the most interesting version of which is David Lewis's best systems account of laws. Lewis writes,

> Take all deductive systems whose theorems are true. Some are simpler, better systematized than others. Some are stronger, more informative, than others. These virtues compete: an uninformative system can be very simple, an unsystematized compendium of miscellaneous information can be very informative. The best system is the one that strikes as good a balance as truth will allow between simplicity and strength.... A regularity is a law iff it is a theorem of the best system. (Lewis 1994, p. 478)

The Humean/Lewisian idea is that the laws must supervene on the local facts, in the sense that given the same local facts, we get the same laws. Moreover, on this picture of laws, the laws are a subset of universal regularities (that subset defined in terms of the best compromise between competing theoretical virtues), and a miracle thus cannot be defined in terms of laws. Instead, we would need to the concept of a near-law, where the near-laws are constructed in the same Lewisian fashion as the true laws, except that the comparison class for a balance between simplicity and strength will be composed of generalizations that are almost exceptionless. In this way, we can have miracles and yet have laws that can't be violated or overridden from forces outside the system in question.

But such a conception of laws does violence to the deliberative model under consideration. What is metaphysically basic on this picture is the local facts; the laws are just a compact and informative summary of these local facts (Beebee 2001). If this coded summary involved equivalence with local facts rather than mere supervenience, one could infer from laws to facts, but since all that is involved is supervenience, the only logical inference possible is from local facts to laws. Thus, even if the system in question were fully deterministic, there would be no necessarily true conditionals taking us from some collage of laws and initial conditions to worlds. At most, what we would get are conditionals from laws and initial conditions to galaxies, where a galaxy is a collection of worlds.

These facts about the Humean account of laws present a difficulty for the model above of divine deliberation. When we are modeling the divine creative act in terms of deliberation, we must assume that the context is one in which God inhabits a particular moment of time and the future relative to that time branches to all the worlds that can result from a divine creative act. If we wish to maintain that God is outside of time, we will treat this feature as an artifact of the model, but it is part of the model nonetheless. The Humean picture of laws has no resources of use in this context, since which generalizations are laws depends metaphysically on the entire history of the actual world rather than being the sort of thing that governs the unfolding of such a history.

So the Humean picture of laws has the following consequences in our context. It allows for the possibility of miracles without requiring *ceteris paribus* clauses in the laws themselves. But it undermines the model proposed, since there will be no necessarily true conditionals connecting given sets of laws and initial conditions with worlds actualized as a result, where the laws and initial conditions can be known in a way that is prior to the unfolding of the mosaic of local, particular fact. Instead, the model of divine creation that would need to be adopted given the Humean conception of laws is one on which God determines immediately and directly the entire sequencing of local facts that are metaphysically basic on this picture. No modeling in terms of inferences using laws and initial conditions is possible, and hence the notion of divine deliberation is present only in the way it is present in occasionalism, as a limiting case of deliberation where antecedent and consequent are identical. There is no deliberation involved in the model employing the normal language of means and ends, but only a sequence of choices about which collection of local facts to create at each moment of time.

My purpose, however, is not to argue about the implications of Humeanism about laws, but rather to pursue the question of how to model the divine act of creation. Humeanism posits that the fundamental explanatory relations go from local facts to laws, so if we want to model creation deliberatively in terms of antecedents that yield specific worlds as outcomes, we will have to abandon Humeanism. In short, the only hope for developing a deliberative model of creation that can sustain a strong view of providence is through a rejection of the Humean story.

As we have seen, however, we can't develop the deliberative model under the assumption of determinism by adopting the Strict Conditional Model above, for such a model yields a deism inconsistent with miracles. Instead, the laws will have to be conceived as containing *ceteris paribus* clauses so that miracles are not violations of laws but rather overridings of them by a power outside the system of nature in question.

But if we cannot use the Strict Conditional Model above, how can we alter it to accommodate the existence of miracles? Here is an idea. One argument standardly used against Humeanism about laws is the failure of that view to give a proper account of the relationship between laws and counterfactuals. If gravity is a law of nature, that law supports the claim that if an object were to be dropped from a ledge overlooking the Grand Canyon, it would fall. In the usual presentation of this relationship, the laws of nature are said to entail the counterfactuals in question, so perhaps, in place of the Strict Conditional Model, we could use counterfactuals entailed by the laws of nature as fodder for the deliberative machine:

> Implied Counterfactual Version: Necessarily, where C is the collection of counterfactuals implied by the laws of nature, given C and initial conditions I, W is actual.

There is a problem with this idea, however. If the laws have *ceteris paribus* clauses in them, why won't the counterfactuals as well? I don't think there is a way out of this problem, if we are claiming that counterfactuals are entailed by laws. Suppose there is a law-like connection between properties F and G. If there is and counterfactuals are entailed by laws, then it will follow that if something were an F it would be a G. As noted above, however, the existence of the law is compatible with a miracle that results in an F that is not a G. Yet, no account of the truth conditions of counterfactuals can stomach the counterfactual coming out true when it has a true antecedent and a false consequent.

A better account here of the relationship between laws and counterfactuals is found by returning to the vague language used earlier: that laws of nature support counterfactuals. That is, they provide strong evidential support for counterfactuals. What they entail is not an unqualified counterfactual, but rather one with a *ceteris paribus* clause, just as is contained in the law itself. But the law provides strong evidence as well for the unqualified counterfactual, so that if we know the laws, we have powerful evidence, though of a defeasible sort, for the unqualified counterfactual.

In the present context, though, the conclusion we must adopt is that the appeal to the relationship between laws and counterfactuals isn't going to help here. Instead, the deliberative model will have to posit weaker conditionals than those used in describing the Strict Conditional Model above—conditionals which include in their antecedent some account of which miracles will be performed and which won't:

> Theistic Strict Conditional Model: Necessarily, given laws of nature L

and initial conditions I and some collection of interventions in the course of nature by God, W is actual.

Thus, in order for the model to generate an account of creation, the conditionals must make reference to which actions God will perform in overriding the laws of nature (hence the qualifier "theistic"). So in deliberating, God will have to know which conditionals describe the course of nature when left to itself, and will also have to know his intentions to intervene in that natural course if he were to create that combination of laws and initial conditionals.

Regarding the former point, knowledge of necessary truths is all that is needed. Given a particular set of laws and initial conditions, then if no over-ridings take place, some particular world is the actual world. Moreover, if some overriding is assumed to occur at some point in history, the course nature would take on its own can be calculated by taking the conditions in place at the point of overriding and assuming that no future overridings will occur. So for this aspect of deliberation, all that is needed is necessary truths and God's knowledge of them.

The pleasing result, if this is the end of the story, is that the model shows how God can exercise full providential control over the history of creation, from first to last, just by picking laws, initial conditions, and his own interventions into the natural course of affairs. Things aren't quite that simple, however, unless it is impossible for God to change his mind about his original creative decisions. The model is designed to have a particular possible world as the consequential outcome of God's creative activity, for such an implication is at the core of the idea that God exercises full providential control over every aspect of his creation. But if we add to the model that God can change his mind, the entailment from laws, initial conditions, and overridings chosen at the moment of creation disappears. The choices at creation and the intentions underlying those choices must thus be assumed to be irrevocable.

It is tempting to describe this feature of God's intentions as being implied by the traditional doctrine of immutability. There is a problem with this portrayal, however, for on the model in question we have a host of possible interventions and a choice by God concerning which to author. If God's intentions and character are immutable in the sense of being incapable of changing, this model cannot be adequate. For on the model, we move from one moment at which there are only possibilities of intervention to another moment at which an intention is formed to make actual one of the possibilities. Perhaps, though, the doctrine of immutability should be taken as implying only that once in place, an intention cannot be altered or abandoned.

If we accept this modified account of immutability as the ground of the irre-vocability in question, a further issue arises concerning the level of generality of the intentions needed. The interventions can be described in terms of types or tokens. In order for the model to explain how a particular possible world is chosen to be the actual world, the interventions in question will have to be thought of in maximally specific fashion, in the way that the language of a token intention implies. Of course, even with maximal specificity, there is still a distinction between type and token, so it is not quite necessary that the intentions be about token interventions. I will be enough that the intentions involve a content that is maximally specific enough that only one token can satisfy the description in question.

The point of noting all these complications about possible interventions by God is to make clear what is required for the model to yield the doctrine of providence, conceived of as requiring a creative decision by God to actualize a particular possible world by choosing a certain collection of laws, initial conditions, and interventions. In order to succeed, the choices themselves have to be irrevocable, and if it is part of God's nature to choose only in this way, then we have an explanation via this model of the doctrine of providence.

It is important to note here that we can't succeed at providing an account of creation in accord with the standard doctrine of providence if we conceive of God as choosing whether or not to make a choice irrevocable. If some of God's choices are irrevocable and some are not, and yet it is thought to be up to God which category a decision falls into, incoherence results. For on this account of an irrevocable choice, God actually chooses two things: first the choice itself, and second the choice to make the first choice irrevocable. But the second choice only counts as making the first choice irrevocable if in fact the second choice itself is irrevocable. On the picture in question, irrevocability is the product of some further meta-choice, so there would need to be a third choice to make the second choice irrevocable as well. This hierarchy of meta-choices goes to infinity without ever succeeding in generating the needed irrevocability. Each choice in the hierarchy is only conditionally irrevocable, requiring a further choice at the metalevel that is itself irrevocable. But at the next level, all we find is further conditional irrevocability, and the conditionality in question is never eliminated, even if the entire infinite sequence of choices were made. The regress is thus vicious, since the conditionality of the irrevocability cannot be eliminated merely by positing more metachoices.

There is, however, a different and better and more standard explanation of such irrevocability in terms of the immutable character of God. It is not that some choices come tagged as irrevocable in virtue of God saying they are, but rather than it is God's nature to make every choice, conditional or categorical, an irrevocable choice. The only question, then, is whether the choices in question are categorical or conditional, and as described, they are clearly categorical. We thus arrive at a model of deliberation that relies only on necessary truths, presupposing a doctrine of immutability and generating a strong doctrine of divine providence resulting from irrevocable choices of laws, initial conditions, and maximally specific interventions.

There are further questions that could be pursued about this model, but we have come far enough to see that there is a relatively straightforward way to fix the problems with the Subjunctive Minimal Model by using substantive strict conditionals referring to laws of nature in place of the contingent counterfactuals that referred only to possible actions of God. A strong doctrine of providence is elicitable from this new model, given the assumption that the laws of nature themselves are deterministic.

What happens, though, when we allow the laws to be stochastic? The most obvious implication is that conditionals with a complete world specified in their consequent will no longer have any claim on being strictly true, so the introduction of indeterminism requires some addition to the antecedent of the conditionals in question if the model is still going to be one that employs strict conditionals.

Here the Strict Conditionalist has few options. Claiming that the doctrine of providence is a contingent one, and that God's exercise of providential control over the course of the world is metaphysically optional undermines the model we are considering, for then, at first glance at least, we lose the picture of deliberation in terms of strict conditionals alone. If we take a collection of laws of nature some of which are purely probabilistic, it looks like we can no longer be guaranteed that a certain complete world will result from such a collection. Instead, all that would be guaranteed is a certain kind of world, with the details left to chance.

So the Strict Conditionalist has, as far as I can see, only two options. One is to insist that there are no possible merely probabilistic laws of nature, and the second is to defend the idea that even if there are merely probabilistic laws of nature, the Strict Conditional Model can be rescued.

The first route is the truly heroic one. How could one argue that it is logically or metaphysically impossible for there to be probabilistic laws of nature? Such an option is at odds with our best science, since it leaves open the possibility of irreducibly probabilistic laws. One might, in response, hang one's hat on *a priori* arguments in favor of some Principle of Sufficient Reason, but there are two problems here. First, philosophers and theologians have a poor track record when it comes to the use of such arguments to rebut developments in science, and second, there are significant philosophical obstacles to a defense of any such principle.[7] So, while more discussion would be needed to rule out this option, there are grounds for skepticism regarding this approach. In light of them, perhaps a less heroic approach would be in trying to rescue the Strict Conditional Model while granting the possibility of probabilistic laws of nature.

There is a "god of the gaps" way to pursue this strategy which may appeal to some. God could choose to intervene precisely in those cases in which chance plays a role and determine which of the chancy directions will actually occur. So, by beefing up the interventions appropriately, we can still model an indeterministic system of nature in keeping with the Strict Conditional Model.

Such a view is hardly plausible, however. The history of "god of the gaps" hypotheses inclines us to be wary of such devices. Moreover, even if we grant the possibility that God could match interventions with chance in a way to generate strict conditionals to use for deliberation, we can't rescue the Strict Conditional Model until we show that every conditional of deliberation is a strict conditional.

---

[7]For a worthy recent discussion and defense of the principle, see (Pruss 2006).

If it is possible for God to intervene in precisely the chancy situations, that is not enough to rescue the Strict Conditional Model. That model would also need the point that it is impossible for God not to intervene in precisely the chancy situations, for if it is possible that he not intervene, then some of the conditionals of deliberation will not be strict conditionals with a complete world specified in their consequent.

Of course, the Strict Conditional Model could be altered in terms of the consequents allowed. Instead of requiring a world specified in the consequent of a deliberative conditional, we could instead allow the specification of a collection of worlds left open by the antecedent in question. We could speak, that is, of a galaxy of worlds implied by a given antecedent, where it is a matter of chance which member of the galaxy is the actual world. Such an option would be rejected by all parties to the discussion at this point, however, for such a revision of the Strict Conditional Model saves it at the cost of a strong doctrine of providence.

Defenders of the Strict Conditional Model who also wish to retain a strong doctrine of providence might try something like the following. What if, even though it is fully stochastic whether E or $\sim E$ occurs in condition C, we try to exploit the conditional relationship between the two? The idea is that even if there is an equal chance between E and $\sim E$, given C, one of the two will occur in C and hence one of two conditionals is true: either if C then E or if C then $\sim E$. Whichever it is, we might try to put the true conditional in the antecedent of the divine conditionals of deliberation, and in so doing, restore full and specific providence to the model even in the face of merely probabilistic laws of nature and no enhancement in terms of "god of the gaps" intervention.

This possibility complicates our model in a couple ways. To this point, we imagine strict conditionals being used, and creation results from irrevokably choosing to make true the antecedent of one such strict conditional. If we add conditionals of the sort noted above, we cannot say that creation results from ir-revokably choosing to make true the antecedent of a strict conditional, for that is the "god of the gaps" view at work. Instead, if there are contingent conditionals in the antecedents of strict conditionals, creation results from irrevokably choosing to make true the antecedent of certain contingent conditionals in the antecedent of our strict conditional, together with the remainder of the antecedent of the strict conditional. That is, the form of a conditional of deliberation will now look like this (where we abbreviate reference to the laws, the initial conditions, and the overridings by God as "LIO":

> Chancy Modified Strict Conditional Model: Necessarily, if $LIO\&((\text{by chance})\ C \supset E)$, then W is actual,

where L is a collection of laws of nature, I is the initial conditionals, O is the set of interventions by God to override the laws of nature, and the material conditional stands in for all the material conditionals needed to close the gap between chance and actuality. God's creative activity is then understood in terms of irrevokably selecting to make true $LIO\&C$. So long as the strict conditional has a specific world as consequent, we still get strong providential control through such irrevokable choosing.

One should be suspicious here, however. We should suspect that the strict conditionals now envisioned will no longer count as deliberative conditionals. We should suspect that such conditionals will be deliberatively useless, on somewhat the same grounds as we used to reject the Minimal Models earlier. The problem we found there is a need for backtracking reasoning to determine which of two conditionals is being used in the account of creation. The same issue is present here, for if there is a chance for both E or $\sim E$ in the presence of C, then there are two necessarily true conditionals:

Necessarily, if $LIO\&((\text{by chance})\ C \supset E)$, then W is actual,

Necessarily, if $LIO\&((\text{by chance})\ C \supset \sim E)$, then W^* is actual,

where W is the world in which E occurs and W^* is the world in which E fails to occur. In order to be true, each of these necessary conditionals must correlate the conditional in the antecedent with the world that is actual in the consequent. We are assuming, however, that there is no "god of the gaps" intervention to make one of the conditionals true, so the conditional in the antecedent needs to be true independently of any divine activity (which is the explanation for including the parenthetical phrase "by chance").

If we recall our discussion of the Material Minimal Model, I think we can detect what is unsatisfying about this proposal. Recall that for a conditional to function as a deliberative conditional in the context of God's decisions regarding creation, we begin with a class of conditionals that are known to be true. Then, by evaluating the desirability of the various outcomes regarding which these conditionals inform, a choice is made about which conditional to rely on in deciding which antecedent to make true. But here, knowledge of what certain features of the actual world are like (namely, those responsible for the truth of the material conditional) replaces an evaluation of the desirability of the outcomes. For a conditional to function deliberatively, God needs to know that it is true. But knowledge of the conditional isn't sufficient, it if takes the place of an evaluation of the desirability of the outcomes. That is what was wrong with the Material Minimal Model, and that is what is objectionable about this alteration of the Strict Conditional Model. Wherever chance has a role to play, evaluation of the desirability of the outcome is replaced by knowledge of actuality.

The point to note here is that the Strict Conditional Model incorporates three elements. First, it contains strict conditionals that we assume are known by God to be true. Second, it maintains that these conditionals are conditionals of deliberation, and this step involves an evaluation of the consequents of the conditionals in question as to their desirability as a precursor to deciding which antecedent to actualize. Third, it claims that creation can be modeled by conceiving of God as irrevocably choosing to make true the antecedent of some strict conditional. This third element of the model is revised on the present strategy for dealing with chance, but in doing so, the second claim is undermined. For if there are two distinct strict conditionals and whatever God irrevocably chooses to make true is the same for these two distinct conditionals, then knowledge intrudes into the story, replacing the evaluation of the desirability of the consequent of the conditional with knowledge of which conditional is true. If so, however, the conditional is no longer suitable to be used as a conditional of deliberation, and is thus incompatible with a deliberative model of creation.

It is important to notice that this difficulty doesn't disappear if we change the connective to a subjunctive one. It is somewhat mysterious to hold that the laws of nature give a 50/50 chance to a particular electron going to the left rather than right when emitted, and yet that if the electron were emitted, it would go to the left. But suppose this is the suggestion: not only is the material conditional true but the subjunctive as well.

Here things remain as before. If there is a chance for both E (going to the left) or $\sim E$ (going to the right) in the presence of C (being emitted by a given machine), then there are two necessarily true conditionals:

Necessarily, if $LIO\&((\text{by chance})\ C \,\square\!\rightarrow E)$, then W is actual,
Necessarily, if $LIO\&((\text{by chance})\ C \,\square\!\rightarrow\sim\!E)$, then W^* is actual,

where W is the world in which E occurs and W^* is the world in which E fails to occur. Here, as before, knowledge of certain features of the actual world (namely, those responsible for the truth of the subjunctive conditional, including whatever similarity relations to other worlds our possible worlds semantics might posit for such subjunctives) replaces an evaluation of the desirability of the outcomes. For a conditional to function deliberatively, it is necessary that God knows it is true. But knowledge of the conditional isn't sufficient, it if takes the place of an evaluation of the desirability of the outcomes. That is what was wrong with the Material Minimal Model, and that is what is objectionable about this last alteration of the Strict Conditional Model. Wherever chance has a role to play, evaluation of the desirability of the outcome is replaced by knowledge of certain features of actuality. As a result, the conditionals are not deliberative conditionals any more, and can't be used in the Strict Conditional Model to understand God's creative activity in terms of deliberation.

These points fit well with the characterization given earlier of deliberationally useless, even though true, conditionals in terms of backtracking reasoning. If we imagine reasoning from God's perspective about which of these subjunctives are true, we have to appeal to foreknowledge of the features of the actual world that are responsible for the truth of the subjunctives in question, and then backtrack to the assumption that God already knows these truths.

This story applies not only to the earlier Minimal Models but also to the modifications proposed to the Strict Conditional Model in light of the possibility of probabilistic laws of nature. The first modification proposed that God could use one of the following conditionals as a deliberative conditional:

Necessarily, if $LIO\&((\text{by chance})\ C \supset E)$, then W is actual,
Necessarily, if $LIO\&((\text{by chance})\ C \supset\sim\!E)$, then W^* is actual.

The backtracking here concerns trying to determine which conditional is being used in deliberation, since by hypothesis both are true and both involving God making true the same exact parts of the antecedents in question. But the central features of backtracking are present here as much as in the case of Sly Pete:

it is only the object about which the reasoning occurs that is different. In the case of Sly Pete, the backtracking reasoning occurs in Sigmund regarding the conditional he asserts. In the case of our deliberative model, the backtracking reasoning occurs to determine which of two competing conditionals is really the one being used in God's creative activity. The reasoning in the latter case goes as follows (whether by us or by God in the model): If it were the first conditional, it would already have foreseen that E would occur by chance, and so it would be the first conditional that is being used. The lesson to learn from this backtracking is that both conditionals above would be deliberationally useless in a model of God's creative activity in deliberational terms.

A similar story must be told about the last attempt to modify the Strict Conditional Model in the face of purely probabilistic laws of nature. On that proposal, the conditional relationship between antecedent and consequent in chancy circumstances is subjunctive:

Necessarily, if LIO&((by chance) $C \mathrel{\square\!\!\rightarrow} E$), then W is actual,

Necessarily, if LIO&((by chance) $C \mathrel{\square\!\!\rightarrow} {\sim}E$), then W^* is actual,

Just as before, however, the question of which conditional is being used is not known except in a backtracking way: we reason that in virtue of knowing how things will or would go in the course of affairs, God would have to have been using the first rather than the second because as a matter of fact, E would be the result rather than $\sim E$. Again, the classic signs of backtracking reasoning are present: first one supposes the antecedent is true, and then one reasons backward to something that would already have been known by God, namely, the counterfactual in question, and then we reason forward to the conclusion that it was, say, the first conditional rather than the second that was being used. Because the conditionals would be functioning in this way, neither conditional is appropriate for deliberational use in our model.

7.4   Molinism and Deliberation

By this point, the implications for Molinism will already be fairly obvious. The Molinist has, in addition to the issue of probabilistic laws of nature, the additional issue of human freedom of the sort that is incompatible with causal determination. As such, the version of Molinism left open by our prior discussion of the Subjunctive Minimal Model offers a minor amendment to the Strict Conditional Models discussed to this point. Such Molinists note that no fixing of the laws of nature, initial conditions, and interventions by God into the course of nature can fix which action a free individual will perform. So they add to the antecedent of a strict conditional a further counterfactual. To this point, Molinists have not addressed the difficulty for a strong doctrine of providence brought on by the possibility of merely probabilistic laws of nature, but if we combine the response above to that problem with the Molinist response to the problem generated by freedom, we get strict conditionals of the following sort:

Necessarily, if LIO&((by chance or freedom) $C \mathrel{\square\!\!\rightarrow} E$), then W is actual.

Of course, just as before, compatible with everything God strongly actualizes in terms of the antecedent of such a conditional, there is a competitor conditional:

Necessarily, if LIO&((by chance or freedom) $C \mathrel{\square\!\!\!\rightarrow} \sim E$), then W^* is actual,

and the question is whether God is using one conditional or the other in his creative activity. And, just as before, the answer to this question appeals to items that are distinctively backtracking: since he would know which of the conditionals was being employed by knowing the course that things will or would take in the course of affairs, he must have been using, say, the first rather than the second conditional because as a matter of contingent fact it is the first counterfactual that is true rather than the second. That is, after assuming the relevant portion of the antecedent, the Molinist reasons backward to what must have already been known by God, and whichever it was, that's the sign for which conditional is being used. Because such backtracking is present, neither conditional is appropriate for use as a conditional of deliberation in a model of God's creative activity.

Such a Molinist may insist that there is no illegitimate backtracking going on, because we should have constructed our model of deliberation giving God access not only to all strict conditionals but all conditionals that are true in a way that is logically prior to God's creative activity. Molinists use the term "middle knowledge" to refer to God's knowledge of such counterfactuals precisely for this reason, to communicate the idea that such knowledge is logically subsequent to God's knowledge of logical necessities (his "natural knowledge") and his knowledge that results from his creative activity (his "free knowledge") (de Molina 1988).

Such a claim doesn't avoid the problem, however, but merely describes it. Moreover, there is a danger to such an appeal here. Once we begin down the path of adding to the model claims about what God "already" knows before deciding to create, we run the danger of eliminating the possibility of modeling creation deliberatively. One might say as well that prior to creating, God already knew all the details of what he would create, since he is omniscient, and this knowledge is logically prior to any creative activity.

If we go down this path, however, we can no longer model God's creative activity with a deliberative model. To model such activity on a deliberative model, we begin with information available to the agent that doesn't include post-decision information. That means, in the case of God, we must bracket any information whose truth depends on which world is created. Then, as noted above, we can see when backtracking is involved in the use of a conditional, and thus whether a conditional is suitable for use in our deliberative model.

7.5   Conclusion

What recourse does the Molinist have at this point? I can imagine a couple of possible responses here. First, one might claim that the backtracking that occurs in the model is an artifact of the model rather than a feature rightly ascribed to God. Thus, even though backtracking does occur in the model, there is no backtracking in reality and hence Molinism remains untouched by this difficulty.

The problem with this response is that if it works, it looks like we could back up to much simpler models and say the same thing about them. We could use one of the Minimal Models, or the first modified Strict Conditional Model that used only material conditionals. None of this guarantees that the strategy of distinguishing features of the model from features of reality can't work, but the task of making it work is a large one indeed.

A second possibility is to reject the idea of modeling the divine creative activity deliberatively. One way to do this is to emphasize God's eternity, and insist that deliberation itself could only effectively model the creative activity of God if he were in time. Here it is very hard to see what story could be told to generate any kind of understanding of the divine creative activity, but even worse, it is not clear how any such story will function to sustain Molinism. Perhaps there are other ways as well to motivate modeling the divine creative activity in non-deliberative ways, but I don't know what they would be at this point.

Perhaps the most promising route is to question the role of backtracking in the account I have given. One might begin by noting that the most common attitude toward the directionality of time among contemporary physicists seems to be that such directionality is a fundamental though contingent feature of our universe. If we suppose that this is the correct view, it brings into question whether backtracking reasoning can be tolerable when we model the divine creative activity that is, by hypothesis, logically prior to the question of the directionality of time. Perhaps further thought about such matters will reveal a way to allow some backtracking in this special context and thus perhaps find a way to defend the use of backtracking in a way in which the Molinist may find comfort. These issues are difficult and complex, and at this point there can be no question but that the hope is, at best, faint. The provisional conclusion to draw, then, is that focusing on deliberative conditionals and the use of conditionals in deliberative contexts reveals a serious problem for Molinism—a problem whose prospects for solving are murky indeed. Once the Molinist insists that counterfactuals of freedom must be pre-volitional, their presence in any conditional threatens the use of that conditional in deliberation, independently of the issue of whether such a conditional is true or necessarily true. The most plausible conclusion to draw, then, is that following up on the suggestion that we focus directly on the concept of a deliberative conditional when sorting disputes among various Molinists is that the details of the view don't really matter much. Once the counterfactuals of freedom are claimed to be pre-volitional, Molinism is in trouble.

onal is true or necessarily true. The most plausible conclusion to draw, then,

AN EPISTEMIC THEORY OF CREATION

8.1 Introduction

A theory of creation plays a central role in a defense of the doctrine of providence, and the central philosophical difficulty faced in such a project is whether and how the doctrine of creation can be reconciled with the doctrine of providence without requiring a construal of human freedom that libertarians must reject. A common assumption is that one can have either full providence or human freedom, but not both. Molinists disagree, but the status of the central explanatory feature used by Molinists to find a way of preserving both providence and freedom—counterfactuals of freedom—remains controversial, both in terms of the existence of true counterfactuals of this sort and whether they can perform the function needed to reconcile providence and freedom.

Here I will argue for a different solution to this problem, addressing first the relation between accounts of creation and providence in order to clear the conditions of adequacy on a theory of creation. In short, I will argue that we want a theory of creation that leaves open the possibility of a doctrine of full and complete providence. I will then show that there that there is such a theory of creation available—one that does not require abandoning libertarianism. Finding such a theory involves, as we will see, a paradigm shift away from the standard semantic-metaphysical approaches to creation in favor of a more epistemic approach.

The key idea of the new approach is that there is no alternative for understanding creation except in terms of a deliberative model of the process God uses in determining what to do. The explanatory focus is thus on whatever goes into moving from an initial state of relative uncertainty to a resolution of that uncertainty into a complete plan for creation. Such an approach is inherently epistemological, and the central element in such an approach must be on the conditionals central to this deliberative model, and, as I will argue, these conditionals are epistemic conditionals. The approach is thus an epistemic one, in contrast to more standard approaches that focus on entailments or counterfactual connections.

By way of preview, the central steps of the model are these. First, the account is developed using epistemic conditionals that involve fully fallible connections between antecedent and consequent. Second, the account will involve suppositional reasoning and update semantics, in contrast to the more common truth-conditional semantics. When this reasoning mechanism, using epistemic conditionals and update semantics, results in a complete suppositional picture of the world, the picture itself will involve fully fallible grounds for moving from an initial possible creative act by God to the total picture. The key moves in the theory will thus require showing how this fallible initial position could be converted to infallibility. Doing so will involve showing that, once the mechanism yields such a complete picture, one can show that fallible justification is undefeated justification, and that undefeated justification, in the context of our model, yields infallible (suppositional) knowledge. We may thus summarize the model by saying that *God knows the beginning from the end*: that is, once the mechanism reaches completion, there is an explanation from this end point as to how God could infallibly know what the future will involve, in every detail, given a particular possible creative act.

In the process of developing such a model, we must be careful to note that language about diminishing divine uncertainty is an artifact of the model rather than a feature of the reality being modeled. Deliberating involves trying to *figure out* what to do and how to do it, but there is little plausibility to the suggestion that God actually goes through such a process in deciding what to do. An intellectually perfect being has no need for any stage of perplexity followed by some later stage at which the perplexity of what to do and how to do it is resolved. We might put this point as follows. God has no need to *deliberate* about what to do or how to do it.

Yet, we have nowhere else to turn in attempting to understand God's creative activity other than attempts that model that activity in deliberational terms. If we are careful to point out that what we are doing is constructing a deliberational model of the reality in question, and careful to point out ways in which the model can mislead as well as enlighten, there is nothing theoretically troubling about such an approach.

Most approaches to the theory of creation emphasize God's sovereignty and providence at the expense of libertarian freedom or emphasize libertarian freedom in a way that is viewed by defenders of the first approach to compromise God's sovereignty. These disputes arise in terms of the types of conditionals available to God prior to any creative activity (where the notion of priority here is supposed to be logical or metaphysically explanatory priority, rather than temporal priority). If we think of a doctrine of full and complete providential control over all of creation (a doctrine of providence, for short), what is needed is an account of creation that allows for God to know in advance, and subsume under his divine plan, every aspect of the created order, down to the minutest detail. Sovereignty, whatever else it involves, will be understood here to include the dependence of everything other than God on God. Full sovereignty thus would require the explanatory dependence of everything metaphysically necessary on some features of the divine intellect, and explanatory dependence of everything contingent on God's will. The theory of creation itself involves only a concern for the category of the contingent, and the story that gets told by those wanting to preserve sovereignty in this sense is a story involving strict, or metaphysically necessary, conditionals in the model of divine deliberation prior to creation. Perhaps the antecedents of these conditionals involve granting secondary causal powers to created things and establishing laws of nature, but whatever is involved in the antecedents of such conditionals, the unfolding of history is a matter of logical consequence from what is made true by the inviolable will of God.

Such a theory of creation is rejected by fans of libertarian freedom, since it leaves no room for the optionality central to such a theory. This optionality is usually expressed by some version of the Principle of Alternative Possibilities (PAP), and there is a large body of literature on whether there is a defensible version of PAP, and if so, exactly how it should be formulated, tracing to the initial attack on it in Frankfurt's 1969 paper on the topic (Frankfurt 1969). I will here use only the vaguer language of optionality, in order to signal the intent of avoiding any particular precise position in response to this body of literature. The point to focus on is, rather, the way in which libertarianism, however precisified, is undermined by a model of creation employing only strict conditionals: optionality disappears in the face of the logical and metaphysical necessities of that model. Those preferring an incompatibilist account of human freedom thus appear to need a model of creation with recourse to conditionals other than strict conditionals.

The standard approach here focuses on subjunctive conditionals, making the nearly universal assumption that such conditionals are the general type of conditional used in deliberation more generally. This assumption is questionable: in considering where to eat, we can use subjunctives ("if we were to go to A, we would spend too much, but if we were to go to B, we would not like the food") but we can just as easily use indicatives ("we spend to much if we go to A, but we get lousy food if we go to B").[1] In our context, however, the issue of the mood of the conditional won't be a central concern. What matters is that they are contingently true or false, in contrast to strict conditionals. By being contingent, either type of conditional leaves in place some possibility for the kind of optionality that is cherished by libertarians concerning human freedom.

Once such optionality is secured, however, there is a concern that such optionality forces abandoning either sovereignty or providence or both. Standard Molinism claims that full providence can be preserved because, among these contingent conditionals are conditionals of creaturely freedom: conditionals that specify in their antecedent something that is under God's complete control, and have as consequent the specification of some freely-performed action. Open Theists challenge the existence of such contingently true conditionals, claiming that there is no adequate story to tell about how these conditionals could be true.[2] Defenders of sovereignty and providence, however, are not happy either way. If there are such truths, they are truths that are independent of God's will, thus

---

[1] For investigation of this standard assumption about deliberation, and an argument for preferring the view that indicatives are the conditionals of deliberation, see DeRose (2010).

[2] This objection, commonly called the Grounding Objection, first appeared in recent literature in Adams (1977). A version of the objection can be found in Hasker (1989), and a sustained response to the objection can be found in Flint (1998).

compromising sovereignty, and if there are no such truths, there is no available theory of creation that leaves open the possibility of providence. Those who reject the possibility of conditionals of freedom (whether indicative or subjunctive) maintain that they are not needed for practical deliberation in the human context. They maintain that all that is needed is "would probably" conditionals: we don't need to know that if angry, Joe will (or would) retaliate; all we need to know is that he probably will (or would). The probability versions are fully adequate, it is claimed, for deciding not to make Joe angry. Moreover, no concerns seem to exist for the probability claims as compared with the unqualified ones.

The problem, of course, is that if God can only use probabilified conditionals in creation, the doctrine of complete providence is lost. And the current state of the literature focuses on this dilemma: if we want sovereignty and providence, we lose the optionality of libertarianism; if we retain optionality, we lose at least sovereignty as specified above and perhaps providence as well.

I believe there is a way around all of the potholes here, and it involves a paradigm shift away from thinking about these issues from the semantic-logical-metaphysical perspective presupposed in the current literature to a more epistemological approach, one that approaches deliberation in terms of epistemic relationships between various pieces of information and suppositional reasoning from one state of information to another. This change in perspective will also involve a change in semantic approaches, away from the standard truth-conditional approach to a dynamic semantics, but before launching into the details of this new theory of creation, I want to explain what such a theory is supposed to accomplish so that we will be in a position to assess whether the new approach is adequate, once it is developed. To see what makes a theory of creation adequate, we need a careful account of the relationship between the theory of creation and the doctrine of providence itself.

8.2   Creation and Providence

The crucial point to note here is the way in which a defense of providence goes well beyond any theory of creation included in such a defense. A full defense of the doctrine of divine providence will include a theory of creation compatible with the doctrine, together with the required metaphysics to undergird the doctrine. In its most robust form, divine providence needs, intuitively, a metaphysics that leaves no holes in the world. Such a metaphysics will include a defense of bivalence and excluded middle together with an account of the nature of propositions that refuses to limit their presence to only certain regions of metaphysical space. In addition, concerns about some essential incompleteness in the world must be addressed by a full defense of the doctrine of providence, whether the incompleteness arises through the incoherence of attempts at unrestricted universal generalization, or deriving from Cantorian worries about the existence of a set of all truths (See, e.g., Grim (1991), Williamson (2003), Grim and Plantinga (1993)). These issues will be bypassed here, however, since they are separate from what is needed in order to provide a model of creation that leaves open a defense of full providence.

In order to determine whether a successful model of creation can be developed, we will assume here what would need defense if the goal were a successful defense of the doctrine of divine providence. Thus, we will assume bivalence and excluded middle, the necessary existence of every proposition, and the completeness of the world. Furthermore, worries about the possibility of inscrutable truths—truths that leave open no possibility of detection whatsoever—will be shelved as well. If it turns out that these assumptions are mistaken, then the doctrine of providence will have to be abandoned together with the model of creation developed here. The goal is thus to show that considerations regarding the nature of God's decision to create do not, of themselves, undermine the doctrine of providence. Hence if the doctrine fails, it will be for other reasons. For this task, we may legitimately assume everything else that needs defense in order to sustain a doctrine of providence, leaving only the question of whether a theory of creation can be developed that is consistent with full providence.

I should caution, however, against overestimating the scope of these initial assumptions. In assuming, for example, that there aren't any inscrutable truths, I am assuming that all truths are knowable or at least capable of being believed rationally on the basis of some indicators of truth. It is important to note, however, that I am not assuming that infallible knowledge of each truth is possible. The assumption is only that every truth leaves discernible tracks, so that evidence of truth, justificatory information, is present for every truth. More precisely, I will assume that in worlds where p is true, there will be internal or external defeaters for any justification that exists in that world for $\sim p$. Such justificatory information is simply the ordinary type of justification involved in fallible human knowledge. Thus, the task for a theory of creation is still quite significant, since this assumption is still a long ways in logical space from the kind of knowledge needed by a defense of providence, and it is part of the task of a theory of creation to show how such knowledge is possible.

Knowledge for present purposes will be understood in terms of undefeated justified true belief.[3] The central difficulty for this approach has been the problem of misleading defeaters (see, e.g., Klein (1981) for a full discussion of this issue and a potential solution). The problem here is that the theory is too strong: some things we know involve a justification that is defeated by misleading defeaters. Hence, the sticking point for this theory is to provide an adequate account of the distinction between misleading and non-misleading defeaters. We can bypass that issue here, however, because we will only be using the other direction of the theory. We will only use the implication from undefeated justified true belief to knowledge, and thus the central concern of the defeasibility theory of knowledge will not affect the use to which we put this account here.

---

[3]More exactly, I'm assuming that the presence of knowledge co-varies across all worlds with the presence of undefeated justified true belief. I do not presuppose here that knowledge is analyzable by this defeasibility approach, or by any other approach.

On the defeasibility theory, the degree of epistemic support for the belief in question needs to be adequate, and to be adequate, no internal and non-overridden defeaters can be present regarding the support in question. Moreover, in order for such justified beliefs to count as knowledge, no external and non-overridden defeaters distinctive of Gettier situations can be present either. The distinction between internal and external here concerns what is within the purview of the individual in question. Information involved in the individual's beliefs and experiences counts as internal; information of which the person is unaware counts as external. In addition to the absence of both types of defeaters, the theory also insists that the belief in question must be properly based in order to be known. To be properly based, the belief must be held for epistemic reasons, not because of, or not simply because of various non-epistemic factors such as self-interest or self-deception.

With this understanding of knowledge, the central task of a theory of creation involves coming to know what plan of creation is the preferred plan, and a successful theory of creation along these lines will leave open the possibility of a defense of full providence. The crucial aspect here is in the "leaving open" language. To insist that a theory of creation do something stronger, such as provide an explanation of why full providence obtains, is to burden the theory illegitimately. A defense of providence is one thing, a theory of creation another. They relate to each other in various ways, but the crucial feature to note for present purposes is the minimal condition of adequacy just outlined: a theory of creation is successful when it leaves open a defense of full providence, even if there turn out to be reasons independent of the theory of creation that make a defense of full providence impossible. Let us turn, then, to the details of the theory of creation to be developed here.

8.3   Conditionals and Dynamic Semantics

In developing our model of creation, we begin by noting the central role that conditionality must play in deliberation. When we deliberate, we use conditionals to connect possible actions with their consequences, and then we sort these consequences into better and worse in order to arrive at a decision regarding which path to follow. Perhaps this conditionality might be developed in terms of conditional probabilities instead of conditionals themselves, but such an approach will diverge in significant ways from the practice of ordinary deliberation if it isn't supplemented by some conditional probability interpretation of how ordinary deliberation proceeds. Here we will begin with conditionals themselves, leaving conditional probabilities to one side—at least for the time being. We thus begin by considering the kinds of conditionals needed for a deliberative model of creation. We can begin here by dividing conditionals into subjunctive and indicative,[4] and at least the latter class into open conditionals and belief- or supposition-contradicting ones. Open conditionals are ones compatible with

---

[4]A rough guide to the distinction between subjunctive and indicative conditionals is syntactic, with paradigm cases as already presented: "if X were to happen, Y would happen" is

background information, while supposition-contradicting ones are not. For example, it is an open conditional for most of us that if Obama is in New York, his family is as well. It is an open conditional because we have no information one way or the other on whether he is in New York. It is a belief- or supposition-contradicting conditional for most of us that if Booth didn't kill Lincoln, someone else did. The antecedent contradicts our belief that Booth did kill Lincoln. (The latter example shows as well why we need to distinguish subjunctives from indicatives, since, while the conditional just stated is true, it isn't true that if Booth hadn't shot Lincoln, someone else would have.)

We start by restricting the conditionals in the model to open conditionals, intending to introduce supposition-contradicting ones only when needed. The major difference between this conditional approach and those that have come before is that the open conditionals central to this model are epistemic open conditionals. Fundamental to conditional relationships of the sort needed to model divine deliberation is an epistemic support between antecedent and consequent: the information in the antecedent provides an adequate reason for the consequent. We can speak of this fundamental epistemic connection in various ways. We can speak in terms of adequate reasons, as I just did. We can also speak in terms of epistemic commitments, where the information in the antecedent epistemically commits an individual (in a given background information state) to the consequent. For the most part, I will suppress reference to the individual, for two reasons. First, I believe the fundamental epistemic relations are abstract relations between propositions and background systems of information. Second, reference to an individual tends to bring to mind the concept of belief, and changes in information states then get thought of in terms of transitions from one total belief state to another. Such a tendency runs the risk of inducing the conditional fallacy, since belief itself can both create and destroy, enhance and diminish, the abstract epistemic support relations central to the model here.[5] So for the most part I will suppress reference to the individual in what follows.

We represent an argument from Φ to Ψ as

$$\Phi \vdash_\epsilon \Psi$$

This formula tells us that the argument from Φ to Ψ is epistemically adequate, that Φ provides an adequate reason to conclude Ψ, that a rational commitment to Φ carries with it a rational commitment to Ψ. All this is relative to a background system of information, which we will leave unstated for present purposes. Relative to this assumed background system of information, we can move freely between adequate epistemic arguments and justified epistemic conditionals. That is, relative to a given background system of information, we should expect the

---

a subjunctive conditional, whereas "if X happens, Y happens" is indicative. Mere syntax isn't sufficient, however, but there is no reason to try to make the distinction precise here. For details on the problems involved in making the distinction precise, see Bennett (2003).

[5]The conditional fallacy was first described as such in Shope (1978). For arguments about the implications of this fallacy regarding the connection between propositional and doxastic justification, see Kvanvig and Menzel (1990), Kvanvig (2003).

following to be true:

DT: $\Phi \vdash_\epsilon \Psi$ iff $\vdash_\epsilon(\Phi \rightarrow \Psi)$

In English, the argument from one claim to another is a good epistemic argument if and only if the conditional between the two is itself epistemically supported, and referred to as "DT" because it an analog of the Deduction Theorem for first-order logic.

This approach to conditionals falls within the general family of evidential support theories of the indicative conditional, as defended by Adams (1966, 1975), Edgington (1995), Lewis (1976), Jackson (1979, 1987) and Douven (2008). Such approaches rely heavily on the conditional probability of the consequent of a conditional on its antecedent. Adams and Edgington do so in a way that denies that conditionals have truth value, claiming that the assertion or acceptance of a conditional does not involve asserting or accepting a proposition (where a proposition is understood to be a bearer of truth value), but instead involves expressing a high conditional attitude toward the consequent given the antecedent. Jackson and Lewis, by contrast, insist that the truth conditions for an indicative are those of the material conditional. For them, the assertibility or acceptability of a conditional requires a high probability for the material conditional together with what they term the "robustness" of the conditional with respect to its antecedent: $Pr(P \rightarrow Q \mid P)$ is high, which Jackson later recognized is just the requirement that the probability of the consequent given the antecedent is high (Jackson 1987, p. 31).

The fundamental problem with these conditional probability approaches is that they are insufficiently epistemic. They fail to impose an any epistemic relationship requirement when the consequent is itself highly probable and the antecedent is probabilistically independent of the consequent. For example, consider the claim that my lottery ticket will lose. This claim is highly probable, but epistemically unrelated to the claim that Ghandi was a great man. Because of this unrelatedness, the conditional *If Ghandi was a great man, my ticket will lose* is not acceptable or assertible, precisely because of the epistemic irrelevance of the antecedent to the consequent.

The obvious solution here is to supplement the conditional probabilities in question with a further epistemic requirement that the antecedent must be evidence for the consequent. This requirement alone is not strong enough either, since it licenses the conditional *If I buy a lottery ticket, it will lose,* and that conditional is no more assertible than is the unconditional assertion that my ticket will lose. One of the virtues of the knowledge account of assertion is its ability to explain why, in usual contexts, such an assertion is objectionable.[6] There is, however, an alternative to the knowledge account of assertion that explains the data equally well, and has the advantage of helping here to supplement the usual epistemic approaches to conditionals. An epistemic justification condition

---

[6] Defenders of the knowledge account include Williamson (2000), Hawthorne (2004), DeRose (2002).

alone explains both why it is usually objectionable to assert that one's ticket will lose and also what is wrong with the conditional *If I buy a lottery ticket, it will lose.*[7] The key point to note here is that there are two quite different types of alethic justification. Ordinary alethic justification tracks well with high conditional probability, so that one has a high degree of ordinary alethic justification for the claim that one's ticket will lose and for the claim that if one buys a ticket it will lose. Epistemic justification, however, does more. It puts one in a position to know, provided only that one's belief is true and unGettiered. In order to do so, it must be good enough to legitimate closure of inquiry on the question at hand, and one's ordinary alethic justification about lottery tickets does not legitimate closure of inquiry. That is why it remains reasonable to check the winning numbers tomorrow to see whether one won, and why it isn't typically reasonable to give away one's ticket.

This approach is similar to Douven's epistemic approach. Douven notes that a number of approaches to the lottery paradox explain away the apparent justification of lottery beliefs in terms of some defeater of the high probability in question. He then requires that an acceptable conditional be one in which the conditional probability of consequent given antecedent is high and that the antecedent is evidence for the consequent that is not defeated in the way in which the high probability for lottery claims is defeated (Douven 2008, p. 30). So, on both his account and the present account, the lottery claim and the lottery conditional get excluded, on roughly similar epistemic grounds. Moreover, on both his account and mine, the theory only applies in typical cases. As I would put it, there are lots of non-epistemic indicative conditionals, but only the epistemic ones will be needed in our model.

Two kinds deserve special mention here: those that involve epistemic limitations in oneself and others, and non-interference ones. Non-interference conditionals are ones that lend themselves naturally to a strengthened form in terms of 'even if' or 'whether or not' or inserting 'still' into the consequent. For example, imagine a scene in which a parent is comforting an adolescent offspring, conveying the idea that the world doesn't turn on the issue of having won a certain honor, saying "Thursday follows Wednesday if you didn't win." Such a remark can be perplexing, and the intention is better communicated by saying "Thursday still follows Wednesday if you didn't win," or "Whether or not, or even if you didn't win, Thursday still follows Wednesday." The point of the strengthening is to signal the fact that the antecedent here is unrelated in the usual way to the consequent, and such conditionals can sometimes be non-misleadingly said without the strengthening. Such conditionals are not epistemic conditionals, and are not needed for our model.

This point may help with an example Jackson uses in rejecting an epistemic account of conditionals. Consider this example: if the President is bald, no one

---

[7]For the application of this approach to the issue of norms of assertion, see Kvanvig (2009*a*, 2011*a*, 2012).

in the press knows it (Jackson 1987, p. 44). Perhaps the underlying idea here concerns the quality of the assurance the press has that the President isn't bald, or more weakly, the total absence of any grounds for thinking that he is bald. In such a case, the example is best thought of as a non-interference conditional, naturally expressed by pointing out that whether or not the President is bald, the press has no information to the effect that he is bald.

A second type threatens the Ramsey test. According to the Ramsey test, the acceptability of a conditional is a matter of first adding the antecedent to one's belief system and then testing the new belief system to see if the consequent is supported. There are counterexamples, however: if Joe is a double agent, he is so smart and clever that we won't be able to tell. Our model need take no stand on whether the Ramsey test can be finessed to escape such examples, since conditionals involving such epistemic limitations can't arise in the divine deliberative context of creation.

Besides these similarities between Douven's account and this one, there are some central differences. First, Douven's model, as with the other epistemic relevance approaches, is explicitly probabilistic and mine is not. This point is important in the context of conditionals with antecedents or consequents having extreme probabilities of either 0 or 1. As noted already, we will initially focus on open conditionals, leaving belief- or supposition-contradicting conditionals until needed. It is important to note, however, that there are such belief-contradicting conditionals and that they are not well-suited to being treated, as Douven does, in terms of non-interference conditionals (Douven 2008, p. 37). Standard examples include the standard assassination examples in the literature: if Booth didn't kill Lincoln, someone else did. But there are other example that are not easily treated as involving some uncertainty regarding the antecedent in question, as Douven does with assassination examples. Consider the claim that if I don't exist, Descartes' cogito argument fails; or if the South Pole is not in Antarctica, my teachers were untrustworthy about more than I suspected. These cases do not involve any degree of uncertainty concerning their antecedents, and are not treatable in terms of "even if" conditionals. Both of these conditionals are epistemic ones, and it is a disadvantage of an epistemic approach to be unable to accommodate such cases. To accommodate them, the present model places no restriction on belief- or supposition-contradicting conditionals, allowing such conditionals even in the face of certainty that the antecedent is false.

Second, Douven endorses the idea that the justification for lottery beliefs must be defeated in some way or other, whereas my approach does not endorse this claim. I take this to be an advantage, since it is fairly obvious that, in some truth-related sense, lottery beliefs are justified. It is for this reason that lottery and preface paradoxes present such a threat to coherentism, since both paradoxes present the intuitive plausibility of a set of rational but inconsistent beliefs and a minimal requirement on coherence would seem to be logical consistency (Foley 1986, pp. 96–102). Distinguishing between ordinary alethic justification and epistemic justification allows the present approach to grant the intuitively plausible point while still insisting that the epistemic relation isn't strong enough for use in an epistemic approach to conditionals.

It is also worth noting that the present approach can remain non-committal on the fundamental divide between propositional and non-propositional accounts of conditionals. The issues between these two camps are deep and complex and are thoroughly discussed in Bennett (2003), but the resolution of this issue is largely irrelevant to our present concerns. Throughout I will talk from the standpoint of the view that such conditionals are true, noting here that if the non-propositional account of conditionals is correct, adjustments to the complete theory would need to be made. It is worth noting that one of the burdens the non-propositional account must shoulder is to give an adequate rendition of the ordinary idea that some conditionals are true and some aren't, and to the extent that no such account can be developed, the non-propositional account is deficient. By talking from the standpoint of a propositional approach, I will not create any additional burdens on the non-propositional account that it doesn't already carry, and thus doesn't imply that the model developed here could be adequate only if the propositional account is correct.

These epistemic conditionals provide the central propositional resources of the model, and the remainder of the model involves an account of the transitions from one state of information to another as deliberation occurs. For the initial state of information for our model, we begin by assuming that God knows all necessary truths, i.e., that the space of metaphysical possibility is not delimited in any way at all. The remainder of the model involves suppositional reasoning by God, taking God from this initial informational state to subsequent ones involving various suppositions. A suppositional chain of reasoning that delimits the space of possibilities to a single complete possibility I'll call variously a "story" or "complete story" or "complete fiction".

In characterizing such suppositional reasoning, we employ the key idea of update semantics in opposition to truth conditional semantics. As Frank Veltmann puts it,

> the slogan 'You know the meaning of a sentence if you know conditions under which it is true' is replaced by this one: 'You know the meaning of a sentence if you know the change it brings about in the information state of anyone who accepts the news conveyed by it'.(Veltman 1996, p. 221).

We begin with a language $L\rightarrow$, which is the language L of propositional logic supplemented with the epistemic conditional. L is thus constructed from the smallest set of atomic propositions $A = \{p, q, r, \dots\}$ and is closed under negation and conjunction. We obtain $L\rightarrow$ by closing under $\rightarrow$ as well.

We will understand a world, for present purposes, in terms of a function from atoms to truth-values. That is, for a set of atomic propositions A, a world w is a function from A to $\{0, 1\}$. Letting W be the set of such worlds, we can understand an informational state s as a subset of W: $s \subseteq W$. S is the set of such ss.

In our context, the original informational state for God, prior to engaging in any suppositional reasoning, is just W itself. It amounts to the information state corresponding to logical omniscience. In the imperfect realm of human cognition, there is the other extreme, of an informational state with no content at all, since it involves an inconsistency. We will have no need of this possibility in our model, but we will have recourse to another limiting case—the case of perfect mastery of a complete story, in which there is some world w identical to the state of information in question: $s = w$.

We can introduce the idea of update rules most easily by thinking in terms of a toy epistemology in which all epistemic reasoning is monotonic and proceeds via the use of only open epistemic conditionals of the sort described above. We can understand transitions from one state of information to a new state of information in terms of an informational state update function.[8] Take any $w \in W$, $s \in S$, $p \in A$, and Φ, $\Psi \in L \rightarrow$; $\uparrow$ is a function on S defined recursively on the following conditions for such a toy epistemology:

1. $s{\uparrow}p = \{w \in s : w(p) = 1\}$
2. $s{\uparrow}{\sim}\Phi = s \setminus (s{\uparrow}\Phi)$
3. $s{\uparrow}(\Phi \& \Psi) = (s{\uparrow}\Phi){\uparrow}\Psi$
4. $s{\uparrow}(\Phi \rightarrow \Psi) = \{w \in s : ((s{\uparrow}\Phi){\uparrow}\Psi = s{\uparrow}\Phi)\}$.

In English: updating by adding a proposition restricts the state of information to worlds where that proposition is true, and updating by adding a negation involves subtracting whatever would have survived updating by the unnegated claim; updating by adding a conjunction is just the sequential updating by each conjunct, and updating by adding a conditional occurs when the epistemic commitments of adding both antecedent and consequent are the same as when the antecedent alone is added.

The most important issue to consider is the relation between the clause for $\rightarrow$ and the clause for $\supset$. The clause for $\rightarrow$ has only two options. It reports about a state of information whether that state of information includes the epistemic conditional in question or not. It is a test on the epistemic structure of the state of information, and the test is run by seeing whether updating by both antecedent and consequent yields the same output state as the output state that results by updating by the antecedent alone. If these output states are the same, the function returns the initial state of information itself. If it doesn't include it, the conditional is inconsistent with that state of information, and returns the absurd state of information, which is the state of information corresponding to the empty set of worlds.[9]

---

[8]I here rely on Gillies (2004). This approach was first presented in Heim (1983).

[9]This explanation shows why clause 4 does not involve a typographical error, even though it may seem to involve one at first glance. It has this appearance because there is no reference to w after the colon, which is atypical but grammatical. In this sense, it is like formulas such as "x(p)", which is a wff but inclines readers to think a typographical error has occurred.

The clause for the material conditional behaves quite differently. Suppose we begin with a state of information s, which is nothing more than proposition r, and consider updating s by $p \supset q$ (where each p, q, and r are all logically independent). We update s by finding the updated s' resulting from updating s by $p \& \sim q$, and then subtracting s' from s. The result of this subtraction is a new state of information corresponding to the union of the $r \& \sim p$-worlds with the $r \& q$-worlds. Where the logical independence assumption holds, this union is neither identical to s itself nor to the absurd state of information, which is the empty set of worlds. Thus, updating by the material conditional does not typically yield as output the same state of information as the epistemic conditional.

Nonetheless, the updating functions in question honor the sacrosanct principle that the epistemic conditional entails the material conditional, in virtue of prohibiting a state of information from containing both the epistemic conditional as well as its antecedent together with the denial of its consequent. The update clause returns the absurd state of information for any state of information containing the antecedent and the denial of the consequent, since updating by both antecedent and consequent won't give the same information state as updating by the antecedent alone. Thus, no state of information that is consistent allows a counterexample to the sacrosanct principle.

This updating function also allows us to say efficiently what it is for a given state of information to make reasonable or to epistemically support some claim. A given state of information contains an adequate rational basis for a given claim just in case updating with that claim returns the very same state of information.

It is worth noting how such conditionals are weaker than strict conditionals. Where $\Rightarrow$ is the symbol for entailment, we can formulate an update clause for strict conditionals as:

$$s{\uparrow}(\Phi \Rightarrow \Psi) = s \text{ if } \sim\exists s^* \exists w((w \in s^*)\&(s^* = (\Phi \& \sim\Psi))) \text{ and } \emptyset \text{ otherwise.}$$

According to this clause, updating by a strict conditional returns the very state of information with which one began. Such a clause reports only whether the conditional in question was already contained in the state of information, and, just as for the epistemic conditional, returns the original state of information if it was so contained and the absurd state of information if not. But the clause used to establish whether the strict conditional in s already is stronger than what is used for the epistemic conditional, designed to show that a strict conditional is contained in every state of information or in none. Hence, the clause shows that there can be information states containing the strict conditional but not the corresponding epistemic conditional, revealing that strict conditionals are necessary if true and epistemic conditionals need not be necessary even if true. Thus, we needn't balk at the clause for $\rightarrow$ on grounds that it is somehow nothing more than a disguised entailment claim.

Of course, our toy epistemology is inadequate. The monotonicity of epistemic reasoning that it presumes is mistaken. When we learn something new, we sometimes lose epistemic grounds for claims that were supported prior to the new learning, whereas on the above update clauses, new learning always involves a contraction of the set of worlds that is the initial state of information in question.

Consider the implications for clause 1 above of honoring the defeasible character of ordinary reasoning. According to clause 1, when we learn (just) p, the new information state is a subset of the old information state. Yet, if learning is better understood to involve defeasible reasons, we must assume that the transition from old information state to new information state might result in losing information already present, once we learn p. In such a case, the set of worlds that is the new state of information might contain members that were not contained in the set of worlds for the initial state of information. What we lose will be a function of which epistemic conditionals are epistemically supported by the relevant states of information. As new information is gained, old information can be lost. Moreover, once information is lost as a result of learning, conditionals will typically be lost as well, since their presence in a system of information is a function of the total state of information in question.

Such defeasibility plays a central role in the logic for epistemic conditionals. For example, it is well-known that for both material conditionals of first-order theory and their strict cousins of standard modal logic, strengthening of the antecedent is valid:

(SA) $\Phi \supset \Psi \vdash (\Phi \& \Theta) \supset \Psi$

(MS) $\Box(\Phi \supset \Psi) \vdash \Box(\Phi \& \Theta) \supset \Psi$.

Not so, however, for the epistemic conditionals involved in our model. Take an ordinary match and the striking strip on the side of the box: if you strike that match on that strip, it will ignite. But if you strike that match on that strip while submerging both under water, it won't ignite. So the analogs of (SA) and (MS) that result from replacing '$\supset$' with '$\rightarrow$' are invalid sequents.

The non-monotonicity of epistemic support will be assumed in what follows, but the details of an update semantics need not be developed beyond the above for our toy epistemology.[10] All that is needed is an idea of how an update semantics works so that the idea can be put to use in the context of suppositional reasoning in the context of deliberation prior to creation.

The idea is to use the dynamics above to move from the original state of information that delimits W in no way at all (i.e., contains no information) in suppositional terms so that full fictions are generated in terms of additions of suppositions and the hypothetical changes to states of information these suppositions yield. We can begin by noting several simplifying features of the context of creation compared with ordinary human contexts.

First, the model begins from a state of no information at all, which corresponds to an assumption of logical omniscience. Though such an assumption is problematic in ordinary human contexts, it is fully appropriate for the context involving divine deliberation concerning creation.

---

[10]For information on what things look like when we put the toys away, see Pollock (1995). For an excellent discussion of various systems of defeasible reasoning, see Koons (2009).

There is another feature of human fallibility that is legitimately ignored in our context as well. Not only are humans fallible about the world, they are also fallible about the nature of epistemic support itself. In the process of learning what the world is like, we also learn how evidence works, and we improve our understanding of what confirms what. The above updating model elides this matter, assuming that each epistemic conditional is either included in a system of information or inconsistent with it. In effect, the model assumes then that God is not only logically omniscient but epistemically omniscient as well: he never makes a mistake or wonders about what is supported by the information in any informational state. In the human context, such an assumption would be a mistake, but in the divine context it is just what we should expect.

The other clauses will still need adjustment to honor the defeasible character of epistemic reasoning, however, but even in the absence of full details about the needed adjustments, we can get an initial glimpse at this point of the advantages of this epistemic approach over the more standard approaches. The metaphysical bent of that literature focuses exclusively on subjunctive conditionals and the question of whether there are true subjunctives concerning human behavior conceived to be free in the sense that libertarians cherish. Such a focus forces a theory to address whether there could be any true conditionals of this sort, as opposed to "would probably" conditionals. It is readily granted that the latter are true: if I were to offer my children a treat, they would probably take it. But is it strictly true that if I were to offer, they would take it? What could explain the existence of that stronger truth, if we are assuming that they are free to do otherwise? Moreover, there is an argument from their conceived freedom to a denial of the unqualified claim: if they are free in the requisite sense, then they might refuse the treat if offered, and to say that they might refuse is just to deny that they would accept.[11] Defenders of robust accounts of providence employing counterfactuals of freedom require a way out of this argument, among other issues facing the view.

Notice that our epistemic approach sidesteps these issues. There is no question that one can have adequate reasons for thinking that one's children will accept an offered gift. To insist that states of information never provide such reasons will generalize too quickly to a more general skepticism, perhaps of the sort that presupposes that states of information never provide adequate reasons for any claim unless those reasons entail the truth of the claim in question. We should reject such a claim, however, and in the process we can endorse the obvious facts we encounter when employing ordinary conditionals. We reason using conditionals both about systems assumed to be deterministic and those not assumed to be deterministic, and arrive at (defeasibly and fallibly) rational conclusions in both types of cases. There is simply no room at this point in the epistemic approach to introduce metaphysical concerns about needed truthmak-

---

[11] There is a disputed premise in this argument which is the definition of subjunctive 'might' in terms of a denial of subjunctive 'would'. David Lewis endorses such a definition in Lewis (1973), while Robert Stalnaker challenges this understanding in Stalnaker (1981).

ers for counterfactuals of freedom in order to sustain this point. In this way, the epistemic approach taken here avoids, at least at first glance, quite a large pool of perhaps needlessly spilled ink.

In order to appreciate further differences between the behavior of conditionals in ordinary contexts when compared with the context of creation, we need to be more explicit about the connection between update semantics and the suppositional reasoning involved in divine deliberation concerning creation, the topic to which we now turn.

8.4 Suppositional Reasoning

In order to move from the apparatus above to a full account of providential control in creation, we need to supplement the dynamic semantics above with an account of how suppositional reasoning can take deliberation from the original information state W to a full fiction or story. We can see how this process can work by dividing the possibilities for divine deliberation into subtypes.

We begin by considering the range of things that God suppositionally considers as candidates for strongly actualizing. Here the understanding of strong actualization involves causal necessitation, whether the object of necessitation is some particular matter of fact or some law of nature governing transitions from one collection of particular matters of fact to another collection. We assume, further, that when God supposes something he also supposes that he will causally necessitate both it and the conjunction of it with everything else being supposed.

Here I part company with Plantinga's definition of strong actualization, which transmits across entailment. Plantinga writes, "God strongly actualizes a state of affairs S if and only if he causes S to be actual and causes to be actual every contingent state of affairs S^* such that S includes S^*." (Tomberlin and van Inwagen 1985, p. 49). Inclusion here is metaphysically necessary, so that S cannot include S^* if there is a possible world in which S obtains and S^* doesn't, which is why the account requires that strong actualization transmit across entailment. Yet, God can make it true that if I don't freely refrain from A-ing, he will do B (just imagine him decreeing that it is so), and he can certainly make it true that he won't do B. So suppose he does both. If strong actualization transmits across entailment, he automatically strongly actualizes both the conjunction of what he strongly actualizes and also what follows from it—that I freely refrain from A-ing. Yet, free actions are just the kind of thing that no one but the individual in question can strongly actualize.[12]

To solve this problem, I will characterize strong actualization only in terms of causal necessitation. Such necessitation may be closed under conjunction, but I will assume here that it is not closed under entailment, thus preventing the problem just noted from arising here. As we shall see, such closure isn't needed for our purposes, so there is no motivation from these purposes for adopting any closure requirement.

---

[12]This difficulty for Plantinga's account was brought to my attention by Alex Pruss in conversation.

Within the suppositional units in question we next distinguish between total and partial suppositional units. A total suppositional unit is one that contains everything that God is considering strongly actualizing in a given piece of suppositional reasoning; a partial suppositional unit is one that contains only some of what God is considering strongly actualizing in a given piece of suppositional reasoning. When the suppositional unit in question is total, I will call the ordered set of suppositions in question a "plan", ordered in terms of the temporal sequencing of the parts of the plan. We thereby imagine the suppositional reasoning possibilities as restricted to those involving plans, since such reasoning shows the greatest potential for showing how full providence is possible.

To pursue the issue about the possibility of full providence, we take each such plan and apply the update semantics above to the conjunction of all suppositions involved in each plan. (It turns out that the sequence of the conjunction matters here, since updating by $p\&q$ need not generate the same result as updating by $q\&p$–that is why the suppositional units involved in plans are ordered). Once such updating has occurred, there is a new state of suppositional information, for each such set of suppositions. The collection of such resulting states can now be divided into various groups.

The most important division here is between those plans that are complete and those that are incomplete. A plan is complete when updating by the semantics in question yields a final state of information that, for every p, includes either p or $\sim p$. In such cases, the total plan in question generates, via the update semantics, a complete fiction or story: the output state of information is a possible world.

Take, then, those total plans that yield complete stories. For each member of the group, the original supposition generates at least one adequate reason for each of the remainder atomic propositions. Some such total plans yield worlds that are fully deterministic, but in our context, the central question is whether some such plans yield worlds which are not deterministic, involving libertarian freedom. For there to be such complete stories, each proposition concerning a free action will form the consequent of some epistemic conditional in the update process, so that the other items already fixed by the informational state provide adequate reasons for concluding that such a free action will occur.

One might worry that this group will be empty. To this worry, a number of points can be made, though none of them provide a conclusive proof that the group has any members. Instead, these points minimize this worry sufficiently that the proper conclusion to draw from them is that it is at least an open epistemic possibility that the group is not empty.

First among these considerations on behalf of the open possibility that the group is not empty is the implausibility of global skepticism about free action. No one should use as an argument that the group is empty that no one can know what a free individual will do. Knowledge doesn't require infallible grounds, and the quality of our ordinary epistemic support regarding the behavior of other humans is regularly as good as our epistemic support regarding the behavior of, say, our favorite espresso machine.

Nor should one reject the possibility in question by embracing global skepticism about the future. In our context, such a position involves claiming that one can never have adequate epistemic grounds for thinking anything about the future. Such a skeptical position is important to consider in general epistemology, but to assume it here would place excessive demands on a model of creation. It would be just as if we assumed global skepticism is true, and then unsurprisingly concluded that foreknowledge of free actions is impossible. Equally important to note, however, is just how counterintuitive skepticism about the future is. I put water into the machine and push the button. Why? Because I want a cup of coffee, and that's how I get it. I turn the faucet at the sink. Why? Because I want to wash my hands, and turning the faucet will give me the water I need to do so. Such means–ends reasoning is ubiquitous, and involves beliefs about the future that are fully reasonable, implying that global skepticism about the future overreaches.

One might insist that God's knowledge needs to be infallible, and that nothing in the model allows such a conclusion at this point. In response, I note that we are not, at this stage in the development of the model, attempting to establish infallible knowledge. Discussion of that issue will come later. At this point, all we are considering is those suppositional information states that include sufficient grounds for concluding what free individuals will do, granting that there are other suppositional information states that don't include such grounds and that the grounds in question are defeasible. Grounds are defeasible when it is possible for those grounds to fully justify a given belief and yet that justification be overturned by further learning. Fallibility involves susceptibility to false beliefs, and the central type of such susceptibility in the human context at least is a by-product of believing on the basis of defeasible reasons. Since we are characterizing the update semantics as generating new states of information from old states in a way that constitutes a defeasible consequence relation, the model begins from a defeasible standpoint in line with the kind of justification displayed by fallible beings. Later on, we will need to show how to get something epistemically stronger into the model.

Once the threat of global skepticism concerning free actions is removed, there is no longer any reason for thinking that the suppositional state couldn't be complete in the way envisioned. No claim is being made here that suppositional states must contain adequate evidence regarding the entire range of free actions, but only that it is possible that they do so. Once global skepticism about free behavior is abandoned, there is no basis for concluding that the group of suppositional states that are complete in this way must be empty if freedom is involved. This 'must' is the 'must' of epistemic necessity, which is the dual of epistemic possibility. So from this 'must' claim, we can infer that it is an open epistemic possibility that the group in question is not empty.

With this result, we can then focus on the last divisions needed for our model. As already noted, for total plans that are complete, the state of information that results from updating by the semantics in question is itself a possible world: it is a state of information that is consistent and includes either p or $\sim p$, for every proposition p. It is a complete story or fiction. Second, every piece of information in such a state of information is rational relative to that state of information. We might describe such states of information as follows: they are potential, or suppositional, belief systems of the divine mind, and as potential belief systems, they specify systems of belief that are complete and consistent, and contain all and only justified beliefs. The system of suppositional belief in question is an epistemic consequence of the suppositions involved, and we can thus say that each of the beliefs that result is epistemically entailed by those suppositions.

We thus have the first step needed for our account of creation. It is to show how to use dynamic semantics and suppositional reasoning to generate the possibility of a freedom-including creation, where everything involved in that creation is epistemically predictable, given the initial supposition concerning what God will strongly actualize. Completing our account of creation will require moving from such epistemic predictability to knowledge, and from knowledge to infallible knowledge. These next two steps are still yet to be completed, but completion of the first step allows an illuminating comparison with standard Molinism.

The fundamental difference between the epistemic model and Molinism concerns the epistemic conditionals used in the epistemic model—conditionals that play the role that Molinists hope to fill with counterfactuals of creaturely freedom. In both approaches, the conditionals specify a free action in their consequent and trace back to conditionals that have states of affairs that are strongly actualizable by God in their antecedents. The role that logically contingent conditionals play in each approach generates a division in logical space between creatable worlds and possible worlds on these accounts. For the Molinist, there are possible worlds where an actually true counterfactual of freedom is false in virtue of having a true antecedent and a false consequent. Such worlds are possible but not creatable. For our epistemic model, something similar occurs. Creatable worlds involve plans that yield complete stories, so that for each free action, that action is epistemically entailed, though not logically entailed, by the information involved in the original plan. That means, however, that there are possible worlds containing the same strongly actualized items but where the action in question is not performed. Such worlds are not creatable worlds.

Some hedging is crucial here, however, since to know more precisely which worlds are creatable and which aren't, we'd need much more information about the update semantics than we have here. Without such further information, though, we can say the following about which worlds are uncreatable. The relevant categories are these. First, some total plans don't yield complete stories, which happens most clearly when Buridan's Ass situations develop. Such a situation develops when it becomes known that there are equally attractive options for some individual, and there is no basis on which to conclude that the individual will take one of the options over the others. Buridan's ass is in such a situation: we know that the donkey must eat from either the bale of hay on its right or the bale of hay on its left, but there is no information available either to the donkey or to the observer for concluding which bale will be consumed. For Buridan's Ass situations, there are two possible worlds—one corresponding to each consumption behavior, and on the present model, one of these worlds is not creatable.

The epistemic model, however, has two important advantages over the Molinist approach. First, an epistemic focus allows us to bypass the grounding objection to Molinism discussed earlier, since the ground of epistemic conditionals is fully explained in the model: it arises in virtue of the relationship between epistemic conditionals in a given context and the necessary principles of rational support that underlie the epistemic validity of various inferences. One may question any particular proposal concerning such a principle, as happened when Roderick Chisholm first presented this approach (Chisholm 1957). Chisholm's earliest approach tied being appeared to F-ly with rational belief that something is F—a proposal that can't work because it ignores the possibility of grounds for doubt. For example, if one has recently taken hallucinogenic drugs, it is irrational to form beliefs based on appearances. Because of this problem, the second edition of *Theory of Knowledge* contained a more refined principle, to the effect that being appeared to F-ly makes rational the belief that something is F only when there are no grounds for doubt present (Chisholm 1977).

Of course, one may still have reasons to think that this principle is not necessarily true. Coherentists will be suspicious of it, perhaps thinking that appearances themselves can't justify, or that when they do, they must have a content which itself passes epistemic muster of some sort relative to the system of beliefs for the person in question. If they are correct, further refinements of these kinds of epistemic principles will be required. The point to note, however, is that the task here is one of refining the principles to find the correct ones, and the correct ones are the ones to be used in our model of creation, governing the updating process from the initial state of information together with the suppositions involved in total plans. For that purpose, we do not need to specify which principles are correct, and I have not tried to do so. Instead, all that I have done and all that needs to be done is to point in the direction where the true principles are to be found, maintaining that the model relies those true principles. To find out which principles are the true ones would require a complete epistemology, but all we need to do here is to presuppose such an epistemology rather than actually construct one.

One might worry, however, that such refinement isn't possible, that epistemic support is so individual-relative that there won't be any truths of the required sort. One might think, that is, that one gets a truth value assignment for an epistemic principle only relative to an individual perspective. If this point were correct, however, our task is made much simpler. If the truth of the epistemic principles underlying our model is relative to an assessor, it would be easier to maintain that the model of creative deliberation leaves open the possibility of full providence. If the truth of such principles were assessor-relative, the range of epistemic principles available for the model increases, since what is true-from-God's-perspective might be different from one plan to another (and might be completely unlike any that are true-from-our-perspective). Our assumption, that there the truth value of epistemic principles is not assessor-relative, is thus more restrictive, imposing a stronger burden on the model, since the truths in question are the same for both divine and human contexts and from one instance of suppositional reasoning to another.

So the first advantage of the epistemic approach is that it suffers from no analog of the grounding objection that is raised against Molinism. The second advantage is that the epistemic approach can exploit the way in which opponents of counterfactuals of freedom, such as Robert Adams (1977), are happy to weaken such "would" claims to "would probably" claims, noting in the process that the latter are sufficient for purposes of practical deliberation. Addressing a favorite example from I Samuel 23 in which David attempts to divine what to do by means of an ephod, and apparently learning that (1) if David were to stay in Keilah, Saul would besiege the city, and (2) if David were to stay and Saul were to besiege the city, the men of Keilah would surrender David to Saul, Adams writes,

> [T]he propositions which may be true by virtue of correspondence with the intentions, desires and character of Saul and the men of Keilah are not (1) and (2) but
>
> > (5) If David stayed in Keilah, Saul would probably besiege the city.
> > (6) If David stayed in Keilah and Saul besieged the city, the men of Keilah would probably surrender David to Saul.
>
> (5) and (6) are enough for David to act on, if he is prudent; but they will not satisfy the partisans of middle knowledge. It is part of their theory that God knows infallibly what definitely would happen... (Adams 1977, p. 111)

Adams here raises a version of the grounding objection, insisting that there must be something that makes true the claims in question, and it can't be found in the character, intentions, and desires of Saul or the men of Keilah. More relevant to our second advantage for the epistemic approach over the Molinist approach, however, is Adams' passing remark that the "would probably" conditionals are "enough for David to act on."

Here two responses are in order. The first is that Adams' remark can be correct only if the "would probably" claim is supplemented by a detachment rule of some sort for the probability operator in question, having the following form:

DR: given context C, $Pr(p) \vdash_\epsilon p$.

Without a version of DR in place, David can only reason in terms of (5) and (6) to the conclusion that he should probably leave Keilah, and that isn't an adequate end point for practical deliberation about what to do. What is needed is a theory that generates advice about what to do and what to think, and thus what is needed for practical deliberation is a theory that tells David to leave

Keilah. Telling him that it is not true that he should leave Keilah, but only that it is probable that he should leave Keilah, won't do.

Perhaps David could get along just fine without using such a detachment rule if he abandoned the approach to practical deliberation relying on the conditionals above and instead used the tools of decision theory. In such a case, all he would need is probabilities and utilities, it might seem, together with the one overarching conditional to do what has the highest expected utility. Notice, however, that this isn't how David reasons, and it isn't Adams' point to recommend rewriting the story in terms of modern decision theory. Refusing to revise the story is wise, since deliberating by using conditionals is commonplace and ordinary, while trying to use the apparatus of decision theory is not commonplace and also involves a distortion of that apparatus. That apparatus can be used in an intentional way to resolve the question of what one should do, but it isn't designed for that purpose and doesn't pretend that doing so is an adequate way to decide what to do. Instead, it is a theory of what one should do, and assesses decisions based on probabilities and utilities. It could be true, compatible with the adequacy of such a theory that it would be a mistake to assess what one should do by trying to apply the theory. Adopting the plan of applying modern decision theory to one's choices might have lower expected utility than using other approaches. So nothing about modern decision theory implies that one can get along without some detachment rule.

Moreover, to use standard decision theory, one still has to embrace the overarching conditional to do what decision theory favors. But that conditional just is a detachment rule: it says that when decision theory favors an action that one should probably perform, one should perform it. So appeals to decision theory merely instantiate DR, rather than avoid it.

In addition, it would be anachronistic to recommend that David apply modern decision theory to his decision problem, and it would be unreasonable to insist that no one approach decision problems using ordinary conditionals in the way David uses them in the story. Thus, we should take Adams at face value: he claims that using conditionals is a fine way to approach the decision problem in question, and maintains that "would probably" conditionals can do the job necessary if they are the only conditionals that are true. In response to that claim, the need for a detachment rule is obvious.

This point about a needed detachment rule doesn't undermine Adams' claims about (5) and (6) compared to (1) and (2), since this point only requires supplementing his account with a suitable detachment rule for the probability operator. Epistemic conditionals and inferences are more efficient routes to the same end, encoding in the conditional and inference pattern itself the suitable detachment rule. If the necessary epistemic principle is that in circumstances C, believing q on the basis of p is rational, the epistemic conditional *if p, q* is included in the state of information involving C, and this conditional itself detaches any epistemic operator involved in the statement of the necessary epistemic principle.

It is worth pointing out that Adams' emphasis on what is needed for practical deliberation is crucial to this entire discussion. If an approach to deliberation has as a consequence that David has no business drawing conclusions about whether to leave Keilah on the basis of his deliberations involving conditionals, that approach is inadequate. Moreover, for deliberation to yield conclusions about what to do, it must yield conclusions about what is rational to believe, and these conclusions will be stark claims about the world itself and how to act in it rather than qualified ones about the epistemic or probabilistic status of claims about the world and our actions. It is of the very nature of the epistemic approach to feed on this point by encoding the relevant support relations in the conditionals central to this model of creation.

So, the epistemic approach has two advantages here. First, it suffers from no grounding objection, and it tells a much simpler and more elegant story about the connection between the conditionals in a deliberative model and the role that such deliberation must play in an account capable of informing agents about what to do and what to think, a need presupposed by critics of Molinism who claim that "would probably" conditionals are all that is needed to figure out what to do and what to think. In short, Adams' passing remark presupposes that we often have adequate reasons concerning the free behavior of others, and the epistemic approach developed here exploits this fact directly, rather than trying to get at it through counterfactuals probabilistically qualified together with some detachment rule for the probability operator.

8.5   From Fallible to Indefeasible

What remains to be shown, then, is how to move from a complete system of (suppositional) justified beliefs to the kind of knowledge needed for an account of creation to leave open the possibility of full providence. If we partition the belief system into the parts involving libertarian freedom and the remainder, the latter part consists not only of justified beliefs but of beliefs (suppositionally) known infallibly. This knowledge result depends only on God's ability to know infallibly what he will and will not bring about by a direct act of will and the logical implications of this knowledge. What remains, then, is to see what can be said about the part of the suppositional belief system concerning the actions of free individuals.

To address the issue here, note first that, given the assumptions with which we began, it is part of the nature of justification and knowledge as it applies in the limited realm of finite cognizers with fallible cognitive capacities that if a given false belief is adequately justified to be a candidate for knowledge, we can show that defeaters of some sort must be present if the belief in question is false. That is because we have assumed that there are no inscrutable truths and thus that falsity leaves traces, and these traces will constitute defeaters of the justification in question. Such defeaters can be either external or internal, and they can be either rebutters or undercutters of justification. With regard to the latter distinction, note that the story of justification for any belief centrally involves two things: the things that provide epistemic support (the justifiers) and the link between these justifiers and what they justify (the principles). Defeaters can attack either of these elements. Rebutters come in the form of additional information that justifies the denial of the claim in question, and undercutters attack the connection between the justifiers and what they justify—they confirm that the evidence in question does not justify the conclusion drawn from it. The common element between undercutters and rebutters is that they are defeaters: in conjunction with the justifiers, the conjunction fails to count as a justifier of the claim in question. Both types of defeaters can be either internal or external. Internal defeaters are ones already with the state of information constituted by the beliefs and experiences of the person in question; external defeaters are outside this state of information. When an internal defeater is present, and not overridden by any further information in the system of information in question, then the justifier in question is a *prima facie* justifier only, and any belief based on that justifier will be *prima facie*, but not *ultima facie*, justified. When a defeater of this sort is external to the state of information in question, it is the stuff of which the Gettier problem is made. It is, that is, a piece of information which prevents a belief from counting as knowledge even when it is both true and *ultima facie* justified relative to the system of information for the believer in question.

Here it is important to note that an inference from p to q is epistemically valid, and the epistemic conditional $p \rightarrow q$ a theorem relative to a given system of information, when and only when basing a belief q on p in that context yields an *ultima facie* justified belief. That is, the truth of the conditional is undermined by the presence of (undefeated) defeaters within the system of information. One way to think about this result is that the epistemic inferences (or transitions) codified by DT ($\Phi \vdash_\epsilon \Psi$ iff $\vdash_\epsilon (\Phi \rightarrow \Psi)$) identify potential proper bases for beliefs, where a belief can't be properly based when it is merely *prima facie* justified. Instead, the epistemic inferences and theorems come and go in the process of updating systems of information, as undercutters and rebutters are introduced or eliminated in that process.

What follows from these points, then, is that if S has a properly based (and hence justified) false belief in p, the system of information relative to which the belief is justified contains no undefeated defeaters of some legitimate epistemic transition from some part of the system of information to p. Thus, the only defeaters that could be present are external ones. So in cases of justified false beliefs, where the justification involves a state of information containing an epistemic conditional recording a conditional relationship between the basis of the belief and its content, there can at most be external defeaters. Moreover, when considering the possibility of such external defeaters for finite human beings and for truths that are not inscrutable, such external defeaters will always be present, since there is some amount of further learning that could reveal the truth. So, given our assumption of excluded middle, if a given justified belief is false, its denial is true and leaves tracks, and these tracks constitute further information which count as external defeaters of the justification for the false claim in question.

This result shares a common feature with a nearly universal view in work on the Gettier problem: namely, that any justified belief that is unGettiered (i.e., subject to no undefeated defeaters) has to be true.[13] Some have dissented, however, arguing that all that is necessary for unGettiered justification is that the person's belief would not be accidentally true for the person in question, if it were true (Howard-Snyder *et al.* 2003). This response, as the authors admit, doesn't show that there can be unGettiered justified false beliefs, it merely blocks certain standard arguments for thinking that unGettiered justified beliefs must be true. Moreover, its reliance on the notion of non-accidentality is troubling without further clarification. Without such clarification, it looks like nothing more than a placeholder for whatever condition solves the Gettier problem, and if so, we might as well have run the entire argument using this counterfactual instead: if the belief were true it would be unGettiered. Then consider a case of a false justified belief that also fails the Gettier condition. The counterfactual then allows us to conclude that if we move to a close situation in which the falsity of the belief is removed, we have also moved to a close situation in which the Gettier failure is removed. We then impose this condition on Gettiered but justified beliefs: such a belief can only be both Gettiered and justified when, in close circumstances where the belief is true, it would also be unGettiered. There is no good reason to think that the closeness relation has any such property. In some cases it may: for example, an epistemic angel might make the closeness relation function in this way, even though a bit careless in allowing lots of justified false beliefs. And perhaps we might ramp up such thought experiments to where the epistemic angel is close enough to a necessary being that the operations in question hold across all worlds in which there are fallible cognizers. All such ruminations can show, however, is some type of possibility of a connection between Gettiered justified beliefs and the counterfactual in question. They cannot show that the connection is even remotely plausible. Hence even if such a conclusion shows that there is no argument available whose premises entail the conclusion that justified beliefs that are unGettiered must be true, the possibility that undermines deductive arguments for this conclusion is either neutral or positive regarding an epistemic, non-deductive argument for this conclusion, since it is so implausible to think that the closeness relation on worlds functions in a way that ties truth to being unGettiered in close counterfactual circumstances. Thus, this assumption in the Gettier literature is strong enough from an epistemic point of view to support the claim made here that justified false beliefs by finite creatures fail the Gettier condition as well.

Even so, this point about the connection between justified false beliefs and failing the Gettier condition doesn't require the stronger assumption of the Gettier literature. As noted already, part of the argument for the connection involved

---

[13]For discussion of this issue, and the variety of perspectives on the Gettier problem committed to the entailment claim, see, e.g., Lehrer (2000), Sturgeon (1993), Zagzebski (1994).

the assumption we are making here that truths leave tracks of truth, that there are no inscrutable truths. It is these tracks of truth that make justified false beliefs for finite creatures fail the Gettier condition, for they present additional information that provides an external defeater for the justification for the belief in question. So even though the standard assumption of the Gettier literature provides support for this claim, this standard assumption is not strictly required.

These features of the finite and fallible human condition change somewhat when we move to the situation involved in the suppositional reasoning in the context of deliberation about creation. What changes is that, by the conclusion of the suppositional reasoning process, no possibility remains for any external defeater. The reason there can't be any external defeaters is that, by the end of the reasoning process in question, the story is complete. Thus, by the end of the process, the only defeaters there could be would be internal defeaters, which by hypothesis are not present. Together with the assumption that there are no inscrutable truths allows us to conclude that, since the entire collection of suppositional beliefs in question are justified and unGettiered, they are all suppositionally true and constitute suppositionally indefeasible knowledge.

In slogan form, then, what the model shows is that *God knows the beginning from the end.* That is, until the story is completed, the suppositional reasoning in question is as subject to fallibility as ordinary human reasoning is. Once the story has been completed, however, things change. Once the point of completion is reached, there is an argument available to show that no mistakes have occurred, and that there are no defeaters available to prevent full and complete suppositional knowledge of every aspect of the world in question. Thus, at the point of completion, we are finally in a position to see that the growing collection of fallible justifications emerges by the end as indefeasible knowledge. It is in this way that God knows the beginning from the end.

8.6   From Indefeasible to Infallible

Indefeasible knowledge, however, is not the end of the story. Perhaps it is enough for purposes of securing a doctrine of full providence, in much the same way that simple foreknowledge is enough (Hunt 1993), but it would be a much more satisfying perspective to be able to defend the possibility of infallible knowledge as well. To see how to do so, we need some groundwork on the notion of infallibility.

8.6.1   *What is Infallibility?*

As a first pass, we might try this: infallibility amounts to being able to rule out every possibility of error. As Lewis says,

> It seems as if knowledge must be by definition infallible. It you claim that
> S knows that p, and yet you grant that S cannot eliminate a certain possi-
> bility in which *not-p*, it certainly seems as if you have granted that S does
> not after all know that p. To speak of fallible knowledge, of knowledge de-
> spite uneliminated possibilities of error, just sounds contradictory.(Lewis
> 1996, p. 549)

Lewis's view, however, remains murky, because of its reliance on the language of "ruling out." A natural interpretation of this phrase is in terms of knowledge itself: one rules out a possibility when and only when one knows, or is in a position to know, that it does not obtain. Yet, once we endorse a plausible closure principle about knowledge—that one can come to know the logical consequences of what is already known by competently deducing them (Hawthorne 2005)–infallibility—on this construal of it, can be a consequence of epistemic closure alone, which is too weak an interpretation.

One might try to avoid this weakness by referring to the evidential basis of the knowledge in question, and require that the ruling out be done by it alone. Fallibilists, however, can still trivialize the view: evidence e rules out all $\sim p$ possibilities when and only when e provides an adequate epistemic basis for believing p. To avoid such trivialization of infallibilism, a retreat into the refuge of logic seems fortuitous: e rules out all $\sim p$ possibilities when and only when e entails p. Thus, it might seem, the heart of infallibilism is found in the demand for logical guarantees of truth in one's evidence base.

This characterization can only work if one insists on excluding p itself from e, but this restriction is appropriate: we don't want an account of knowledge that allows knowledge of p to arise in virtue of the fact that p entails p. Even so, this account of infallibility remains too easy to satisfy. It leaves open the possibility of Cheap Infallibilism.

One obvious example of Cheap Infallibilism arises from a disjunctive account of the contents of perception. One might hold that one is in a different perceptual state when one is actually seeing an elephant from the state one is in when no elephant is present but one's perceptual state is indiscriminable by reflection from the former state (for representative literature on this view, see Byrne and Logue (2009)). If we include the contents of experience in the body of evidence available, then this disjunctive approach is a version of Cheap Infallibilism, since the body of evidence in question could not obtain without the belief in question being true.

Another example of Cheap Infallibilism arises from the Williamsonian identification of knowledge and evidence (Williamson 2000). If one's evidence is exactly what one knows, then one's evidence entails anything known to be true.

These infallibilisms are cheap because no self-respecting skeptic would allow that such an infallibilism is enough to solve the skeptical challenge. We don't need a careful account of exactly what it takes to solve that challenge to notice that the above infallibilisms do not solve it. Such approaches may be part of an adequate response to the skeptic, but they can't do so in the straightforward and satisfying way that, say, success of the Cartesian project in the *Meditations* would provide. In that sense, the infallibilism they provide is *cheap*, leaving any responsible epistemologist even slightly inclined toward skepticism wishing for more.

It is worth noting that the model developed here sustains Cheap Infallibilism as well. Suppose e is adequate evidence for p. Then the epistemic conditional

$e \rightarrow p$ is contained in the relevant system of information for beings who are logically and epistemically omniscient. Even for the rest of us, reflection can make this conditional available as part of our total evidence. Once present, however, we have evidence available that entails p, and thus generates infallibility by the above standard.

Even though one's evidence, including epistemic conditionals, entails the belief in question, it needn't soundly entail it, if we allow false claims to be in the set of evidence (as I believe a sensible epistemology should). There is no refuge here, however, for avoiding cheapness in one's infallibilism in terms of sound entailments, for once we build in the assumption of no inscrutable truths, we can still get Cheap Infallibilism here in the case of God by noting that once a story goes to completion, the elements of the story can only be justified if they are also true. So, given the assumption of no inscrutable truths (which, by hypothesis, God knows to be true), it follows on our model that God's indefeasibly justified beliefs in complete stories are also (cheaply) infallible, since the informational system in question contains evidence to soundly entail the content of each belief.

One might try to save the evidential approach to infallibility by adopting a restrictive condition on proper basing. In the case above, one might insist that it isn't the total system of evidence that matters, but rather only the part that confers justification on p—namely, e itself.

This approach cannot succeed, however, for there simply is no legitimate restrictive requirement on proper basing. Note first how this point holds with respect to ordinary, fallible justification. Recall that, underlying instances of epistemic support are general epistemic principles. A good example of such is Chisholmian: if S is appeared to F-ly and lacks grounds for doubt that something is F, then it is reasonable for S to believe that something is F (Chisholm 1977). I'm not endorsing this principle, but only using it for purposes of illustration, since its antecedent makes reference to both a *conferrer* of justification—the appearance state in question—and an *enabler*—the lack of grounds for doubt. Given such a principle, the above restriction on proper basing insists that, relative to such a principle, one can only base a belief properly on the appearance state in question. That restriction is mistaken, however. S might, for example, reflect on whether there are grounds for doubt concerning the claim in question, and might come to believe that there are no such grounds for doubt, and might then come to believe that something is F, basing that belief on the appearance state in question together with the belief that there are no grounds for doubt concerning it.

S needn't so base the belief after reflection, but may do so legitimately. S might reflect and come to believe that there are no grounds for doubt, and still might rationally believe that something is F by basing it only on the appearance state in question. The additional reflective belief is allowed to be part of the basis of the belief that something is F but it is not required to be part of the basis even when it exists. The proper conclusion to draw here is that proper basing comes in a variety of flavors, and any account of infallibility that restricts these options is bound to fail.

Not only can a belief be properly based on more than a minimal conferrer of justification, it can also be based on a minimal basis when something stronger is available. Consider the Cartesian project of restoring confidence in our standard belief system in the face of the skeptical doubts in the *Meditations*. Descartes' desire is to provide an argument for the conclusion that mistakes in our system of beliefs occur when and only when our will outruns our understanding—put colloquially, when our non-alethic interests, desires, and motivations could our purely intellectual judgment. In attempting to restore confidence, Descartes provides an argument for this conclusion. The argument fails, but let's ignore that issue for the moment and suppose it had succeeded. Moreover, suppose it were transparent to us whether we were motivated by non-alethic factors. If these assumptions held, the Cartesian project of defending our systems of belief against skepticism would succeed. Our present system of beliefs (properly adjusted to include nothing ill-motivated) would be a system in which we could place full confidence, and it would meet the most stringent infallibilist strictures. But nothing in this story requires that we base our beliefs on the Cartesian system itself in order to satisfy infallibilist strictures. The system must withstand scrutiny, and perhaps those with the secure knowledge undergirded by this system must be aware of the arguments involved in it, but there is no reason to insist that ordinary beliefs, formed in the ordinary way, are not infallibly known just because they are not also based on the system itself. The reflective knowledge about how the system works and why it is adequate is enough when one bases, say, a perceptual belief on an appearance state while recognizing that the belief is motivated by a concern for understanding alone.

One might hold out hope that infallibility could be defined in terms of entailing minimal conferrers of justification. Instead of thinking in terms of a proper basis of justification, one might think of all the proper bases and select the minimal one available, and insist that it entail the truth of the belief in question. Or, if one is concerned that there may be no unique minimal one available, we can speak instead of one's basic evidence, and insist that it be in virtue of one's basic evidence that infallibility obtains.

Such a restriction has implausible consequences. One's basic evidence will consist either of beliefs or something else, such as experience and its contents. If infallibility is a product of entailment from the set of basic evidence, then any belief included in the set of basic evidence will itself be infallible. Such a conclusion once again makes certain instances of infallible belief too easy to come by: mere basicality of belief shouldn't ensure infallibility. So one's basic evidence can't include any beliefs, or any other item that is itself capable of being justified or unjustified.

Moreover, there is no good reason to restrict the evidence to which an account of infallibility can appeal in a way that will avoid this problem. For human beings in ordinary circumstances, basic evidence will involve some collection of beliefs and experiences, and if beliefs are excluded from the set of basic evidence, infallibility would then depend solely on the justificatory power of experience itself. Note that in such a case, the Cartesian project was hopelessly confused from the beginning. Had that project succeeded, our ordinary conception of the world would have been shown to be infallible, but nothing in the Cartesian strategy hoped to demonstrate this point from experiential inputs alone. So it is an objectionable account of infallibility that it must result solely from some logical connection between experience and belief.

The problem, then, for the evidential approach to infallibility is to find a way to distinguish cheap evidence from non-cheap evidence, so as to avoid Cheap Infallibilism. Because of the difficulties noted above, it is unclear how to draw the needed distinction, and in the face of this issue, an alternative is to conclude that we shouldn't expect to find an adequate account of infallibility solely in terms of evidence and what it entails. Instead, we might turn to modal dimensions of knowledge, looking for an account of infallibility in terms of epistemic modal notions such as safety and sensitivity.[14] A belief is safe when it would normally be true when held (Sosa 2007), and a belief is sensitive when it would not be held when false (Nozick 1981). Mere counterfactual connections are clearly too weak for infallibility, so the inclination is to look for necessary connections instead: in some sense, the belief not only wouldn't, but couldn't, be held while false; not only would the claim be true if believed, it would have to be true.

It would be too strong, however, to interpret the necessity needed here in terms of metaphysical necessity. On such an account, infallibility would require immunity from error concerning the claim in question in every world in which the individual in question exists. One reason such a requirement is too strong is that some cognitive interests are optional, in the sense that there are worlds where the person in question need not consider the claim in question, and should not be disbarred from being infallible about it simply because in some worlds the individual never considers the issue. Another reason arises because of possibilities of massive disability and mental incompetence or confusion. Descartes thought that some beliefs not even an evil demon could render believed yet false, but that is compatible with a demon getting one to believe that the claim is false even though it isn't. So if we impose a modal constraint on infallibility, it will have to be restricted to something less than perfect correlation between truth and belief across all metaphysical possibilities.

The Cartesian project is useful for pointing us in the right direction when looking for such a modal dimension. We want an account of infallibility such that if the Cartesian project had succeeded we would all be in a position to have a wide range of infallible beliefs: avoiding error would be totally up to us, requiring only that we don't let our wills outrun our understanding when it

---

[14]This conclusion is importantly similar to that defended in Dutant (2007). Dutant, too, distinguishes between evidential and modal approaches to infallibilism, but his modal approach differs slightly from the present one, focusing on the basis of belief rather than the informational system in question. Because of the points raised earlier about the optionality involved in basing, I think the latter approach has more hope of success here.

comes to belief. If it were transparent to us whether our will were outrunning our understanding, then we would have an argument available that guarantees the truth of our belief—an argument that would be accessible in a wide range of worlds. Some individuals will access such available arguments across all the relevant worlds, and others will be more spotty, noticing the argument in some worlds but not others. What to say about the latter group isn't quite clear, but it is clear that those individuals that access the available argument across all the relevant worlds will have infallible beliefs for the conclusions supported by the available arguments (the ones available on the assumption that the Cartesian project succeeds).

The central points to note here, then, are these. First, there is no legitimate requirement on infallibility that requires safety and sensitivity across all metaphysical possibilities. Second, we want an understanding of infallibility that allows for it to be present if the Cartesian project had been successful. One way to achieve such a result is to find arguments available from premises that are infallibly known for each belief that is held, but our earlier discussion of Cheap Infallibilism raises a cautionary flag to avoid appeals to "cheap" arguments for the beliefs in question. We have not succeeded in finding out what makes arguments and evidence cheap as opposed to non-cheap, but even in the absence of such an account we can recognize that some arguments are cheap and some aren't. Uncertainty about cheapness and uncertainty about the scope of an appropriate modal dimension for infallibility each show that we don't have a precise understanding of infallibility. Even so, the discussion has given us a clear enough idea of the notion to show that the suppositionally indefeasible knowledge generated in our epistemic model yields infallibility as well. To a defense of this claim we now turn.

8.6.2 *Divine Infallibility for Complete Stories*

To develop our argument, we begin with an epistemically basic set of suppositions about what God might strongly actualize. When we move from the suppositional context to the context of creation, what will be basic to God's knowledge of the unfolding of the created order is reflective knowledge of the divine will. Those who might wonder whether infallibility can be sustained on our model will not have a concern at this point: God's ability to infallibly know the divine will is not the locus of concern (if it were, full providence would have been abandoned before any investigation was undertaken concerning how knowledge of future contingents is possible). Nor is there a concern about infallible knowledge of what is causally or logically determined by the original total creative act. Instead, the concern is about what is left undetermined by God's acts of will. Thus, for present purposes, we can assume a recursive account of infallibility, resting on an infallible base clause—one that can be assumed to be satisfied in virtue of God infallibly knowing his own will. Our focus is then on how to get infallibility into the picture as we move from this basis to non-basic pieces of information, already shown to constitute indefeasible suppositional knowledge. The issue to consider is how to show that this indefeasible knowledge is also infallible.

We can begin by noting the possibility of what we might term "limited infallibility", where the modal dimension involves quantification only over worlds resulting from complete plans. If we suppose that the actual world is one that results from a complete plan, and also conclude that the modal dimension for infallibility involves all worlds resulting from complete plans, we are already in a position to see that God's suppositional beliefs satisfy this modal dimension. On this rendition of the modal requirement for infallibility, God's indefeasible knowledge has a modal stability that extends beyond mere safety and sensitivity, since some such worlds will be quite dissimilar from the actual world and the assumption in question couldn't be acceptable if the close worlds were not worlds all of which result from complete plans.[15] God's beliefs in such a case would then be modally secure enough to fall within the vague characterization above concerning infallibility, allowing the intermediate conclusion here that the model allows for the possibility, at least, of strong enough modal security for infallibility. In addition, the argument for how to move from the initial state of fallible justification for suppositional beliefs to indefeasible knowledge will be available in every such world, satisfying the evidential demand for non-cheap arguments for the truth of belief across all the worlds required to satisfy the modal dimension. So, given this account of the modal dimension, infallibility follows.

One could ask for more, however, noting that infallibility follows only on this understanding of which worlds are relevant for satisfying the modal dimension for infallibility. It is worth noting that this understanding is not wholly implausible, but I will not press this point here, since stronger results are possible that do not depend on this understanding. The next section shows how to get such results.

8.6.3 *God's Nature: The Rest of the Story*

In order to move from this limited infallibility result to full, unrestricted infallibility, the nature of God, in terms of risk-taking, plays an essential role. To see it, consider Einstein's claim that God doesn't play dice with the universe. This remark is not a modal one, but still might be intended to convey the modally strong idea that it is incompatible with the divine nature to take risks with creation. In the context of our model, what that would show is that the class of feasible worlds is limited to those resulting from complete plans, limited by the divine nature itself.

One might endorse the quote, however, holding that it only expresses a contingent truth. In such a case, the class of feasible worlds includes worlds resulting both from complete plans and from incomplete plans. It is just that the actual world is claimed to be a feasible world resulting from a complete plan. When the plan is a complete one, we can call the world that results a *divine accomplishment*; when the plan is an incomplete one, the world that results is a *divine*

---

[15]The argument here appeals to a possible worlds semantics for safety and sensitivity requirements: that a belief is safe when in every close world the belief is true if held, and a belief is sensitive if in every close world the belief would not be held if false.

adventure. For God to display full providential control, the actual world must be an accomplishment rather than an adventure. God takes risks with creation, plays dice with the universe, begins an adventure, by adopting an incomplete plan.[16]

In either case, however, an argument from limited infallibility to unrestricted infallibility is available. If God can't play dice with the universe, this fact will be known to the divine mind, and hence God will know, prior to creation, that only worlds resulting from complete plans will be feasible worlds. If those are the only worlds that can be actualized, then God's cognitive state is modally stable in a such a way that infallibility follows. If God can't play dice with the universe, God knows that divine risk-taking isn't possible, and knows as well that no mistakes are possible in any world that can be created. Such modal stability goes way beyond the kind of modal stability necessary for infallibility, arising as it does from knowledge of what could be actualized and what could not. It is a modal stability stronger than anything that would be present given success of the Cartesian project, for such success could yield infallible beliefs even if there are creatable worlds in which ordinary humans display weakness of the will, allowing it to outrun our understanding concerning certain claims. So, if God can't play dice with the universe, the inference from indefeasible knowledge in complete stories to infallible knowledge across feasible worlds is secure.

Moreover, even if rolling the dice is possible, God will know whether such has occurred, once the totality of suppositional reasoning described in this model has been completed. Thus, if God isn't playing dice with the universe, there will be available an argument for this conclusion, and that argument will be part of the system of information characterizing the divine mind prior to creation. Thus, even if there are feasible worlds in which some future contingents are not known and not knowable prior to creation, there are also feasible worlds in which God will know infallibly the totality of what the future holds, on the basis of the information generated in the model. Once again, the Cartesian project provides a useful reference point in establishing this result. Success in that project would allow infallibility even when there are other worlds in which one allows one's will to outrun one's understanding. So long as one can tell infallibly whether one's will has interfered, it is compatible with infallibility that there are other worlds where one displays intellectual weakness of the will.

The key point to note about this result is that it arises once the suppositional reasoning involved in our model has been completed. So long as God can infallibly know the divine will and nature, God can reason in the ways just adumbrated. In doing so, the divine mind arrives at a state of information that involves the kind of modal resistance to error that, together with the fact that the state of information contains evidence that entails the entirety of the future, is stronger

---

[16]Perhaps Einstein meant to affirm the stronger claim that playing dice happens wherever determinism is false. If so, that's a mistake, as the present model shows. Playing dice arises from incomplete plans, and a plan can be complete even for indeterministic worlds, just as it can for worlds involving libertarian freedom.

than what is needed for infallibility. We thus complete the journey in our model from fallible beginnings, to indefeasible justifications, and finally to infallible knowledge, thus yielding the possibility of full and complete providential control.

8.7 Is Essential Omniscience Lost?

One might suspect, however, that the results come only at the cost of essential omniscience. To see why, consider a complete story w that includes some free action: S's A-ing. Then there is another world w^* in which God strongly actualizes exactly what he strongly actualizes in w and yet in which S doesn't A. So in w^*, God has no grounds on which to know that S doesn't A; in fact, it looks as if God will have a false belief in w^* about what S will do. Hence, the epistemic model developed here appears to yield infallibility only at the cost of essential omniscience.

This conclusion overreaches, however. God's total epistemic situation with respect to whether a free individual A's or not is not exhausted by the information about what God strongly actualized. Since all conditionals obey the sacrosanct principle that they can't be true when their antecedent is true and consequent false, the conditionals can't be the same for w and w^*. Yet, surely, the epistemic conditionals are central elements in God's total epistemic situation. Given the assumption here that there are no inscrutable truths, it follows that the total epistemic situation in w cannot be the same as in w^*. Hence the argument just given for the loss of essential omniscience is not compelling.

Compare, on this score, the standard Molinist response to a similar argument that Molinism is incompatible with essential omniscience. The argument claims that if S is free, then there are two worlds w and w^* which look the same to God prior to creation, since both worlds count as an unfolding of the same totality that God strongly actualizes. The Molinist response is that there is a difference between the worlds: namely, the counterfactuals of freedom have to be different in the two worlds, and this information is available to God prior to creation. The argument for claiming that the counterfactuals of freedom have to be different appeals to the sacrosanct principle above: if the same counterfactuals were true in both worlds, then it would be possible for a counterfactual to be true while having a true antecedent and false consequent. Since that can't happen, the information available to God isn't the same in the two worlds.

If one thinks of these responses as providing an explanation of how God is essentially omniscient, both accounts are subject to the same objection. In the case of Molinism, counterfactuals of freedom are supposed to be true prevolitionally. That is, in the explanatory order, they come before God's decision to create. Appeal to the sacrosanct principle to reveal their content is to appeal to features of the world in question that arise, in the explanatory order, after God's decision to create. Hence, it would seem, the Molinist account of essential omniscience involves explanatory backtracking, and adequate explanations need to avoid such backtracking.

Similarly, the epistemic conditionals arise earlier in the explanatory story than do the features that allow appeal to the sacrosanct principle to tell us which conditionals are true. So backtracking is involved here as well. In the context of the epistemic model, however, backtracking dimensions are part of the model itself, and thus not as troublesome as they might be on the Molinist story. Epistemic connections run both forward and backward in time, revealing to us both what the future will be and the mistakes we've made in the past. As the machinery of suppositional reasoning progresses through the machinery of update semantics, the revisions to suppositional opinion that can result can proceed both in terms of adding new information and in terms of correcting earlier mistakes. So the mere fact that backtracking is involved isn't, by itself, problematic here.

Notice the difference here between the epistemic model and standard Molinism. On standard Molinism, the relevant conditionals are given, prior to any deliberation about what will happen in the future, should God make certain decisions. There is thus, in standard Molinism, an explicit endorsement of the explanatory priority of the relevant conditionals. In our epistemic model, there is a sense in which the conditionals are prior to what is learned about the future, but the way in which backtracking is allowed in the system shows that revision can occur in the process of updating. Because such revision can occur, the conditionals do not constitute *givens* as they do for standard Molinists.

Thus, if this objection concerning explanatory priority has force, it appears to present a greater problem for Molinism than for Philosophical Arminianism. Even so, the issues involved in the notion of explanatory priority are deep and complex, and leave open the possibility that, in some way or other, the above accounts fail to sustain the doctrine of essential omniscience. Even so, there is a way of blunting this worry by denying that the claims made above concerning the doctrine are meant to offer an explanation of the truth of that doctrine. A weaker way to understand these claims is simply to deny that they are explanations of the truth of the doctrine, but are instead only consistency proofs that there is nothing in either the Molinist model nor the epistemic model that rules out the essential omniscience of God. Understood in this way, both approaches are silent on the issue of how to understand or explain God's essential omniscience, and arguments relying on the notion of explanatory priority to show that some problem exists would be irrelevant. Such arguments are relevant when the question is whether these approaches can explain the possibility of essential omniscience, but are irrelevant when the issue is mere consistency. When the issue is mere consistency, the claim being advanced is that there is no contradiction between the doctrine and either Molinism or Philosophical Arminianism, and this claim is compatible with these viewpoints having no explanation of this possibility.

Moreover, there is an argument that such silence is appropriate. A model showing how it is possible for God to exercise full and complete providential control even in a world containing indeterminisms of various sorts should not also need to show that there is no world in which such complete providence is not possible. Not even theological determinists can claim such a result for their model of divine providence: that would require their model of providence to rule out the possibility of God playing dice with the universe. If it is essential to the divine nature that God not play dice with the universe, this point will not be elicitable even from an deterministic account as to how the entirety of the future can be calculated from the laws, initial conditions, and divine decisions concerning which miracles to perform. What makes a model adequate for purposes of explaining providential control is one thing; what makes for essential omniscience another. Or, to put the point differently, aspects of the divine nature are one thing, and that which shows the possibility of providential control in an indeterministic world another.

Notice that if one's theological stance inclines one toward an account of deity on which loss of essential omniscience is a devastating consequence, one needs only the consistency proof above to allow combining Philosophical Arminianism with essential omniscience. I want to suggest, however, that such a deep commitment to the doctrine of essential omniscience is a mistake unless such consistency proofs work. For, if they don't work, then one can affirm the doctrine of essential omniscience only by committing to the unattractive claim that creating an indeterministic world is simply impossible for God. There is no good reason why perfect being theology should side with the doctrine of essential omniscience on this score, for it would seem to be a great-making feature of a being to be able to create both deterministic and indeterministic worlds. Once we see that essential omniscience isn't needed for full and infallible providential control, there won't be an argument available for abandoning the possibility of indeterministic worlds in favor of preserving essential omniscience.

8.8 Conclusion

In closing, it is worth addressing a concern that the task undertaken here is too minimal. One might put the worry this way: the model might leave open full providence, but it fails to accomplish what a middle way between compatibilist approaches and Open Theist approaches is supposed to accomplish. Molinists attempt to show not only that full providence is possible, but that it is guaranteed by the Molinist picture of creation. Anything short of such a guarantee isn't a genuine competitor of Molinism and isn't adequate to the task of finding a middle way between two extremes.

It is true that Molinism aims to provide a guarantee of full providence through the Molinist picture of creation, but it is a mistake to make this the standard for an adequate middle way. For one thing, aiming for such a guarantee forces standard Molinists to endorse the Law of Conditional Excluded Middle for subjunctive conditionals, but the only available defense of LCEM preserves it only at the cost of abandoning the principle of bivalence (Stalnaker 1981, Cross 2009). And properly so, since it is a bizarre and counterintuitive idea to suppose that if this never-to-be-flipped fair coin were flipped, it would come up heads, or that it would not come up heads. Neither claim is true, though LCEM could still be maintained in spite of this admission if we give up the idea that either claim has a truth value. Moreover, such cases can be found regarding free actions as well. There are Buridan's Ass possibilities: ;situations in which explanatory considerations are equally balanced between two competing courses of action. Suppose a person will never rest in a given bed at a certain hotel, but that if that person were to rest there, it would be a Buridan's Ass Situation for that person concerning whether to get up on the left or right side of the bed. Just as in the coin-flip case, it is a considerable cost to a theory to insist that the person would exit from the left side, or that the person would not exit from the left side.

If LCEM can be rescued only at the cost of bivalence, however, LCEM provides no comfort to some hope of guaranteeing full providential control through a model of creation. What should be rejected here is the standard in question. A model of creation need not guarantee full providence, since it is obvious that there are metaphysical presuppositions needed in addition to whatever the model might involve in order to provide a defense of the doctrine of providence.

Even given this more limited role for a model of creation, however, Molinism remains controversial, since the standard objections to Molinism threaten not only the hope that it can guarantee full providence but also that it can account for the possibility of full providence. The standard objections attack the central ideas of Molinism that there are true counterfactuals of freedom that are outside God's volitional control, and if those criticisms are correct, there is no Molinist model of creation that can meet even the more minimal standard adopted here. For that reason, the present approach to finding a middle way between compatibilist accounts of creation and providence and Open Theist approaches to creation that deny full providence is superior, even if the present approach leaves open the possibility of creation unfolding in a way that does not involve full providence.

One might try to characterize this result by claiming that the picture developed here entails that God could have created a non-providential world, but that characterization would not be correct. What is true is that nothing in the model of creation guarantees full providence. It remains possible, however, that there is something about the nature of God that could close the gap between the model of creation developed here and the doctrine of providence. Here are some options. Perhaps God simply won't create in a way that results in a failure of full providence. Alternatively, perhaps God wouldn't create in this way, where the "wouldn't" claim is supposed to have stronger modal implications than the "won't" claim. Strongest of all, there is nothing presented here that eliminates the possibility that there is something about the essential and perfect nature of God that metaphysically closes off any creative option that doesn't involve full providence. My suggestion to those who want a modally strong doctrine of providence is that they should seek a ground for such a doctrine in the nature of God, not in the model of creation itself.

The beauty of this result is that it allows a theory of creation that leaves open the possibility of a defense of the strongest doctrine of divine providence, even a metaphysically necessary one, while at the same time allowing libertarian freedom a place in the model. One might put this point in a way that would be enigmatic by many apart from the explanation offered here: there are entailments of God's knowledge regarding which free actions will be performed, but the presence of such entailments does not, by itself, reveal any impossibility of explaining creation in a way that allows full providence and libertarian freedom to co-exist.

Bibliography

Adams, Ernest (1965). "A Logic of Conditionals". *Inquiry*, **8**, 166–197.

Adams, Ernest (1966). "Probability and the Logic of Conditionals". In *Aspects of Inductive Logic* (ed. J. Hintikka and P. Suppes), pp. 165–316. Amsterdam: North-Holland.

Adams, Ernest (1970). "Subjunctive and Indicative Conditionals". *Foundations of Language*, **6**, 89–94.

Adams, Marilyn (1975). "Hell and the God of Justice". *Religious Studies*, **11**, 433–447.

Adams, Robert M. (1977). "Middle Knowledge and the Problem of Evil". *American Philosophical Quarterly*, **14.2**, 109–117.

Adams, Robert M. (1986). "Time and Thisness". *Midwest Studies in Philosophy*, **11**, 315–329.

Adams, Robert M. (1989). "Reply to Kvanvig". *Philosophy and Phenomenological Research*, **50.2**, 299–301.

Adams, Robert M. (1991). "An Anti-Molinist Argument". *Philosophical Perspectives*, **V**, 343–353.

Arntzenius, Frank and Hall, Ned (2003). "On What We Know about Chance". *The British Journal for the Philosophy of Science*, **54**, 171–179.

Barth, Karl (2004). *Church Dogmatics*. Edinburgh: T. and T. Clark.

Beebee, Helen (2001). "The Non-Governing Conception of Laws of Nature". *Philosophy and Phenomenological Research*, **61.3**, 571–594.

Beilby, James K. and Eddy, Paul R. (ed.) (2001). *Divine Foreknowledge: Four Views*. Downers Grove: InterVarsity Press.

Bennett, Jonathan (1988). "Farewell to the Phlogiston Theory of Conditionals". *Mind*, **97**, 509–527.

Bennett, Jonathan (1995). "Classifying Conditionals: the Traditional Way is Right". *Mind*, **104**, 331–344.

Bennett, Jonathan (2003). *A Philosophical Guide to Conditionals*. New York: Oxford University Press.

Bigelow, John (1988). *The Reality of Numbers: A Physicalist's Philosophy of Mathematics*. Oxford: Oxford University Press.

Bigelow, John, Collins, John, and Pargetter, Robert (1993). "The Big Bad Bug: What are the Humean Chances?". *The British Journal for the Philosophy of Science*, **44**, 443–462.

Brunner, Emil (1954). *Eternal Hope*. Philadelphia: Fortress Press.

Byrne, Alex and Logue, Heather (ed.) (2009). *Disjunctivism: Contemporary Readings*. Cambridge, Mass.: MIT Press.

Chisholm, Roderick (1957). *Perceiving*. Ithaca: Cornell University Press.

Chisholm, Roderick (1977). *Theory of Knowledge* (2 edn). Englewood Cliffs: Prentice-Hall, Englewood Cliffs.

Collins, John, Hall, Ned, and Paul, L. A. (ed.) (2004). *Causation and Counterfactuals*. Cambridge, Mass.: MIT Press.

Crisp, Thomas M. (2007). "Presentism and the Grounding Objection". *Noûs*, **41**, 90–109.

Cross, Charles (2009). "Conditional Excluded Middle". *Erkenntnis*, **70**, 173–188.

de Molina, Luis (1988). *On Divine Foreknowledge*. Ithaca: Cornell University Press.

DeRose, Keith (2002). "Assertion, Knowledge, and Context". *The Philosophical Review*, **111**, 167–203.

DeRose, Keith (2010). "The Conditionals of Deliberation". *Mind*, **119**, 1–42.

Douven, Igor (2008). "The Evidential Support Theory of Conditionals". *Synthese*, **164**, 19–44.

Dudman, Victor Howard (1984). "Parsing "If"-Sentences". *Analysis*, **44**, 145–153.

Dudman, Vernon Howard (1988). "Indicative and Subjunctive". *Analysis*, **48**, 113–122.

Dutant, Julien (2007). "The Case for Infallibilism". In *Proceedings of the 4th Latin Meeting in Analytic Philosophy* (ed. C. Penco, M. Vignolo, V. Ottonelli, and C. Amoretti), pp. 59–84. Genoa: University of Genoa.

Edgington, Dorothy (1986). "Do Conditionals Have Truth-Conditions". *Crítica*, **18**, 3–30.

Edgington, Dorothy (1995). "On Conditionals". *Mind*, **104**, 235–329.

Fischer, John Martin (ed.) (1989). *God, Freedom, and Foreknowledge*. Stanford, CA: Stanford University Press.

Fischer, John Martin (1994). *The Metaphysics of Free Will*. Oxford: Blackwell Publishers.

Flint, Thomas P. (1998). *Divine Providence: The Molinist Account*. Ithaca: Cornell University Press.

Flint, Thomas P. (2003). "The Multiple Muddles of Maverick Molinism". *Faith and Philosophy*, **20.1**, 91–100.

Foley, Richard (1986). *The Theory of Epistemic Rationality*. Cambridge, Mass.: Harvard University Press.

Fox, John F. (1987). "Truthmaker". *Australasian Journal of Philosophy*, **65**, 185–207.

Frankfurt, Harry (1969). "Moral Responsibility and the Principle of Alternative Possibilities". *Journal of Philosophy*, **66**, 829–839.

Gibbard, Alan (1980). "Two Recent Theories of Conditionals". In *Ifs: Conditionals, Beliefs, Decision, Chance, and Time* (ed. W. Harper, R. Stalnaker, and G. Pearce), pp. 211–247. Dordrecht: D. Reidel.

Gillies, Anthony S. (2004). "Epistemic Conditionals and Conditional Epistemics". *Noûs*, **38.4**, 585–616.

Gould, Stephen Jay (1980). *The Panda's Thumb*. New York: W.W. Norton.

Grice, Paul (1968). "Logic and Conversation". In *Studies in the Way of Words*. Cambridge: Cambridge University Press.

Grim, Patrick (1991). *The Incomplete Universe*. Cambridge, Mass.: MIT Press.

Grim, Patrick and Plantinga, Alvin (1993). "Truth, Omniscience and Cantorian Arguments: An Exchange". *Philosophical Studies*, **71**, 267–306.

Hall, Ned (1994). "Correcting the Guide to Objective Chance". *Mind*, **103**, 504–517.

Hall, Ned, Paul, L. A., and Collins, John (ed.) (2004). *Causation and Conditionals*. Cambridge, Mass.: MIT Press.

Hasker, William (1989). *God, Time and Knowledge*. Ithaca: Cornell University Press.

Hawthorne, John (2004). *Knowledge and Lotteries*. Oxford: Oxford University Press.

Hawthorne, John (2005). "The Case for Closure". In *Contemporary Debates in Epistemology*, pp. 26–42. Malden, MA: Blackwell.

Heim, Irene (1983). "On the Projection Problem for Presuppositions". In *Second Annual West Coast Conference on Formal Linguistics* (ed. D. F. M. Barlow and M. Westcoat), pp. 114–126. Stanford, CA: Stanford University Press.

Howard-Snyder, Dan, Howard-Snyder, Frances, and Feit, Neil (2003). "Infallibilism and Gettier's Legacy". *Philosophy and Phenomenological Research*, **66.2**, 304–327.

Hunt, David (1993). "Simple Foreknowledge and Divine Providence". *Faith and Philosophy*, **10.3**, 394–414.

Jackson, Frank (1979). "On Assertion and Indicative Conditionals". *Philosophical Review*, **88**, 565–589.

Jackson, Frank (1987). *Conditionals*. Oxford: Blackwell Publishers.

Jackson, Frank (1990). "Classifying Conditionals I". *Analysis*, **50**, 134–147.

Jeffrey, Richard (1964). "If". *Journal of Philosophy*, **61.21**, 702–703.

Joyce, James (1999). *The Foundations of Causal Decision Theory*. Cambridge: Cambridge University Press.

Kane, Robert (1996). *The Significance of Free Will*. New York: Oxford University Press.

Keller, Simon (2004). "Presentism and Truthmaking". In *Oxford Studies in Metaphysics I* (ed. D. Zimmerman), pp. 83–106. Oxford: Oxford University Press.

Klein, Peter (1981). *Certainty: A Refutation of Skepticism*. Minneapolis: University of Minnesota Press.

Koons, Robert (2009). "Defeasible Reasoning". Stanford Encyclopedia of Philosophy.

Kvanvig, Jonathan L. (1986). *The Possibility of an All-Knowing God.* London: MacMillan Press.

Kvanvig, Jonathan L. (1989*a*). "Adams on Actualism and Presentism". *Philosophy and Phenomenological Research*, **50.2**, 289–298.

Kvanvig, Jonathan L. (1989*b*). "The Analogy Argument for a Limited Acccount of Omniscience". *International Philosophical Quarterly*, **29**, 129–138.

Kvanvig, Jonathan L. (1993). *The Problem of Hell.* New York: Oxford University Press.

Kvanvig, Jonathan L. (1994). "He Who Lapse Last Lapse Best: Plantinga on Leibniz' Lapse". *Southwest Philosophy Review*, **10**, 137–146.

Kvanvig, Jonathan L. (2002). "On Behalf of Maverick Molinism". *Faith and Philosophy*, **19.3**, 348–357.

Kvanvig, Jonathan L. (2003). "Propositionalism and the Perspectival Character of Justification". *American Philosophical Quarterly*, **40.1**, 3–18.

Kvanvig, Jonathan L (2009*a*). "Knowledge, Assertion, and Lotteries". In *Williamson on Knowledge* (ed. D. Pritchard and P. Greenough), pp. 140–160. Oxford: Oxford University Press.

Kvanvig, Jonathan L. (2009*b*). "Religious Pluralism and the Buridans Ass Paradox". *European Journal for Philosophy of Religion*, **1.1**, 1–26.

Kvanvig, Jonathan L (2011*a*). "Norms of Assertion". In *Assertion* (ed. J. Brown and H. Cappellan). Oxford: Oxford University Press.

Kvanvig, Jonathan L. (2011*b*). "The Rational Significance of Reflective Ascent". In *Evidentialism and Its Critics* (ed. T. Dougherty). Oxford: Oxford University Press.

Kvanvig, Jonathan L. (2012). "Two Approaches to Norms of Assertion". In *Epistemic Normativity* (ed. J. Turri). Oxford: Oxford University Press.

Kvanvig, Jonathan L. and Menzel, Christopher P (1990). "The Basic Notion of Justification". *Philosophical Studies*, **59**, 235–261.

Lehrer, Keith (2000). *Theory of Knowledge* (2nd edn). Boulder: Westview Press.

Levi, Isaac (2004). *Mild Contraction.* Oxford: Clarendon Press.

Lewis, C.S. (1944). *The Problem of Pain.* New York: MacMillan.

Lewis, David (1973). *Counterfactuals.* Oxford: Blackwell.

Lewis, David (1976). "Probabilities of Conditionals and Conditional Probabilities". *Philosophical Review*, **85**, 297–315.

Lewis, David (1980). "A Subjectivist's Guide to Objective Chance". In *Studies in Inductive Logic and Probability*, pp. 263–293. Berkeley: University of California Press.

Lewis, David (1983). "New Work for a Theory of Universals". *Australasian Journal of Philosophy*, **61**, 343–377.

Lewis, David (1994). "Humean Supervenience Debugged". *Mind*, **103**, 473–490.

Lewis, David (1996). "Elusive Knowledge". *Australasian Journal of Philosophy*, **74.4**, 549–567.

Lewis, David (2001). "Truthmaking and Different-Making". *Noûs*, **35**, 602–615.

Lycan, William G. (2001). *Real Conditionals*. Oxford: Oxford University Press.

Mackie, J. L. (1974). *The Cement of the Universe: A Study of Causation*. Oxford: Oxford University Press.

Macquarrie, John (1966). *Principles of Christian Theology*. New York: SCM.

McCarthy, Cormac (2006). *The Sunset Limited*. New York: Random House.

McGee, Vann (1989). "Conditional Probabilities and Compounds of Conditionals". *The Philosophical Review*, **48**, 485–541.

McTaggart, John (1906). *Some Dogmas of Religion*. London: Edward Arnold Press.

Nozick, Robert (1981). *Philosophical Explanations*. Cambridge, Mass.: Harvard University Press.

Pinnock, Clark (1987). "Fire, Then Nothing". *Christianity Today*, **March 20**, 40–41.

Plantinga, Alvin (1967). *God and Other Minds*. Ithaca: Cornell University Press.

Plantinga, Alvin (1977). *God, Freedom, and Evil*. Grand Rapids, Mich.: Eerdmans.

Plantinga, Alvin (1978). *The Nature of Necessity*. Ithaca: Cornell University Press.

Pollock, John L. (1995). *Cognitive Carpentry*. Cambridge, Mass.: MIT Press.

Pruss, Alexander R. (2006). *The Principle of Sufficient Reason: A Reassessment*. Cambridge: Cambridge University Press.

Ramsey, F.P. (1990). *F.P. Ramsey: Philosophical Papers*. Cambridge: Cambridge University Press.

Robinson, John (1950). *In the End, God*. London: James Clarke & Co.

Russell, Bertrand (1912). "On the Notion of Cause". *Proceedings of the Aristotelian Society*, **7**, 1–26.

Schaffer, Jonathan (2003). "From Contextualism to Contrastivism". *Philosophical Studies*, **119**, 73–103.

Schaffer, Jonathan (2009). "On What Grounds What". In *Metametaphysics: New Essays on the Foundations of Ontology* (ed. D. J. Chalmers and R. Wasserman), pp. 347–383. Oxford: Oxford University Press.

Shope, Robert (1978). "The Conditional Fallacy in Contemporary Philosophy". *Journal of Philosophy*, **75**, 397–413.

Sosa, Ernest (2007). *A Virtue Epistemology*. Oxford: Oxford University Press.

Stalnaker, Robert (1968). "A Theory of Conditionals". In *Studies in Logical Theory*, Volume 2 of *American Philosophical Quarterly Monograph Series*, pp. 98–112. Oxford: Blackwell.

Stalnaker, Robert (1981). "A Defense of Conditional Excluded Middle". In *Ifs* (ed. W. L. Harper, R. Stalnaker, and G. Pearce), pp. 87–104. Dordrecht: D. Reidel.

Stalnaker, Robert (1984). "The Problem of Deduction". In *Inquiry*. Cambridge, Mass.: MIT Press.

Stump, Eleonore (1986). "Dante's Hell, Aquinas's Moral Theory, and the Love of God". *Canadian Journal of Philosophy*, **16**, 181–196.

Sturgeon, Scott (1993). "The Gettier Problem". *Analysis*, **53**, 156–164.

Sturgeon, Scott (2002). "Comments". Rutgers Epistemology Conference, April 19, 2002.

Suppes, Patrick (1994). "Some Questions about Adams' Conditionals". In *Probability and Conditionals: Belief Revision and Rational Decision* (ed. E. Eells and B. Skyrms), pp. 5–11. Cambridge: Cambridge University Press.

Swinburne, Richard (1977). *The Coherence of Theism*. Oxford: Oxford University Press.

Swinburne, Richard (1983). "A Theodicy of Heaven and Hell". In *The Existence and Nature of God* (ed. A. J. Freddoso), pp. 37–54. Notre Dame: University of Notre Dame Press.

Talbott, Thomas (1999). *The Inescapable Love of God*. Boca Raton: Universal Publishers.

Talbott, Thomas (2001). "Freedom, Damnation, and The Power to Sin with Impunity". *Religious Studies*, **37**, 417–434.

Talbott, Thomas P. (1990). "The Doctrine of Everlasting Punishment". *Faith and Philosophy*, **7.1**, 19–43.

Timpe, Kevin (2008). *Free Will: Sourcehood and Its Alternatives*. London: Continuum.

Tomberlin, James E. and van Inwagen, Peter (ed.) (1985). *Profiles: Alvin Plantinga*. Dordrecht: D. Reidel.

van Inwagen, Peter (2008*a*). "How to Think about the Problem of Free Will". *Journal of Ethics*, **12**, 327–341.

van Inwagen, Peter (2008*b*). "What Does an Omniscient Being Know about the Future?". In *Oxford Studies in Philosophy of Religion* (ed. J. L. Kvanvig), Volume 1, pp. 216–230. Oxford: Oxford University Press.

Veltman, Frank (1996). "Defaults in Update Semantics". *Journal of Philosophical Logic*, **25**, 221–261.

Walker, Daniel P. (1964). *The Decline of Hell*. Chicago: University of Chicago Press.

Walls, Jerry (1992). *Hell: The Logic of Damnation*. Notre Dame: University of Notre Dame Press.

Walls, Jerry (2004*a*). "A Hell of a Choice: A Reply to Talbott". *Religious Studies*, **40.2**, 203–216.

Walls, Jerry (2004*b*). "A Hell of a Dilemma: Rejoinder to Talbott". *Religious Studies*, **40.2**, 225–227.

Ward, Barry (2002). "Humeanism without Humean Supervenience: A Projectivist Account of Laws and Possibilities". *Philosophical Studies*, **107**, 191–208.

Wierenga, Edward (1997). "Review of *The Openness of God*". *Faith and Philosophy*, **14.2**, 248–252.

Williamson, Timothy (2000). *Knowledge and Its Limits*. Oxford: Oxford University Press.

Williamson, Timothy (2003). "Everything". *Philosophical Perspectives*, **17.1**, 415–465.

Williamson, Timothy and Douven, Igor (2006). "Generalizing the Lottery Paradox". *The British Journal for the Philosophy of Science*, **57.4**, 755–779.

Zagzebski, Linda (1994). "The Inescapability of the Gettier Problem". *Philosophical Quarterly*, **44**, 65–73.

INDEX